THE INDUSTRIA
Volume

THE RAILWAY INTERCHANGE TRADE

This book deals with the traffic generated by the railway interchange basins. It is now a forgotten trade, but one which was important at the time.

It is generally assumed that the canals went into decline after the railways became established. Indeed, many rural canals may have suffered this fate, but canals such as the Birmingham Canal Navigations and adjoining waterways prospered. Industry had developed alongside these waterways and the canal continued to provide competitive transport for many firms and factories.

Railway companies found that working with the canal proprietors increased traffic on their lines. Transhipment basins and wharves were established where goods could be transferred between boat and railway wagon. The peak years were between 1900 and 1910, where over a million tons were handled annually at these interchange points. This trade accounted for about a seventh of the total tonnage carried by the Birmingham Canal at that time.

Each railway company operated themselves, or through an agent, a boatage service which worked to a strict timetable. These railway, or station, boats were once common sights on the canal. They were often noted on the Dudley Canal and the Netherton Tunnel Branch where they worked between the boatage depots and the interchange basins. Most craft were horse worked open wood or iron boats with no protection against the weather. It is remarkable that this type of boat and service continued through to 1958!

Although interchange basins exist elsewhere in the country, the largest concentration of basins was to be found in the West Midlands. It is the intention of the author, Tom Foxon, to explain the factors responsible for the establishment of this trade, its development and final decline. There is also a complete gazetteer of all basins and interchange wharves complete with a brief history and location maps.

Reference is made in this book to other volumes in THE INDUSTRIAL CANAL series. At the date of publication (2023), these other volumes are out of print.

THE INDUSTRIAL CANAL
Volume 2

THE RAILWAY INTERCHANGE TRADE

Tom Foxon

THE INDUSTRIAL CANAL
Volume 2

THE RAILWAY INTERCHANGE TRADE

Tom Foxon

CANALBOOKSHOP

First edition published 1998 by Heartland Press
Second edition published 2023 by CanalBookShop
Audlem Mill Limited The Wharf Audlem Cheshire CW3 0DX

ISBN 978-1-7399896-2-0

Tom Foxon has asserted his rights under the Copyright, Designs and Patents Act 1988 to be identified as the copyright owner of this work.

Subject to very limited exceptions, the Act prohibits the making of copies of any copyright work or of a substantial part of such a work, including the making of hard or digital copies by photocopying, scanning or similar process. Written permission to make a copy or copies must be obtained from the publisher. It is advisable to consult the publisher if in any doubt as to the legality of any copying which is to be undertaken.

CONTENTS

Preface	vi
Foreword by Tom Foxon	ix
Abbreviations and Acknowledgements	x
Introduction	xii
Chapter 1, The Coming of the Railways	1
Chapter 2, Early Interchange Basins	6
Chapter 3, The 1850s, A Time of Expansion	13
Chapter 4, Traffic and Operation	23
Chapter 5, 1863-1914 Development and Consolidation	36
Chapter 6, 1914-1969 Years of Decline	52
Conclusion	80
Appendix 1, Traffic Statistics	81
Appendix 2, Railway Traffic at BCN Wharves, September 1928	82
Appendix 3, List of Railway Basins	83
Gazeteer of West Midlands Interchange Basins & Boatage Depots	85

PREFACE

Trade on British canals and navigable waterways is a complex subject, for each canal and waterway had its own customers and its own special types of traffic. Some waterways were quiet backwaters where traffic was light. Others were busy with boats passing back and forth even through the night.

Previous studies of transport along waterways have explained their history and reason for existence. The purpose of this book and others in the series is to pay particular attention to types of traffic carried along the canals and navigable waterways of Britain.

One canal, in particular, has been chosen to demonstrate the variety of traffic that was carried on the canals. This canal lies at the heart of the canal system and is known as the Birmingham Canal Navigations.

There is certainly no other line of canal where industry and commerce was so concentrated along its banks. Even at the time when other canals were in decline, traffic on the Birmingham Canal actually increased. Ultimately it was to become the busiest canal in the country. No better description can be made than to call the Birmingham Canal, THE INDUSTRIAL CANAL.

It will be the aim of this study to examine the traffic patterns for the different types of goods carried. It also will attempt to explain the reasons behind each trade, why it started and why it ceased.

The first in the series tackled the coal trade, which provided the greatest traffic on the Birmingham Canal Navigations.

That volume investigated the variety amongst the types of coal traffic which changed as modern mining techniques were adopted. The early gin pits that were once numerous in the Black Country were replaced by deeper and more productive collieries around the perimeter. Such changes had a dramatic effect on the patterns of the coal trade along the waterway. There is a chapter that examines the role of the coal merchants, factors and carriers and deals with both the export and import of coal from the region. It also examines the rise of the gas and electricity industry with particular reference to the coal trade.

In this second volume the subject of railway basin traffic is studied. Railways provided serious competition for the canals. Often it was an unequal struggle and many canal owners lacked the resources to compete effectively. One, the Lancaster Canal, firmly grasped the nettle and took over the running of the railway between Preston and Lancaster. For many others, however, the reverse was the case.

Powerful railway companies such as the London & North Western and the Great Western Railway gained vested interests in the canals and came to own or control an important and strategic number.

Where the canal remained useful, traffic was allowed to continue. In other cases the canal was filled in and sometimes the bed was converted into a railway. Parts of the Aberdeen, Carlisle and the Hereford & Gloucester Canals suffered such a fate. Some canals, such as the Birmingham, actually gained traffic.

When the railways came to the West Midlands, industry was already concentrated along the banks of the canals. This was particularly noticeable in the district that was known as the Black Country. Although the railway companies found it easy to bring merchandise into and out of the district by rail, the short haul to the manufacturing works was better achieved by water. Thus it was that railway exchange basins were established along the waterways so that the goods could start or finish their journey by canal boat.

The Birmingham Canal was one of a group of waterways that came to be controlled by the London & North Western Railway. The LNWR was bound to guarantee a dividend for the canal shareholders under an 1846 agreement. It was a partnership that was to benefit this canal. The waterway was regularly maintained and new canal branches constructed with LNWR consent.

It is the purpose of this volume to discuss the origins of this trade, its rise and ultimate decline when the waterways were nationalised. Tom Foxon will describe the traffic associated with the exchange basins in the West Midlands. Particular emphasis will be made to the trade on the Birmingham Canal Navigations, but traffic to and from basins on adjacent waterways will also be mentioned.

An important part of the railway basin traffic was iron and steel to foundries and ironworks. These works had hitherto been supplied from the locality, but as this dwindled an increasing amount was carried into the district by rail. Details of the reasons behind this demand will be discussed in the Volume 3, The Metal Trades.

Ray Shill
Birmingham
1997

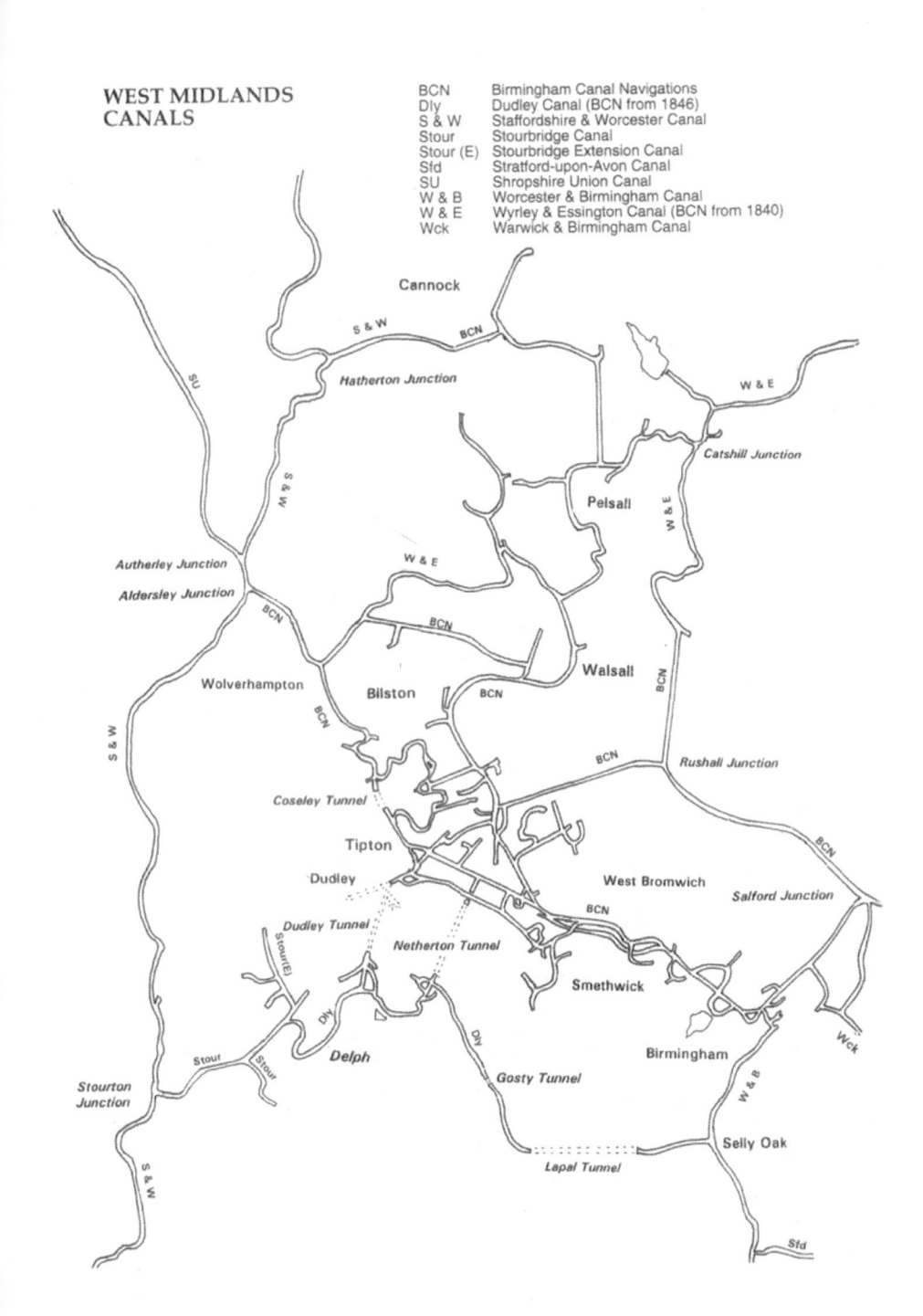

WEST MIDLANDS CANALS

BCN	Birmingham Canal Navigations
Dly	Dudley Canal (BCN from 1846)
S & W	Staffordshire & Worcester Canal
Stour	Stourbridge Canal
Stour (E)	Stourbridge Extension Canal
Sfd	Stratford-upon-Avon Canal
SU	Shropshire Union Canal
W & B	Worcester & Birmingham Canal
W & E	Wyrley & Essington Canal (BCN from 1840)
Wck	Warwick & Birmingham Canal

FOREWORD
by Tom Foxon

When I first became acquainted with the Birmingham Canal and its adjoining waterways in 1950, railway boats and railway basins (known to boatmen as Station Boats and Station Arms) were still an important part of a fascinating and busy transport system.

On my way to Bellis & Morcom's works at Ladywood to deliver my first cargo, our boat passed an awning covered arm, flanked by railway sidings. Inside lay two wooden boats without cabins which were being loaded with reels of paper. I was told that this was Monument Lane station arm and that the boats belonged to British Railways (London Midland Region). After we had unloaded and were on our way to Wolverhampton, we met a Guest, Keen & Nettlefold boat at Winson Green bound for the Western Region basin at Hockley.

I soon came to realise that there were several railway basins and many railway boats operating in the area, although, as our journeys were mainly confined to the main line, I failed at that time to appreciate the full extent of this traffic. We would meet L.M.R. boats, low loaded with steel or piled high with wheelbarrows or dustbins in Tipton Locks or encounter them in the Netherton Tunnel, their towlines shortened to keep the horse close to the boat, and a flaming light on each fore-end. When we went down the Staffs and Worcester Canal to Stourport, there were ex-Shropshire Union flyboats to be seen trading between the L.M.R. basin at Mill Street in Wolverhampton and the railway boatage depots at Kidderminster and Stourport, and Western Region boats running from Stourbridge to Baldwins Iron Works at Swindon.

Many years later, after I had retired from boating, I read a lot of canal history and found that the subject of railway boatage had barely been touched upon. The only way to find out more about it seemed to be to research it myself. So began a most interesting period of my life and I hope the reader of this book will find as much enjoyment as I had in researching it.

So many people have helped me in writing this book that I cannot name all of them. In particular, my thanks go to Roy Jamieson, Archivist of the British Waterways collection at Gloucester and to the staff of the Public Records Office at Kew and the Birmingham Central Library. The assistance of fellow members of the Railway & Canal Historical Society, especially Joseph Boughey, Alan Faulkner, Ray Shill, Michael Hale and Pat Thorn was invaluable. Among those with personal reminiscences of the subject, I am particularly indebted to George and Margaret Wood, John Whittington, Keith King and Kevin Gripton.

Tom Foxon
Tewkesbury, Gloucestershire

Abbreviations and References

It is the intention of the author to keep abbreviations to a minimum. The following have been used and are common in the text for this book and others in the series.

General Terms

C & D	Collected and Delivered
PRO	Public Record Office, Kew

Railway & Canal Company Abbreviations

B&DJR	Birmingham & Derby Junction Railway
B&WJC	Birmingham & Warwick Junction Canal
BCN	Birmingham Canal Navigations.
B&G	Birmingham & Gloucester Railway
B&OJR	Birmingham & Oxford Junction Railway
BSWR	Birmingham West Suburban Railway
BW&D	Birmingham Wolverhampton & Dudley Railway
GJR	Grand Junction Railway
GWR	Great Western Railway.
Hal	Halesowen Railway
Har	Harborne Railway
L&B	London & Birmingham Railway
LMR	British Railways (London Midland Region)
LMS	London, Midland & Scottish Railway.
LNWR	London & North Western Railway.
MR	Midland Railway
Old	Oldbury Railway
OWWR	Oxford, Worcester & Wolverhampton Railway
SBR	Shrewsbury & Birmingham Railway
STBC	Stourbridge Canal Company
Stour	Stourbridge Railway
SSR	South Staffordshire Railway
SU	Shropshire Union Canal Carrying Company
SUR	Shropshire Union Railway & Canal Company
SVR	Birmingham, Wolverhampton & Stour Valley Railway
WMR	West Midland Railway
W&WR	Wolverhampton & Walsall Railway

Maps

Maps are either free drawn or are reproduced from other sources. In the case of the free drawn maps, there are numerical references to locations or firms mentioned in the text.

Measurements (all Imperial Measurements)

Cwt.	Hundredweight
ft.	Feet
in.	Inch
ton	Ton

Money

d	Old Pence (pre- Feb. 1971)
p	New Pence
S	Shilling (pre- Feb. 1971)
£	Pound

Acknowledgements

In preparing this series, grateful thanks are given to the following whose help and assistance were invaluable in assembling the information:

Joseph Boughey
Nigel Chapman
Alan Faulkner
Michael Hale
Roy Jamieson
Alan Smith

Patrick Thorn
Alan Price
Jack Haddock
Martin O Keeffe
Ned Williams

Also the Staff of:-

Birmingham Public Library and Archives Departments
Derby Record Office
Dudley Archives Centre, Coseley
Public Records Office, Chancery Lane
Public Records Office, Kew
The Boat Museum, Ellesmere Port
The British Museum
The Joint Record Offices of Lichfield and Stafford
The National Waterways Museum, Gloucester
Sandwell Libraries and Archives Centre
Smethwick Walsall Archives Centre
Wolverhampton Archives Centre
Black Country Living Museum

INTRODUCTION

Before entering into a description of railway basin traffic, some details need to be given concerning the histories of the different railway companies that served the West Midlands.

Early railways, like canals, were conceived for the carriage of goods and materials. They often reached places where it was inappropriate to construct a canal and also frequently served as canal feeders. Most were owned by the people who either wanted to carry their minerals to market, or derived revenue from the tolls generated by that traffic.

These early railways were most diverse. There were different shapes and weight of rail, and the track could be carried on stone blocks, wooden or iron sleepers. Some of the earliest lines even used wooden rails. So diverse were these early railways that different names are applied to them: Dramroad, Gangway, Plateway, Tramroad, Tramway or Wagonway. Generally, tramroad or tramway have remained the preferred name for railways whose track is lightly laid.

Within the West Midlands, many local mine owners used tramways to move materials from the pit head, whilst ironworks had them for loads within the foundry. The track usually comprised light weight rails laid on wooden or metal sleepers. The distance between the two rails, that is the gauge, usually varied between one and three feet, but there were a few notable exceptions. Haulage was sometimes by hand but more generally with the help of a horse. In later years, rope haulage became common and most local collieries used the endless rope to move tubs to canalside wharves. Many tramways had short lives, and tramway systems, particularly within the Black Country, would change and alter as pits closed and new pits opened.

The term railway was usually reserved for the permanent lines of track used for the carriage of goods and passengers. In the early years there was little standardisation of gauge, which led to some interesting problems when they met other railways.

The carriage of passengers set in motion a process that led to the establishment of a national network of railways. It is generally accepted that this development began when the Stockton & Darlington introduced a horse drawn passenger service in 1825. The first passenger trains hauled by steam locomotives began on the Liverpool & Manchester Railway in 1830.

It was the building of the Liverpool & Manchester Railway that really set the whole process in motion. Out of their line grew other railways that eventually forged a link to London in 1838.

On these lines needs of the passenger were paramount. Goods were carried but it was left to established carriers to convey them. People like the Hargreaves family had been carriers for generations. They had built up an important road and canal network in the North West and it was left to them to carry the goods on these new passenger railways. John Hargreaves Junior had a fleet of railway locomotives that plied the Liverpool & Manchester, North Union and associated railways.

Within the midlands, two public railways met in Birmingham, the Grand Junction and the London and Birmingham. They formed a junction in 1838 which cemented the link with the North West and created the embryonic national network.

Although cattle, mail and parcels were carried in addition to passengers, it became the policy again to invite established carriers to convey goods and merchandise. Pickford and Crowley commenced rail traffic within the midlands, but continued to send the bulk of their trade by canal or road. It may be said of these early railway companies that they received traffic at the whim of these powerful carriers.

Slowly the railway companies began to take control of their own affairs and began to carry goods themselves. One of the earliest to do so was the Birmingham & Gloucester Railway. In 1843 they decided to appoint a traffic manager and started a service in February 1844.

Birmingham became an early focus point for new railways. By 1842, four lines converged on the town, but none served Black Country industry. The Grand Junction came the closest, but still gave Wolverhampton a wide berth and passed through countryside to the east of West Bromwich to reach Birmingham via Aston. The Chillington Iron Company was one a select group of firms that benefited from early traffic on this railway.

The first few months of 1844 heralded negotiations for the first of a number of important railway amalgamation. The Birmingham & Derby Junction Railway was to merge with the North Midland Railway and the Midland Counties Railways to create the Midland Railway. There was also support for a merger between the London & Birmingham and the Grand Junction railways. However, a bitter difference of opinion between the respective boards prevented a union at this time.

From April 1844, local newspapers began to publish details about new railway schemes. A railway was proposed from Stourbridge to Birmingham and three schemes were mooted to connect Shrewsbury with Wolverhampton.

The biggest support came for the Oxford, Worcester and Wolverhampton Railway in May 1844. This scheme attracted many influential ironmasters, as it intended to serve an important part of the Black Country. The route through Bilston, Tipton, Dudley, Brierley Hill and Stourbridge passed close to important clay, glass and ironworks.

Between 1845 and 1850, many other schemes were proposed which led to the establishment of the basic West Midland railway network. For those that were granted an act of parliament, most were absorbed by larger companies. Eventually there were three main companies; Great Western, Midland and London & North Western who operated services throughout the region.

These companies operated on a national scale. Their lines pervaded many other industrial districts and greatly enhanced the interchange of goods traffic between the West Midlands and other places. Their names will be mentioned many times in this book, but for those who might have difficulty in relating to their West Midland constituent railways some relevant details are reproduced below:

Unless otherwise stated, all railways were built to standard gauge 4ft 8½in. Companies which owned their own locomotives are indicated by an *.

Birmingham & Derby Junction Railway, B&DJR *

Opened between Derby and Hampton-in-Arden on 12 August 1839. Traffic, both passengers and goods, was directed from Curzon Street to Hampton and vice-versa. The direct railway from Whitacre to Birmingham (Lawley Street) was completed on 10 February 1842. This became their main goods depot in Birmingham. A spur, or siding, joined the Grand Junction Railway south of Vauxhall. Another siding crossed Landor Street and passed under the London & Birmingham Railway to a wagon lift that enabled wagons to pass onto and from the LBR. The B&DJR amalgamated with the North Midland and Midland Counties railways in May 1844 to form the Midland Railway.

Birmingham & Gloucester Railway, B&G *

Opened between Gloucester and Birmingham (Camp Hill) in sections. The part from Cofton to Camp Hill first saw a passenger service on 17 December 1840. The line was extended to Gloucester Junction (LBR) and passenger trains commenced running to Curzon Street on 17 August 1841. Goods trains commenced to run on the B&G from October 1840 and from 23 May 1842 their carrying establishment was transferred from Camp Hill to Curzon Street. In January 1845, the Birmingham & Gloucester entered into an agreement that was to lead to their amalgamation with the Bristol & Gloucester Railway. They formed a joint board of management that was known as the Bristol & Birmingham Company. Both companies were absorbed by the Midland Railway in August 1846. The Bristol & Gloucester was a broad gauge (7ft 0¼in.) railway which involved transhipment of all goods travelling to and from Bristol at Gloucester. By the end of December 1853, the Bristol & Gloucester had been regauged to standard, and goods could be consigned directly to Bristol in the same wagons.

Birmingham & Oxford Junction Railway, B&OJR

Gauge Mixed: Standard and Broad (7ft 0¼in.). They obtained the Act of Parliament to build the railway from Fenny Compton to Birmingham in 1846 where it was to join the Oxford and Rugby Railway. At Birmingham a junction was to be made with the LNWR near Curzon Street. Authority was also given for an extension from Bordesley to a separate terminus at Great Charles Street (Snow Hill), Birmingham where a junction was to be made with the Birmingham, Wolverhampton & Dudley Railway. The B&OJR was absorbed by Great Western Railway in 1848 who constructed the line. Opened Leamington to Birmingham (Snow Hill) on 1 October 1852. The intended railway from Bordesley to Curzon Street was never finished.

Birmingham West Suburban Railway, BWSR

Constructed as single track railway between Kings Norton and Birmingham (Granville Street) and opened on 3 April 1876. The company, although promoted by the Worcester & Birmingham Canal, was vested in the Midland Railway on 1 July 1875. It was rebuilt with two lines of track between 1882 and 1885 to a new junction at Kings Norton. Granville Street Station was closed and demolished. The line was also extended from Church Road to Birmingham New Street with goods lines to Birmingham Central. The old route through Lifford was retained as sidings that served the canal interchange wharf.

Birmingham, Wolverhampton & Dudley Railway, BW&D

Gauge Mixed: Standard and Broad (7ft 0¼in.). Obtained Act for a railway from Birmingham (Snow Hill) and Priestfield where a junction was to be made with the Oxford, Worcester & Wolverhampton Railway. BW&D trains had running powers over the OWWR track to the Low Level Station in Wolverhampton. Low Level Station was a joint station shared by both the BW&D and OWWR. A number of branches into the iron district were contemplated which included a railway towards the Brades. Only one branch, that to Dudley, was authorised by the Act. The BW&D was absorbed by Great Western Railway on 31 August 1848, who constructed the line. The railway was to be finished by 1 September 1854, but due to the collapse of Winson Lane Bridge a postponement was announced. The line was finally opened for passengers to Priestfield on 14 November 1854, the same day the Radstock Branch was opened. Freight services did not run until the following year because most goods stations remained unfinished. Goods traffic officially commenced on 1 June 1855. The Dudley Branch was only part completed. It terminated near the interchange basin with the Balls Hill Branch Canal.

Birmingham, Wolverhampton & Stour Valley Railway, SVR

This company was authorised to make a railway from Birmingham (Navigation Street) to Wolverhampton (Queen Street) Station and Bushbury (junction GJR). The plans included a branch from Smethwick to Stourport along the Stour Valley that was not built. Authority was also given for a branch to Dudley from Dudley Port and the Birmingham Extension Railway from Curzon Street (junction L&B). Construction of the railways and works were organised and financed by the committee of the SVR and was completed from Curzon Street to Bushbury in 1851. Unfortunately various problems (see chapter 1) led to the opening being delayed twice. A goods service began during February 1852, whilst the passenger trains commenced running on 1 July 1852. The line was leased from 1850 by the LNWR who also worked the railway from the start. The Shrewsbury & Birmingham Railway also had the right to use it, but were initially prevented from doing so by the LNWR. Physical and legal barriers were frequently put in their way. The SBR, finally exercised that right, albeit briefly, during 1854. During 1853 a branch was made between Dudley Port and the South Staffordshire Railway (Sedgley Junction) that enabled through working into Dudley. The BW&SVR was vested in the LNWR on 15 April 1867.

Grand Junction Railway, GJR *

Opened between Warrington and Birmingham (Vauxhall) on 4 July 1837. The GJR also absorbed the Warrington & Newton Railway and thus were able to run trains directly onto the Liverpool & Manchester Railway. Their line was extended to Birmingham (Curzon Street) adjacent to the L&B station, by November 1838. On 8 August 1845, the Bolton & Leigh, Bolton & Kenyon and Liverpool & Manchester railways were absorbed by the GJR. They, in turn, merged with London & Birmingham and Manchester & Birmingham companies on 1 January 1846 to form the London & North Western Railway Company. A projected branch from Friar Park to Dudley was not built.

Halesowen Railway, Hal

First conceived as the Halesowen & Bromsgrove Branch Railways. Completed from Longbridge to Halesowen on 10 September 1883. It was a railway that was worked jointly by the MR and GWR. At Halesowen it formed an end on junction with the GWR branch from Old Hill (completed in 1878).

Harborne Railway, Har

Opened from Harborne Junction (LNWR) to Harborne on 10 August 1874. All services were worked by the LNWR. The line crossed the BCN main line near Harborne Junction.

London & Birmingham Railway, L&B *

The London & Birmingham Railroad Company was formed in 1823. They made several surveys of line between Birmingham & London which were opposed at the time by the canal companies.

The Act, for the revised title London & Birmingham Railway, finally received Royal Assent on 6 May 1833 (the same day as the Grand Junction Company). The railway was constructed in three stages from London (Euston) to Birmingham (Curzon Street). The section between Rugby and Birmingham (Curzon Street) was opened on 9 April 1838 and by September 1838, the L&B was complete to London. There were a number of branches that included a line from Coventry to Leamington that was finished on 9 December 1844 and the railway from Blisworth, through Northampton, to Peterborough was completed in 1845. The L&B merged with the Grand Junction and Manchester & Birmingham to form the London & North Western Railway on 1 January 1846.

Oldbury Railway, Old

Originally proposed as the Dudley and Oldbury Junction Railway. Completed from Langley Green to Oldbury Goods and Canal Basin on 7 November 1884. The GWR agreed to work the railway, but did not take over this line until 1 July 1894.

Oxford, Worcester & Wolverhampton Railway, OWWR *

The OWWR united the towns of Wolverhampton, Worcester and Oxford and passed through some of the heaviest industrialised parts of the Black Country. A number of rival schemes were proposed to compete with this railway. They included the London, Worcester, Rugby and Oxford that was to join the L&B near Tring and the Dudley & Sedgely. Neither line was built. The OWWR was completed between Oxford and Wolverhampton in stages. By May 1852 the line had reached Stourbridge. It was extended to Dudley (December 1852) and Tipton (December 1853). The last section from Tipton to Bushbury (junction LNWR) was opened to goods on 15 May 1854, and passengers from 1 July 1854. The section between Priestfield, Wolverhampton and Cannock Road Junction was shared with the GWR and was mixed gauge (4ft 8½in / 7ft 0¼in). Both lines of track from Priestfield to Dudley were also mixed gauge and one track from Dudley through to Oxford was mixed gauge by April 1854. The branch to Walsall Street Goods, finished in 1855, was standard gauge only. The OWWR became known as the West Midland Railway from 1 July 1860 after vesting the Worcester & Hereford Railway and Newport, Abergavenny and Hereford Railway within its organisation.

Shrewsbury & Birmingham Railway, SBR *

The Shrewsbury & Birmingham was a small concern born out of bigger ambitions. By 1844 two companies proposed rival schemes along a similar route. The

Shrewsbury, Wolverhampton, Dudley & Birmingham included branches to Newtown and Wem in their plan, while the rival Shrewsbury & Wolverhampton had a branch to Ruabon. Each line followed the other closely between Shrewsbury & Wolverhampton. A third line, the Shrewsbury & Stafford, followed their route to Wellington before diverging off towards Stafford. The Shrewsbury & Birmingham was the final outcome of the Wolverhampton route. It was authorised on 3 August 1846 to construct a railway between Shrewsbury and Wolverhampton and running powers were granted for SBR trains to use the BWSVR into Birmingham. The line was completed between Shrewsbury and Wolverhampton on 12 November 1849. The section between Shrewsbury and Wellington was shared with the Shropshire Union Railway.

Trains originally terminated at a temporary station at Wednesfield Road, Wolverhampton, but by 1851 were running into Queen Street Station. The SBR amalgamated with Great Western Railway on 1 September 1854.

Shropshire Union Railway & Canal Company, SUR

An act passed in May 1845 enabled the Ellesmere and Chester Canal to absorb the Birmingham and Liverpool Junction Canal, and heralded further canal amalgamations. Plans were also considered to convert parts of their waterway to a railway, although this was not proceeded with. In 1846 the Montgomery Canal, the Shropshire Canal and the Shrewsbury and Stafford Railway Company were absorbed, and the name of the canal undertaking was changed to the Shropshire Union Railway and Canal company. During the autumn of 1846, an offer was received from the LNWR to lease the whole operation. It was accepted, and the lease was ratified by Act of Parliament on 2 July 1847. Amalgamation with the LNWR followed in October 1847. It was to prove an important acquisition for the LNWR particular with respect to the canal carrying operations. The canal carrying side was organised under the title of the Shropshire Union Canal Carrying Company. Their boats plied the length of the Shropshire Union Canals and also had depots on the BCN. The railway part was completed between Wellington & Stafford in June 1849. A joint section between Shrewsbury and Wellington was shared with the Shrewsbury & Birmingham Railway.

South Staffordshire Railway, SSR *

Formed out of two other railway schemes; South Staffordshire Junction Railway and the Trent Valley, Midlands and Grand Junction Railway. Completed from Wichnor Junction to Bescot and Dudley in stages. The final section to Dudley opened officially, though incompletely, on 1 May 1850. It was a railway that forged a link with the LNWR, MR and OWWR. Leased and worked by J. R. McClean from opening. A branch to Cannock was completed on 1 February 1858. McClean transferred the operation to the LNWR in 1852, who also maintained their fleet of engines. In 1859 they took the SSR fleet into their stock and replaced them with their own. The line was finally absorbed into LNWR on 15 July 1867.

Stourbridge Railway, Stour

Railways had been conceived to link Birmingham with Stourbridge before 1845, but all failed to be built. A new company received parliamentary powers in 1860 to construct a railway from Stourbridge to Old Hill with a branch to Congreaves. But further powers were sought for an extension railway to Galton Junction (LNWR) and a branch to Stourbridge Town (not built). The line was opened in stages. Cradley was reached on 1 April 1863; Old Hill, 1 January 1866; Galton Junction, 1 April 1867. An agreement was signed with West Midland Railway to work the line from opening and this working agreement passed to the GWR who took over after they had amalgamated the WMR within their organisation. The Stourbridge Railway was absorbed by GWR on 1 February 1870. The GWR applied for fresh powers to build the Stourbridge Town Branch and commenced running trains on this branch on 1 October 1879.

West Midland Railway, WMR *

Formerly known as the Oxford, Worcester & Wolverhampton Railway, this line was amalgamated with the Great Western Railway on 1 August 1863.

Wolverhampton & Walsall Railway, W&WR

Constructed from Wolverhampton to Walsall via Wednesfield and opened on 1 November 1872. Both LNWR and MR trains used the line, but it was finally purchased by the Midland Railway on 1 July 1876.

All of the above named railway companies were absorbed into three larger concerns:

> GWR - Great Western Railway
> LNWR - London & North Western Railway
> MR - Midland Railway.

These were responsible for the operation of the railway basins when the trade was being developed. Each company competed for the maximum share of the trade.

The 1921 Transport Act, which came into force from 1 January 1923, led to the grouping of railway companies into four major units. The LNWR and MR were merged together as part of the LMS, London Midland & Scottish Railway. Their interchange basins then became LMS property. The GWR remained separate and continued to compete with the LMS for canal trade, which at this time was in decline.

The 1947 Transport Act merged the four companies into one national network, British Railways, and all surviving railway basins passed into British Railways (British Transport Commission) hands from January 1, 1948. For a while, the former

GWR and LMS identities were simply transferred to British Railways Western Region and British Railways London Midland Region. Most interchange traffic ceased during their tenure. From 1 January 1963 all Western Region lines in the West Midlands became the responsibility of the London Midland Region. The remaining interchange traffic ceased in BR(LM) days. Some basin properties stayed in railway ownership, but most have been now disposed of.

The deregulation of British Railways began in April 1994 with the formation of Railtrack. Their responsibility was the land and associated track formerly owned by British Railways. The track and depots are now leased by Train Operating Companies. A number of companies serve the West Midlands but only one still owns a railway interchange basin. English, Welsh & Scottish Railways, which are responsible for freight carrying, still use the railway sidings at Monmore Green.

With the coming of the railways, several canal companies came under railway control. In some cases the canal was simply purchased by the railway company, in others the involvement was more subtle.

The Birmingham Canal Navigations became closely involved with the London & North Western Railway Company. The LNWR sent representatives to BCN committee meetings and gradually came to have more control over BCN affairs.

How this came about was quite complex. The BCN proprietors being wary of railway competition, first proposed to build a railway themselves along the banks of their canal between Birmingham and Wolverhampton, but then formed an alliance with other interested parties as the scheme developed. The new line was sanctioned by Parliament as the Birmingham, Wolverhampton and Stour Valley Railway. It was a partnership between the directors of the SVR, the BCN and the L&B. In order to carry this proposal through, the London & Birmingham Railway and Birmingham Canal Arrangement Act was passed on 27 July 1846. It included the statement which appears to encourage interchange facilities:

And whereas the existing canals of the Birmingham Canal Company communicate with the London & Birmingham Railway and the mutual transmission of traffic to and from such Canals and railways respectively would be facilitated, and it would promote the public Convenience if the working and Management of the Canals and Works of the Birmingham Canal Company were under the Control and Superintendence of a Committee to be appointed by the said Canal & Railway Companies. And whereas the said two companies have entered into mutual arrangements for effecting the purpose aforesaid, and also with reference to the Construction of certain other railways in connection with their respective Undertakings...

Powers were granted for the LBR to appoint five members to the committee of management of the BCN, and from there after the BCN ceased to have a truly independent existence. As part of the deal, the LBR was to guarantee a minimum dividend of four per cent on the share of the company. So BCN shareholders could expect at least a 4% return on their investment. The LNWR inherited the LBR commitment in 1847. At first, profits ensured that the dividend was paid, but gradually these profits fell and the LNWR acquired an increasing financial burden.

Railway interchange, as previously stated, was not just confined to the public railway. There were many more private basins and wharfs within the West Midlands where railways or tramways ran to the canalside.

Volume 1, The Coal Trade, provided various examples where coal was transhipped into boats. Future volumes will demonstrate that clay, ironstone, limestone and sand were commonly brought down to the canal by tramways.

This book is dedicated to the boats and basins associated with the public railway companies. Here there was free interchange of goods between railway and canal. At the private basins, it was often one way trade where minerals were brought onto the canal to be boated elsewhere.

The following photographs provide comparative examples of private basins where rail interchange occurred.

The BCN had their own railway interchange basin at Hednesford where coal was brought down the standard gauge Littleworth Tramway from Cannock & Rowley Collieries and the Cannock Chase Collieries by locomotives. RAWNSLEY from the Cannock & Rugeley Collieries is seen on the wharfside behind a number of coal boats awaiting their next load *Cannock Library*

Ashwood Basin, on the Staffordshire & Worcestershire Canal, is a typical example of a private basin where coal was delivered to the waiting boats

Black Country Living Museum

High Bridge Basin, Dudley No 2 Canal. Doulton & Company boats await their loads of clay brought down from the Saltwells Clayfield

Dudley Libraries

Short Heath Branch, Wyrley & Essington Canal, has had a long history of railway and canal interchange. There was a narrow gauge tramway owned by the BCN that brought coal and ironstone on to the canal. The branch was extended in 1900 when a new standard gauge railway was made from the Hollybank Collieries to new interchange facilities beside the canal

Jim Evans

xxiii

CHAPTER 1

THE COMING OF THE RAILWAYS

By the 1830s, the Birmingham and Black Country area was already highly industrialised. In 1830, 213,000 tons of pig iron were produced from 123 blast furnaces, and the region was the largest producer of wrought iron. Most iron making took place in the district bounded by Walsall, West Bromwich, Stourbridge and Wolverhampton. In Birmingham itself a report of 1839 stated that there were 70 steam engines and 124 wharves and works on the banks of the Birmingham & Fazeley Canal between Farmer's Bridge and Aston (a distance of about two miles). These works were mainly engaged in manufacturing goods from iron and non-ferrous metals and in food processing. Brick (including firebrick) making was important and glass was produced around Stourbridge.

At this time, the region was virtually self sufficient in the principal iron making raw materials of coal, iron ore, limestone and moulding sand. Copper and zinc for the Birmingham brass industry came from Wales and Somerset.

Most of the products of the West Midlands were consumed outside the region, London being the main market, but the trade route to the Mersey was important as this was the main port of export, not only for overseas but for Ireland and for coastwise traffic particularly to Scotland. Canal communication with London and Liverpool was good but the water routes to Bristol and Hull suffered from the poor condition of the Severn and Trent rivers. The iron industry was exposed to competition from South Wales, Cumberland and Scotland, all situated near the coast and having the advantage of cheap transport by sea. West Midland traders were not slow to perceive that the newfangled railways would not only offer competition to the canals and give better access to places not conveniently served by them, but appeared to lack their disadvantages of slowness and uncertainty.

Transport improvements to be achieved by the construction of railways were deemed to be essential to the continuing prosperity of the region, yet the first railways to reach the West Midlands were something of a disappointment. The London & Birmingham (opened for goods in April 1839) terminated at Curzon Street, Birmingham, while the first railway communication to Liverpool and Manchester, the Grand Junction, from a terminus adjoining that of the L & B, bypassed the mining and manufacturing district to the east, penetrating the Black Country only between Darlaston and Wednesfield Heath, the latter sufficiently distant from the centre of Wolverhampton as to infuriate traders.

As early as July 1839, only 15 months after the opening of the GJR, the canal carrying firm of Worthington's, agents for the Trustees of the Duke of Bridgewater, were reporting to their principals that they had been forced to withdraw from the Birmingham hardware trade, finding that "all the best paying goods between Birmingham and Manchester and Liverpool are going by railway"[2]. In contrast to this early penetration of the Birmingham light goods trade, it is not until four years later that we hear of the railways being involved in the heavy end of the iron trade.

In September 1841, the Bridgewater Trustees, at that time important carriers between the Midlands and the North West, had made an agreement with the Grand Junction Railway for the transhipment of traffic from railway to canal at Preston Brook on the Bridgewater Canal or Walton on the Trustees' Mersey & Irwell Navigation, from where it was to be forwarded to Liverpool by the Trustees' barges. The Trustees hoped, by this means, to regain the traffic in South Staffs iron lost to the Shropshire Union route via Ellesmere Port. When this iron traffic failed to materialise, the Railway Directors excused themselves on the grounds that they did not possess the necessary links to the iron works. At the end of 1842 it was reported that a "shed for transhipping iron" from canal to railway was in course of erection and a trade in iron goods began to pass from the GJR to the Bridgewater in February 1843.[3] The location of this transhipment point remains a matter for conjecture but this is the earliest indication that, for the railways to gain a substantial share of the heavy iron trade, connections with the canal were essential.

The Need for Canal and Railway Interchange

The experience of the Grand Junction Railway was not lost on the other railways which were soon to penetrate the Black Country and they planned connections with the canal before their lines were completed. In 1855, the Traffic Manager of the Oxford, Worcester and Wolverhampton Railway was urging the completion of the railway basins at Tipton and Wolverhampton "as it would be impossible to secure the heavy weight of traffic from the works on the canals until we have the means of loading to and from boats into the railway wagons".[4]

Why was this the case? The Black Country iron industry was characterised by a large number of small works which had been sited so as to receive their raw materials and forward their products by canal or by tramways connected to the canal. The railways were not slow to build sidings where they could be justified but in most cases it was uneconomic to connect relatively inaccessible individual works producing fairly small amounts of traffic to the main line. Difficulty of access and cost of construction were not the only considerations. Even at this early date in railway operation it was recognised that numerous connections to the main line and the proliferation of short distance workings would interrupt the more profitable long distance operations and fragmented small traffic arisings would be costly to service.

Road cartage was a possibility. In 1845, one-seventh of local goods in the Black Country were conveyed by land at an average cost of 1s 3d (6p) per ton mile[5], but boatage was much cheaper with charges averaging 4d (1.75 p) per ton mile[6]. The canals existed and the works had been laid out to use them. All that needed to be done was to construct a basin or wharf (a few "railway basins" were, in fact, linear wharves), put sidings alongside, provide a shed, (the extent of covered accommodation varied from an overall roof to nothing) and cranage for heavy lifts. Most goods, including pig and bar iron, were transhipped by hand. One basin, which could be sited to suit the railway's convenience, would deal with the traffic from many works and thus have an economic throughput. In 1898, the 20 transhipment basins then open on the BCN averaged 60,418 tons each, a very respectable amount. This represented about twenty boats per day per basin over a six day week[7].

The main drawbacks to using a canal are ice, drought, and congestion. Except in the very early years, the vast majority of railway boatage in the Black Country was carried out over short distances and on one level which made ice-breaking relatively easy. The heavy and constant traffic on the BCN tended to keep the ice broken in any case, but, if necessary, the company had the ice-breaking resources to keep its routes open. Water supplies were reliable, if somewhat expensive to provide. Only in a few cases did large flows of boatage traffic have to negotiate congested flights of locks.

The iron and brick trades were highly suitable for boatage, usually producing economically sized loads for the 20-30 ton boats used; but, having made their connections with the canal, the railways were not slow to supplement full load boatage direct to and from works with part load and general merchandise services into each others territory. In the 1850s, Great Western Railway boats competed with the OWWR in the carriage of butter and cheese between Wolverhampton, Brettell Lane and Brierley Hill. Boats operated on behalf of the LNWR penetrated to railway Boatage Depots at Kidderminster, Stourport, Stourbridge, Brierley Hill[8] and Netherton, and Midland Railway boats to depots at Old Hill, Netherton and Smethwick. Goods would be carted to and from these Boatage Depots and part loads consolidated for boatage to a canal / railway interchange basin.

The economic rationale behind the use of Railway Basins has its counterpart in the present day where "Steel Terminals" have superseded the use of individual sidings throughout the Black Country, although nowadays distribution is done by road haulage rather than boats. Strangely enough, some of these Steel Terminals occupy (or have occupied) the sites of the old canal / railway transhipment basins at Wolverhampton (Monmore Green), Wednesbury and Great Bridge.

For the very early transhipment basins, the entire BCN, Stourbridge Canal and parts of adjoining canals were their oyster. Darlaston Basin, opened by the LNWR in 1845 enjoyed five years as the only Railway Interchange to serve the BCN outside the immediate Birmingham area. Wolverhampton's Hay and Victoria Basins and the South Staffordshire Railway Interchange at Great Bridge also enjoyed a few years of covering places as far away as Birmingham, Stourbridge and Stourport[9]. It was only from 1855 that large numbers of interchanges were opened and boatage distances reduced.

FOOTNOTES

1. Raybould T.J. THE ECONOMIC EMERGENCE OF THE BLACK COUNTRY David & Charles 1973
2. Case in support of the Birmingham Canal Bill 1839. Birmingham Public Library 177408
3. Mather F.C. AFTER THE CANAL DUKE Oxford 1970 p.148
4. OWWR Report, 21 February 1855 PRO RAIL 558
5. Minutes of Evidence taken before the Select Committee on the OWWR 184. Dudley Public Library LD/625
6. Northern Alliance Agreements 1854 -56 PRO RAIL 250/752
7. RC on Canals 1907 Vol III Appendix 16/14
8. OWWR Goods Agents Meetings 1859/61 PRO RAIL 558/18
9. GWR Agreements PRO RAIL 252/22

EARLY RAILWAY BASINS 1851

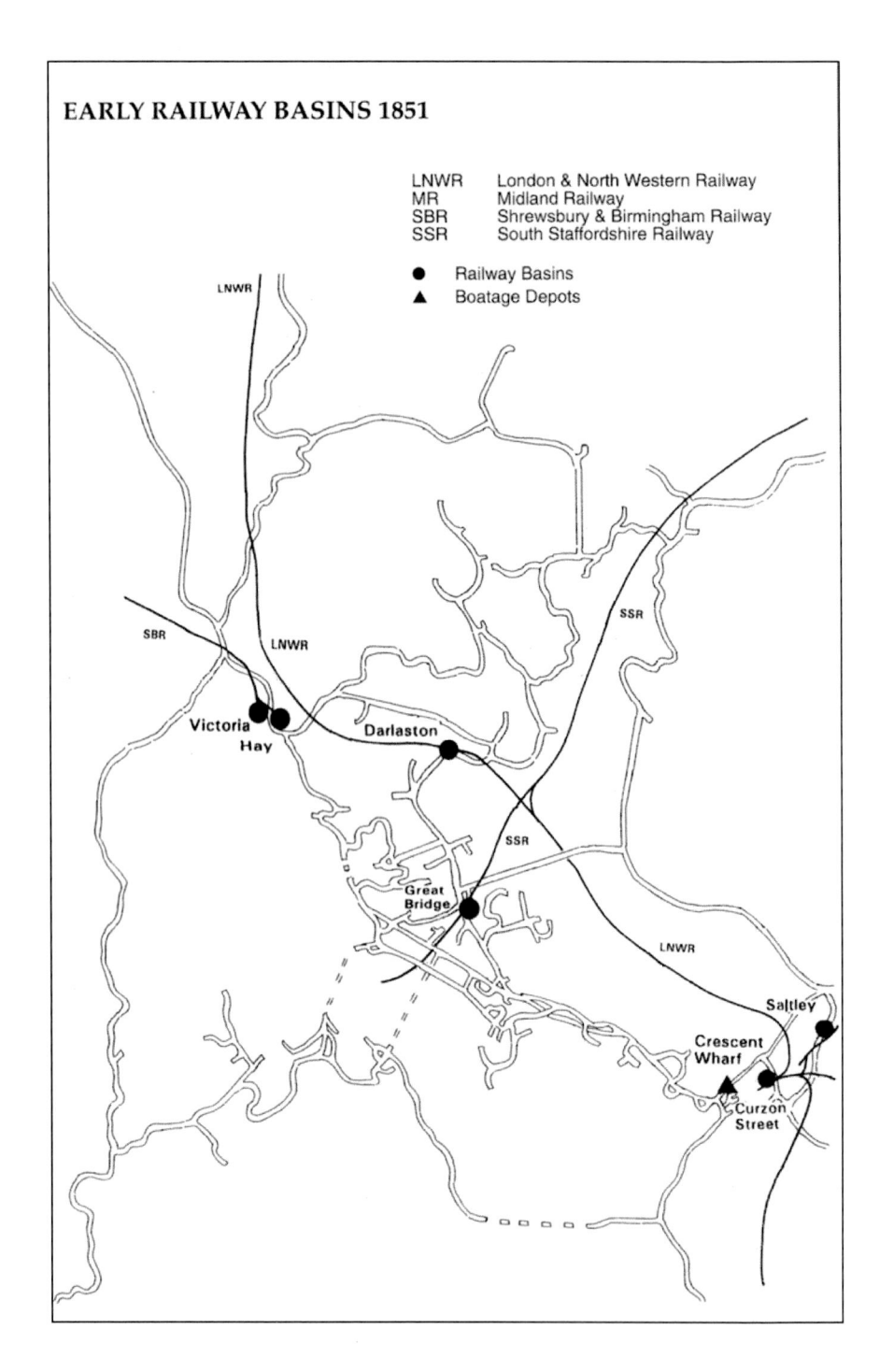

LNWR	London & North Western Railway
MR	Midland Railway
SBR	Shrewsbury & Birmingham Railway
SSR	South Staffordshire Railway

● Railway Basins
▲ Boatage Depots

CHAPTER 2

EARLY INTERCHANGE BASINS

The Birmingham terminus of the Grand Junction (GJR) and London & Birmingham (L&B) railways at Curzon Street was adjacent to the Digbeth Branch of the BCN, and each company had a wharf on the canal. It is possible that these wharves were initially used for the transfer of construction materials from canal to railway and the L&B wharf was certainly used for unloading coke which the early locomotives used as fuel.

The extent to which revenue earning goods were transferred at Curzon Street is uncertain. Although the GJR was opened for goods in February 1838, traffic had to be handled at Vauxhall. The GJR was extended to Curzon Street in November 1838 but Vauxhall continued for some time as the main goods station. As we have seen, within 18 months the GJR had taken from the canal the light, high value traffic between Birmingham and Liverpool & Manchester. The short distances involved and the nature of the traffic would, in my opinion, indicate the use of road cartage from the works to the railway. Curzon Street was very badly sited for canal feeder services, being surrounded in every direction by flights of heavily congested locks and this would tend to favour cartage for most goods.

The L&B was not fully operational for goods until April 1839, so, from the opening to goods of the GJR, for a period of 14 months rail traffic from Merseyside to London had to be transhipped to the canal at Birmingham. The principal carrier between Lancashire and London was Pickfords, whose policy was to transfer their traffic to rail as and when suitable arrangements could be agreed.

By 1841, Pickfords had arranged an integrated system whereby they acted as carriers on the L&B, traffic which employed both canal and rail being transhipped at Camden, Rugby or Birmingham. Pickford's relationship with the GJR was so unsatisfactory that, as far as possible, traffic passing from London to Liverpool was taken to Birmingham by rail and sent on from there by canal.

In 1847, the new London & North Western Railway (LNWR), instituted a policy to exclude carriers from its goods traffic. Prevented from carrying by rail on its most important route and faced with an overwhelmingly powerful competitor to its through canal services, Pickfords was in a difficult position.

However, the LNWR needed terminal agents with the necessary stock of horses,

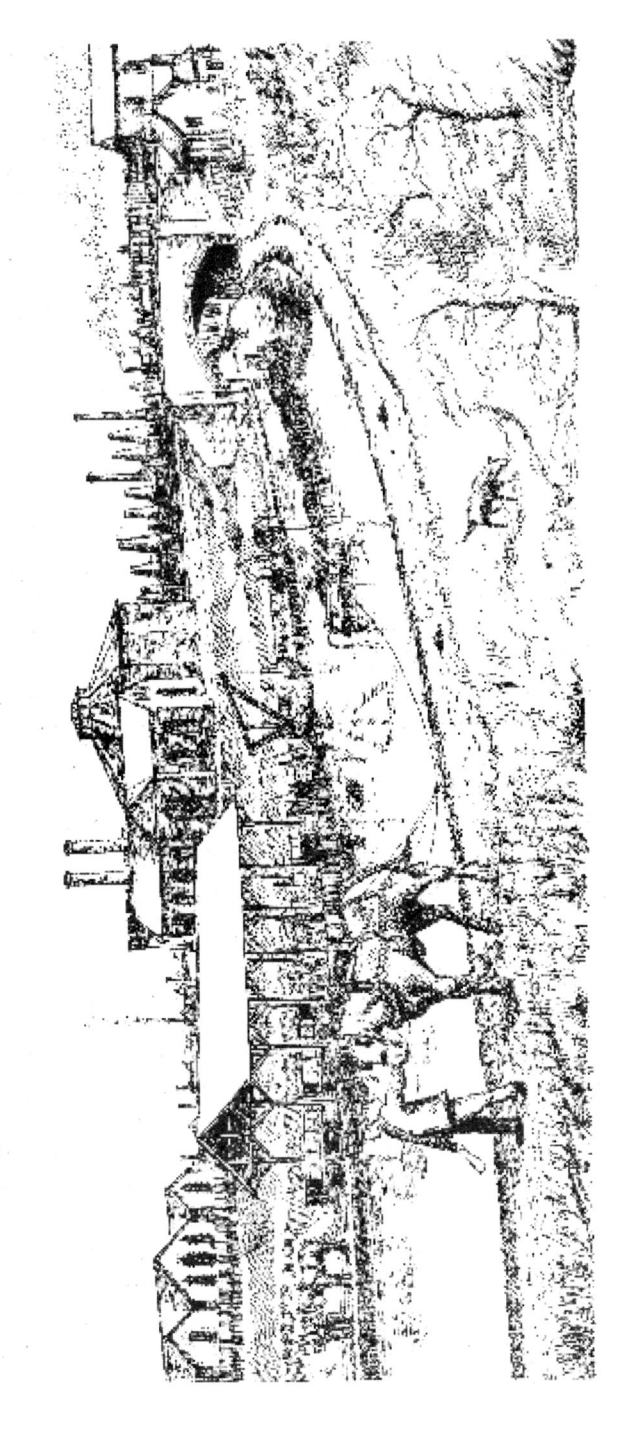

Curzon Street (London and Birmingham Railway) was the first railway interchange in the Midlands. The view above is an artist impression based on Ackerman's lithograph of Birmingham prepared in 1845. A Pickford's boat is depicted passing the covered L&B wharf. Behind the wharf is the L&B station (left) and the L&B engine shed (centre)

Edward Paget-Tomlinson

carts and boats and in-town receiving premises. Pickfords had all these so they became LNWR agents in that year. As such, they performed boatage services for that company until 1901[1].

Both the L&B and GJR wharves were small, being able to accommodate only one boat at a time. The L&B wharf was provided with a covered landing in 1845 but this had to be taken down and the tracks removed when the railway was extended to New Street in the following year. Thereafter, all transhipment took place at the small GJR wharf which had no shed in 1846, but had acquired one by 1852, when it was superseded by the opening of Monument Lane Basin on the Wolverhampton to Birmingham Stour Valley line.

The site of the GJR basin can still be seen alongside the bottom lock of the Ashted flight although the shed has long since gone and the railway land alongside has been raised well above its original level.

───────◆───────

On 30 June 1843, the BCN Minutes record "On the opening of the Bentley Canal, Shipton's put on a daily service between Walsall and Wolverhampton via the Bentley Canal for conveying loads formerly taken by the Railway Co's wagons[2]."

The "Railway Co." can only have been the GJR but where could this traffic have been transferred between boat and rail? Could it perhaps have been carted between the canal and Heath Town Station? Like the "shed for transhipping iron" (page 2), brought into use in February of the same year and with which there may be a connection, the details of this traffic transfer between the canal and the GJR remain, for the time being at least, a mystery.

───────◆───────

The Birmingham & Derby Junction Railway (B&DJR) was opened to traffic on 12 August 1839. It became part of the Midland Railway (MR) on 10 May 1844 and gave the mineral wealth of Derbyshire access to the Birmingham district. This line was unable to make a connection with the canal system at the Birmingham end until the construction of the Birmingham & Warwick Junction Canal (B&WJC), opened on 2 February 1844, after which Saltley Wharf (known to boatmen as Saltley Sidings) was built.

The B&WJC provided a new link between the BCN at Salford Bridge and the Warwick & Birmingham Canal at the bottom of Camp Hill Locks. Traffic originating on this waterway could easily reach the centre of Birmingham as well as industrial heart of Black Country via the newly completed Tame Valley Canal.

Saltley Wharf extended for 200 yards to the south of Aston Church Road Bridge. It was well sited to supply railborne coal to the numerous canalside factories in the district.

◆

On 18 August 1845, the GJR entered into an agreement with the Birmingham Coal Co. who had a basin on the Walsall Level of the BCN at Bughole Bridge, Darlaston. The agreement proposed the construction of a second basin separated from the existing one by a wharf 70 yards long, "so that there may be a basin on each side of the wharf for the use of the Birmingham Coal Co and the GJR, the GJR to have preference of use". The GJR was to pay ½d per ton on goods to and from the wharf[3].

The wharf was made, but not, apparently, the second basin. A 300 yard long siding connected the wharf and basin to the main line. A goods shed spanned the original basin and a siding.

Darlaston was located on the Walsall Level of the BCN, giving lock-free access from Walsall, via Darlaston and Wednesbury, to Great Bridge. Walsall Locks had opened in 1841, giving access to the Bloxwich iron district and Bentley Locks provided a short route to Wolverhampton. Direct access to Bilston still awaited the construction of Bradley Locks (1849) but boats could reach Tipton and the Dudley Tunnel via the Tipton Green & Toll End Communication and Oldbury, Smethwick and Upper Birmingham via Riders Green Locks.

For the next five years, Darlaston was to be the only Railway Basin in the Iron District and could, therefore, have been expected to feed the railway from a wide area. Little is known about its traffic in its early years but it is recorded as dealing with iron ore inwards in 1855 and could be expected to be handling mainly the products and raw materials of the local iron works by that time.. The opening of the Stour Valley line to goods in 1852, enabling interchanges to be built on the Wolverhampton and Birmingham Levels of the BCN, left Darlaston with little more than the Walsall Level for a catchment area, on which it was soon to be in competition with basins at Great Bridge (South Staffordshire Rly.) and Wednesbury (GWR).

FOOTNOTES

1. Turnbull G. TRAFFIC AND TRANSPORT Allen & Unwin 1979
2. BCN Minute Book, 30 June 1843 PRO RAIL 810
3. GJR Darlaston Basin Agreement PRO RAIL 220/17
4. SSR Minutes PRO RAIL 638/2

CANAL & RAILWAYS
CENTRAL BIRMINGHAM (1844-1854)

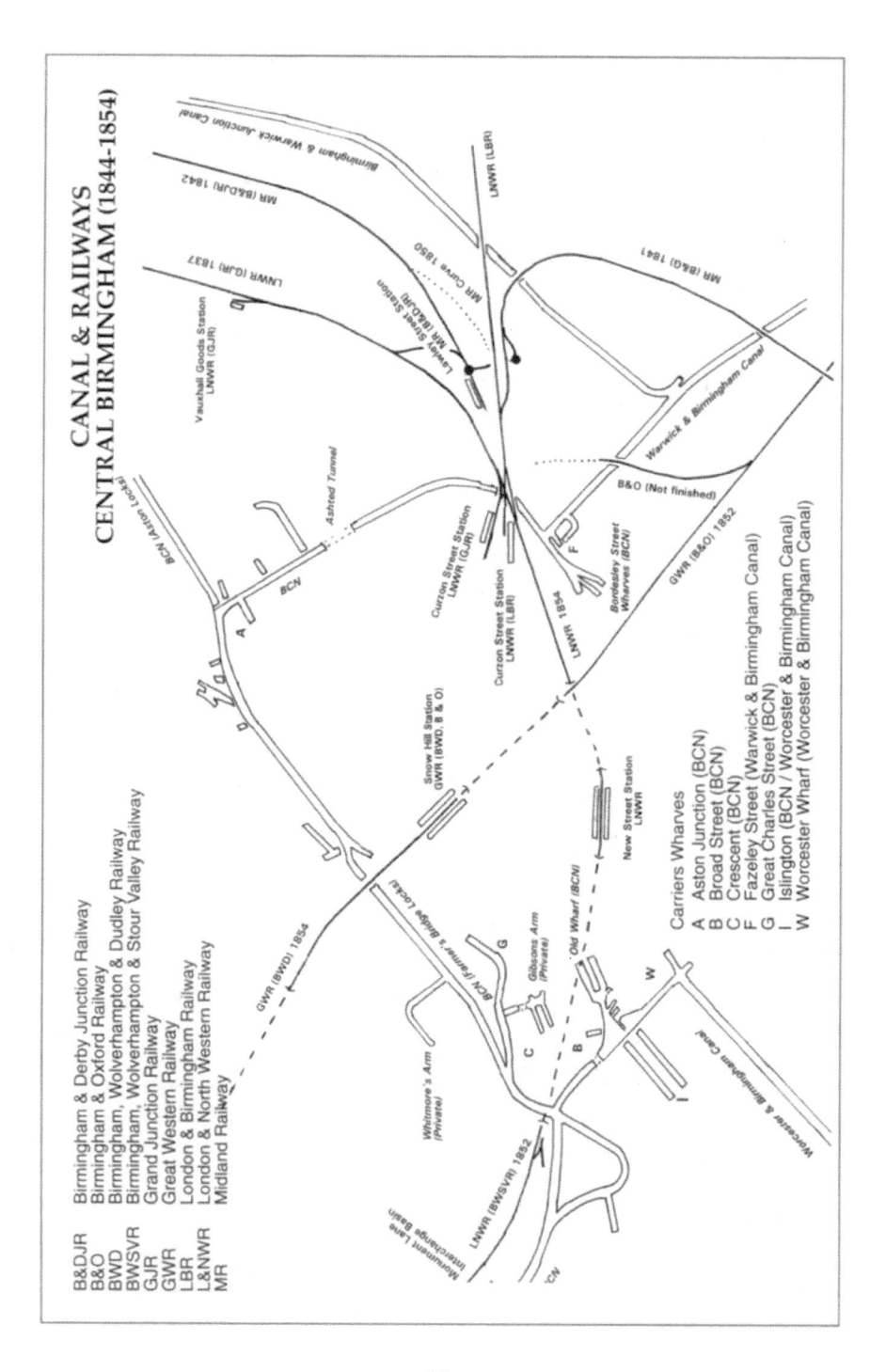

B&DJR   Birmingham & Derby Junction Railway
B&O   Birmingham & Oxford Railway
BWD   Birmingham, Wolverhampton & Dudley Railway
BWSVR   Birmingham, Wolverhampton & Stour Valley Railway
GJR   Grand Junction Railway
GWR   Great Western Railway
LBR   London & Birmingham Railway
L&NWR   London & North Western Railway
MR   Midland Railway

Carriers Wharves
A   Aston Junction (BCN)
B   Broad Street (BCN)
C   Crescent (BCN)
F   Fazeley Street (Warwick & Birmingham Canal)
G   Great Charles Street (BCN)
I   Islington (BCN / Worcester & Birmingham Canal)
W   Worcester Wharf (Worcester & Birmingham Canal)

WOLVERHAMPTON RAILWAYS AND CANALS 1849-1855

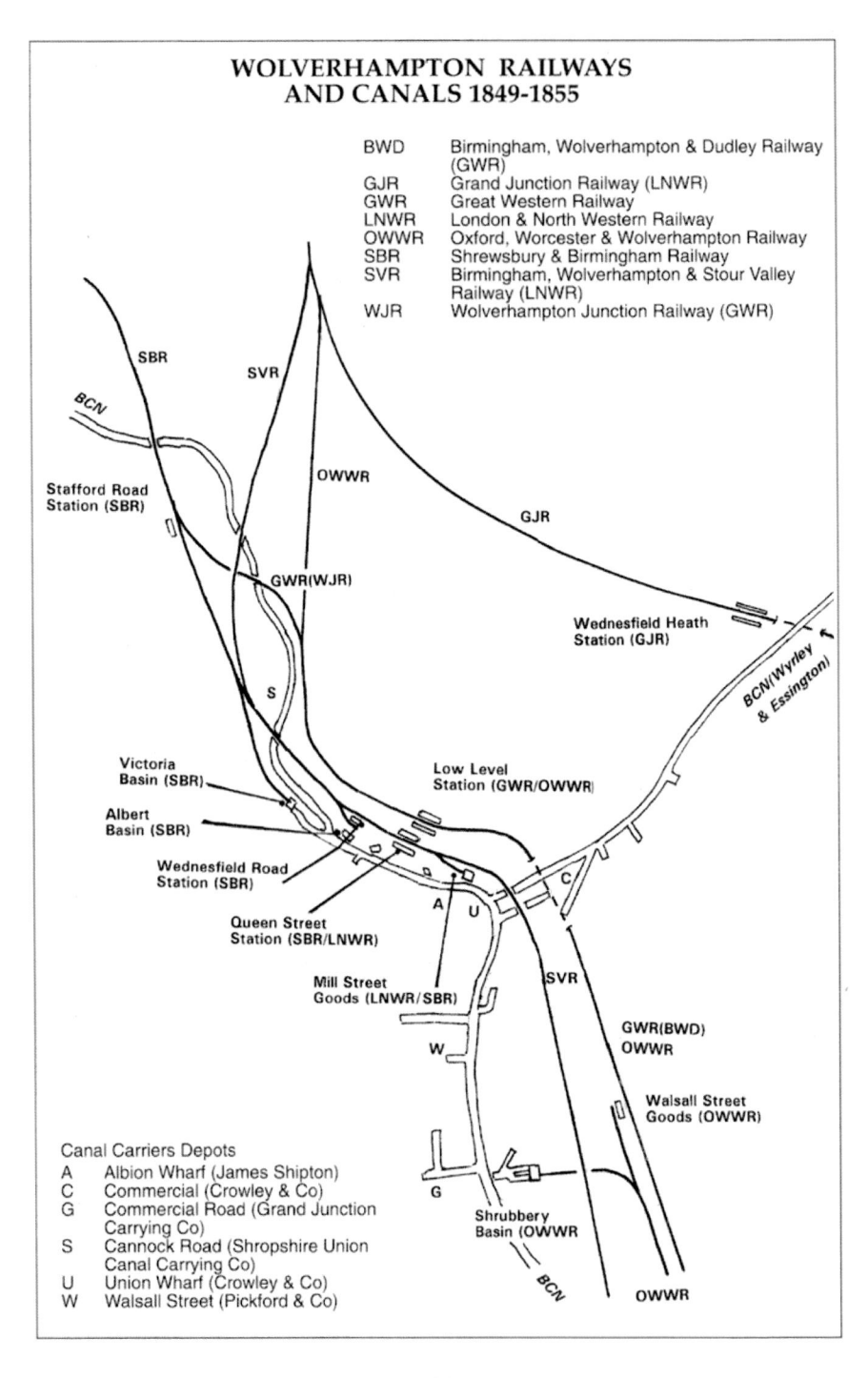

BWD — Birmingham, Wolverhampton & Dudley Railway (GWR)
GJR — Grand Junction Railway (LNWR)
GWR — Great Western Railway
LNWR — London & North Western Railway
OWWR — Oxford, Worcester & Wolverhampton Railway
SBR — Shrewsbury & Birmingham Railway
SVR — Birmingham, Wolverhampton & Stour Valley Railway (LNWR)
WJR — Wolverhampton Junction Railway (GWR)

Canal Carriers Depots
A Albion Wharf (James Shipton)
C Commercial (Crowley & Co)
G Commercial Road (Grand Junction Carrying Co)
S Cannock Road (Shropshire Union Canal Carrying Co)
U Union Wharf (Crowley & Co)
W Walsall Street (Pickford & Co)

The above reproduction of a lithograph of Darlaston Green Furnaces produced in 1872 shows a Crowley boat alongside the wharf

CHAPTER 3

THE 1850s — A TIME OF EXPANSION

The South Staffordshire Railway (SSR), whose line from Wichnor Junction to Dudley was completed in 1850, was aware of the desirability of connections with the canals and was actively planning these during the course of construction. The Coventry Canal was invited to construct a wharf at the point where the railway approaches the canal at Brook Hay but there is no record of this having been done. Connection with the BCN was first envisaged at Walsall by means of a tramway from the station. In January 1849 the Traffic Committee recommended formation of two junctions with the BCN, at Brownhills and Walsall. Brownhills Basin was eventually to be built but the Walsall scheme was abandoned in June of that year, the Engineer being directed..." to submit an estimate of a sufficient Goods Station at Great Bridge in connection with the Birmingham Canal there."

The line from Great Bridge to Dudley was reported complete on 4 August 1849, and Great Bridge Basin was opened on 1 March 1850[1]. The facilities appear to have been too small for the traffic, as three months later tenders were being sought "for the construction of a wharf and basin at the Great Bridge Station". Messrs Hoof and Hill's tender of £2367-17s-9d for this work was accepted on the 11 July, work to proceed forthwith. The "iron shed over the canal at Great Bridge Station" was constructed by Mr F. Morton and payment of £506 was authorised on 11 July 1850.

It is possible that the SSR had some temporary arrangements for transhipping goods from and to the canal before the opening of Great Bridge basin as payments to two canal carriers, Price and Pickfords were recorded as early as 17 January 1849. Although these unspecified payments could have been in respect of construction materials both these carriers were involved in boatage work for the SSR.

The land used for the construction of Great Bridge Basin had formerly been owned by the Eagle Furnace Company, whose furnaces were demolished to make way for the new railway. The name has, however, survived in the street name, Eagle Lane, and the signalbox there was called Eagle Crossing.

In November 1858, agreement was reached between the SSR and John Jones of Ruckley, Salop to rent land near Bloxwich Mill at a point where the canal had been diverted to cross the railway. The company was empowered to construct wharves, canal basins, railways, tramroads, cranes, warehouses etc. The lease ran until 1879 but there is no record of any transhipment facilities having been built here[2].

Brownhills Basin was completed in March 1856. The Wolverhampton Chronicle published the following advertisement announcing its opening:

> SOUTH STAFFORDSHIRE RAILWAY.
> BROWNHILLS CANAL BASINS.
>
> THE Public are respectfully informed that the CANAL BASINS at BROWNHILLS STATION are now completed, and ready for exchange of Mineral and other Traffic to and from the Railway. The Basins will be found very convenient for the Furnaces at Pelsall, Birchalls, and other Works in the neighbourhood of Walsall.
>
> For rates and further information apply to JOHN N. BROWN, General Manager.
>
> Walsall, March 10, 1856.

Brownhills Basin was situated near Brownhills Station, but the original intention had been to make a connection with the canal at nearby Pelsall. The earliest reference to the latter was in August 1853. A basin at Pelsall would have served the needs of Bloomer & Davis, proprietors of the Pelsall Ironworks. Evidently the new Brownhills Basin intended to do the same.

The SSR list of Canal Basins was completed when Churchbridge Basin was opened, the Staffordshire & Worcestershire Canal contributing to the cost.

◆

On 12 November 1849 the Shrewsbury & Birmingham Railway (SBR) was opened to Wolverhampton. This line, part of a through route from the Mersey, was intended to reach Birmingham over the Stour Valley Railway (SVR) which closely parallels the main line of the BCN who owned much of the land needed for its construction.

The Stour Valley was to have been financed jointly by the SBR, L&B and BCN. There were, however, several changes to this arrangement before work began. The chief alteration was the involvement of the LNWR. The L&B was merged into the LNWR in 1846 and the L&B / BCN Arrangement Act of 1846 also gave the LNWR influence over BCN affairs. In 1847, the Stour Valley obtained authority to lease or sell its line to the LNWR.

The LNWR, which wanted to prevent the SBR reaching Birmingham, used its influence to delay the construction of the Stour Valley line and did not take a formal lease of it until 1 January 1850. The Wolverhampton station was joint property of the SBR and SVR. Although SBR trains could reach the Joint Station they were denied access to the track beyond the joint property.

As far as goods traffic was concerned, the S&B hoped to overcome this problem by transferring its goods to the BCN at a point on the joint section of the line. This was the Albert (or Hay) Basin, specially excavated by the BCN for the purpose. In April 1850, they attempted to lay a siding to it whereupon their men were forcibly prevented by their late Engineer, William Baker, who now worked for the Stour Valley, on the plea that the plan had not been sanctioned by the Wolverhampton Joint Station Committee.

The Committee met on 7 May and referred the plan to the Engineers of the two companies. As no representative of the Stour Valley appeared at this meeting, no business could, according to the Committee's bye-laws, be done.

Unable to construct the siding, the SBR attempted to transfer minerals from wagons using barrows wheeled down planks only to be stopped by the SVR contractor's navvies. On the following day a battle between several hundred navvies employed by the two companies took place, those of the SVR under the command of Baker, accompanied, in the rear, by the LNWR lawyer. The Mayor of Wolverhampton called out the Military (with fixed bayonets) and read the Riot Act[3].

An injunction from the Court of Chancery put a stop to the illegal violence and, under its protection, the SBR made the siding. Due to its cramped site, between the Wednesfield Road Bridge and the top lock of the Wolverhampton flight, Albert Basin was small and could not be extended and the arrangements meant that goods and mineral traffic could only be carried on with difficulty. The SBR then decided to build a larger basin on their own land on the opposite side of the canal. The contract was signed on 8 August 1850 and, in the grandiloquent style of the time, it was dignified by the name of Victoria Basin. Payment of £4,200 to the contractor was authorised on 7 March 1851, so it is probable that work had been completed by then. The basin was later enlarged, water being let into the extension on 5 March 1853. On completion, the basin was over 1,000 yards long with a maximum width of 40 feet. Four of the lines on the East side were serviced by a travelling crane which also went over the canal. A smaller basin was made alongside the second lock and chutes were provided for the easier transhipment of minerals from wagons to boats below the second lock[4].

The later history of Albert Basin is somewhat obscure. In March 1852, Richard Smith, agent for Lord Dudley & Ward, attempted to lease it for the transfer of red iron ore from the SBR on the canal. In August of that year the BCN decided it should be a public wharf, but, in 1855, it is described as an LNWR basin. In later years, the name Hay Basin was more commonly used and most maps refer to it as such. During 1878 the LNWR purchased the basin and its surrounding buildings. In 1912 it is mentioned as a Shropshire Union (SU) basin. By 1928 it was used as a coal wharf by Beebee Bros.

Before railway politics intervened, it had been intended that the SBR and SVR would have shared transhipment facilities with the canal at Wolverhampton Mill Street, the Joint Station Committee having resolved on 19 December 1849 that a communication should be made from the canal to the underpart of the Goods Warehouse. It is believed that Mill Street was completed in 1850 although it remains to be determined how much use the SBR made of it. The SBR appears to have used Mill Street chiefly as a railway goods station.

The SBR amalgamated with the Great Western Railway (GWR) in 1854 but the GWR remained partners in the Joint Station Committee until 1858, when they sold their share to the LNWR. Mill Street was used by the SBR and the GWR until 1859 when Herbert Street Goods was finished.

Mill Street had two covered arms but limited transhipment capacity, and dealt mainly with merchandise traffic. This leads me to suppose that the LNWR may have continued to use Albert Basin for mineral transhipments, at least until Monmore Green (Chillington) Basin was opened in 1902. LNWR transhipment capacity in Wolverhampton was small compared to that acquired by the GWR from the SBR and West Midland Railway (WMR).

The Stour Valley Company originally planned canal interchange basins at Soho, Tipton (above and below the locks) and Deepfields. When construction commenced these plans were altered. By September 1851, basins at Steward's Aqueduct and Monument Lane had been considered. Plans for basins at Deepfield and Soho were not proceeded with at this time[5].

Tenders were invited for the construction of sheds over the basins at Tipton (below the locks), Steward's Aqueduct and Monument Lane. Work on the other Tipton basin was delayed until the railway construction was finished[6].

The BCN had been diverted at Bloomfield to enable the railway to be constructed. The new course enabled a larger group of basins to be made there. In April 1852 the SVR announced plans for the enlarged basin for the accommodation of mineral traffic and Northamptonshire Ironstone in lieu of the one already sanctioned.

Three basins appear to have been operational when the railway opened to goods traffic in February 1852; Tipton (Watery Lane), Spon Lane (Steward's Aqueduct) and Monument Lane. They were followed shortly afterwards by Bloomfield. Albion was in use by 1863. Further canal links were made at Ettingshall (1881) and Monmore Green (1902).

Monument Lane, situated at the nearest place accessible to the canal on the Stour Valley line out of Birmingham, effectively superseded the former GJR basin at Curzon Street.

◆

West of the Dudley Ridge another railway was heading towards the Black Country. Dogged by financial difficulties, the Oxford, Worcester and Wolverhampton Railway (OWWR) desperately needed to get traffic on to its line at the earliest opportunity and by whatever means were expedient.

As soon as their line reached the Stourbridge Canal at the obscure industrial hamlet of Brettell Lane, the OWWR organised collection and delivery services on the canal. Topographical difficulties prevented laying in a canalside siding so goods had to be carted between boat and railway wagon. An early contractor was W. Walker, who also used his wharf at Stourbridge to feed the railway in a similar manner[7].

The Stourbridge Canal Company did not look kindly on the abstraction of their traffic by the railway but could not legally prevent any person or company from operating boats on their waters. The difficulties of transhipping at Brettell Lane caused the OWWR to come to an agreement with Messrs Wheeley Bros., local ironmasters and mine owners, to use their basin and crane on the opposite side of the canal to the station. The annual rent of £75 per annum included powers to erect a shed or warehouse[8].

The Stourbridge Canal Co. then sought compensation for all goods transhipped off the canal by the OWWR. The railway rejected both this claim and the suggestion that they might buy the canal and added insult to injury by offering an allowance for any traffic which the canal company would voluntarily relinquish to the railway.

Transhipment at Wheeley's Basin began on 1 June 1854 and the demand by customers seems to have exceeded capacity. In September of that year the Stourbridge Canal Company threatened to block off the basin entrance on the grounds that Wheeley's had been granted a private easement for the use of the canal which precluded them from handling any other traffic than their own. Wheeley's immediately gave notice to the OWWR to give up their tenancy and the railway company had to come to terms, offering 1d per ton on raw materials and 1½d per ton on manufactured goods transhipped at "any place situate at the Brettell Lane". It was not until 1 January 1856 that the Clerk to Stourbridge Canal gave formal assent to the agreement[9].

Brettell Lane was an unsuitable transhipment point. As soon as it could do so, on

14 November 1858, the OWWR opened a commodious transhipment depot on its own property at Bromley, served by its Kingswinford Branch and the Stourbridge Extension Canal of which it was the owner. Thereafter Brettell Lane was only used for the transhipment of minerals, which, because the railway was higher than the canal, could conveniently be tipped down chutes into boats. The chutes and their attendant sidings were adjacent to the main line railway bridge on the station side of the canal.

Bromley was always known as Bromley Basin although it was, in fact, a linear wharf. The railway there was on the same level as the canal.

In 1858 the OWWR built a 1:14 incline to the head of the Stourbridge Branch of the Stourbridge Canal and established a transhipment station there. There had been earlier efforts to tap the canal traffic via Walker's Wharf and the Stourbridge Waterworks Co. Wharf at Stourbridge, using cartage between there and the railway at Stourbridge Junction from 1852.

The OWWR transhipment basins at Shrubbery (Walsall Street, Wolverhampton) and Tipton Factory were opened in June and August 1855. Shrubbery was twice extended, in 1857 and 1862. In 1863 the OWWR, by now renamed the West Midlands Railway, became part of the GWR.

The determination of the LNWR to try to prevent any other company from using the Stour Valley Line prompted the promotion of the Birmingham, Wolverhampton & Dudley Railway between the Birmingham and Oxford Railway at Birmingham and a junction with the OWWR at Priestfield from where it would have running powers over the OWWR to Wolverhampton. In 1851, the Shrewsbury & Birmingham had entered into a traffic agreement with the GWR, to whom the BW&D was leased.

Canal basins were an early priority in view of the fact that the neighbouring SVR and SSR had already commenced interchange traffic. In August 1852 it was resolved that the basins and station accommodation for the junction with the canal at Swan Village, Wednesbury and Pothouse Bridge, Bilston to be made at once[10].

The BW&D opened on 14 November 1854, the same year in which the SBR amalgamated with the GWR. The works included transhipment basins at Hockley and Wednesbury, both in use by August 1855. They were followed in August 1856 by Swan Village.

The wharf at Pothouse Bridge was not connected to the railway but was three quarters of a mile from the BW&D's Bilston Station. It is known that, by 1855, this was being used for railway traffic. What has not come to light are the details of operation or the Railway Companies concerned.

Bantock, who by 1857, were boatage agents for the GWR and OWWR had three boats based at Swan Village in May 1860 and a further three boats at Pothouse Bridge[11].

Details of how railway traffic was operated at Pothouse Bridge have not come to light, but there are two possibilities. Goods could have been brought to and from Pothouse Bridge Wharf by canal and carted between there and Bilston Station, a system known to have been used between the BCN's Halesowen Wharf and Halesowen Station; or goods could have been brought to Pothouse Bridge by canal in traders boats, there to be stored and subsequently despatched by railway boats to a railway interchange. This latter type of operation took place at a number of wharves, e.g. Izons Wharf (West Bromwich) and might have included road cartage from works not on the canal to Pothouse Bridge for subsequent boatage. It would not have excluded use by other railway companies as Pothouse Bridge was a Public Wharf.

FOOTNOTES

1. SSR Minutes PRO RAIL 638/2
2. SSR Minutes PRO RAIL 638/12
3. S&BR Minutes PRO RAIL 615
4. Hale M. A SHORT HISTORY OF VICTORIA BASIN Dudley Canal Trust Bulletin March 1987
5. SVR Minutes PRO RAIL 45/2, 2 September 1851
6. SVR Minutes PRO RAIL 45/2
7. OWWR Traffic Commmittee Minutes, 23 April 1853 PRO RAIL 558/12
8. OWWR Traffic Committee Minutes, 22 October 1853 PRO RAIL 558/12 (ex 6)
9. Stourbridge Canal Minutes PRO RAIL 874/14 (ex 7)
10. BWD Minutes, 13 August 1852 PRO RAIL 44/4
11. GWR Agreements PRO RAIL 252/25 (ex 8)

BLOOMFIELD.
(TELEPHONE No. 30, TIPTON.)

The **London and North Western Railway Company** have accommodation for dealing with Goods and Mineral Traffic.

COLLECTION AND DELIVERY.

The extensive Wharves (covered and uncovered) of the Company in connection with the Birmingham Canal are conveniently arranged for transferring Traffic to and from Boats; and the Agents of the Company (the Shropshire Union Railways and Canal Company) collect and deliver by Boat from and to works in Bilston, Bradley, Bloomfield, Dudley Port, Princes End, Tipton, Tividale, Wednesbury Oak, and neighbourhood.

Communications respecting Goods or Mineral Traffic should be addressed to—

Mr. A. V. IFE, *Goods Agent*

LONDON AND NORTH WESTERN RAILWAY,

TIPTON.

TELEGRAMS: "IFE, NORTHWESTERN, TIPTON."

Traffic should be addressed—
"Per **LONDON AND NORTH WESTERN RAILWAY.**"

SPON LANE

FOR

WEST BROMWICH AND WEST SMETHWICK.

Telephones—
SPON LANE STATION No. 43, WEST BROMWICH.
SPON LANE BASIN No. 95, OLDBURY.

The **LONDON AND NORTH WESTERN RAILWAY COMPANY** have accommodation for dealing with Goods, Minerals, and Live Stock, and have extensive Warehouses for the storage of Grain and other Traffic.

Furniture Vans can also be dealt with.

A Crane, capable of lifting 10 tons, is provided for dealing with heavy weights.

COLLECTION AND DELIVERY.

The Company have a Cartage establishment for the Collection and Delivery of Goods and Parcel Traffic in West Bromwich, West Smethwick, and Spon Lane.

CANAL TRAFFIC.

The Company's Wharf, in connection with the Birmingham Canal, is conveniently arranged for transferring Traffic to and from Boats; and the Agents of the Company (the Shropshire Union Railways and Canal Company) collect and deliver Traffic by Boat from and to works in Spon Lane, Langley, Oldbury, Soho, and Smethwick Districts.

Communications respecting Goods Traffic should be addressed to—

Mr. E. TURNER, *Goods Agent*,

LONDON AND NORTH WESTERN RAILWAY,

SPON LANE, WEST SMETHWICK.

Telegrams; "*NORTHWESTERN, WEST SMETHWICK.*"

Traffic should be addressed—

"**Per LONDON AND NORTH WESTERN RAILWAY.**"

TIPTON.

(Telephone No. 30 Tipton.)

The **LONDON AND NORTH WESTERN RAILWAY COMPANY** have accommodation for dealing with Goods, Mineral, and Live Stock Traffic, and have a large Warehouse for the storage of Grain and other Goods.

Furniture Vans can also be dealt with.

A Crane is provided capable of lifting 10 tons, and will be found convenient for dealing with Boilers and other heavy articles.

COLLECTION AND DELIVERY.

The Company have a Cartage establishment for the Collection and Delivery of Goods and Parcel Traffic.

CANAL TRAFFIC.

The Company's Covered Wharf, in connection with the Birmingham Canal, is conveniently arranged for transferring Traffic to and from Boats; and the Agents of the Company (the Shropshire Union Railways and Canal Company) collect and deliver from and to firms in the neighbourhood.

Arrangements also exist for the Boatage of Traffic between Tipton and Works upon the Canal in the following districts:—

Brettell Lane	Cradley	Rowley
Brierley Hill	Lye	Stourbridge
Brockmoor	Netherton	Withymoor
Bromley	Old Hill	Woodside

Communications respecting Goods, Mineral, and Live Stock Traffic should be addressed to—

Mr. A. V. IFE, *Goods Agent,*
LONDON AND NORTH WESTERN RAILWAY,
TIPTON.

TELEGRAMS—"IFE, NORTHWESTERN, TIPTON."

Traffic should be addressed—

"Per LONDON AND NORTH WESTERN RAILWAY."

CHAPTER 4

TRAFFIC AND OPERATION

The opening of Stourbridge and Churchbridge basins in 1860 brought to an end the main period of railway interchange construction. Birmingham and the Black Country was, by now, well covered, with the exception of the line of the Dudley Canal from Brierley Hill through Netherton, Old Hill and Halesowen to Selly Oak, which lacked any railway/canal transhipment facilities. The Midland Railway was disadvantaged by the location of its only interchange at Saltley Wharf on the fringe of the area.

The railway companies did not attempt to operate canal feeder services themselves, although some of them built boats for rent to their contractors. They relied on the stock and expertise of existing canal carriers who, finding themselves under severe competition from the railways on their long distance services, were glad to find a use for their equipment by providing boatage and cartage.

As we have seen, Pickford became cartage and boatage agents for the LNWR as early as 1847. Geo. Price of Great Bridge was receiving payments from the SSR in Jan 1849 and, although he signed a contract with the SBR for boatage to and from Victoria Basin in 1852, he was still receiving payments from the SSR in April 1854[1]. Like Geo. Price, Pickford had been in receipt of payments from the SSR in Jan 1849 and Pickford entered into a five year agreement to provide boatage services for the SSR to run from 1 June 1852, with boats running as far as Wolverhampton, Birmingham and beyond the Dudley Tunnel. Who performed the boatage in the early years of Darlaston (GJR) Basin is not known but it is likely that, after 1847, Pickfords would have been involved there, as they would have been when the LNWR Stour Valley basins opened after 1852. They were also, at this time, agents for the OWWR and Midland Railways.

The LNWR had another major boatage agent, Crowley. This business started as long distance canal carriers under the name of Crowley, Hicklin & Co. They became agents for the LNWR on 12 August 1847, disposing of their London stock to the Grand Junction Canal Co. from the beginning of 1849.

Crowley retained their regular canal service between Wolverhampton (Union Wharf), Kidderminster and Stourport. They were still operating this service in 1861[2] but, by 1864, they had integrated it with their railway boatage, the boats then running to and from Wolverhampton Mill Street Basin. Crowley were also agents for the OWWR and Midland Railways.

BOATAGE RATES ON UNDAMAGEABLE IRON - May 1852	
FROM GREAT BRIDGE (SSR): Pickford & Co.	
Wednesbury, Moxley & Darlaston	1/-
Bromford, Oldbury & Tipton	2/-
Bloomfield, Wednesfield	2/3
Wolverhampton, Birmingham	2/6
South of Dudley Tunnel	2/6
PRO RAIL 201 / 66	
FROM VICTORIA BASIN (SBR): Geo. Price.	
Bilston	1/6
Tipton	2/-
West Bromwich & Bromford	2/-
Muntz & Co.	2/6
Birmingham	3/6
Dudley Canal	2/9
Stourbridge Canal	3/6
Works on Staffs. & Worcs. Canal and to Kidderminster Whf	3/6 3
PRO RAIL 252 / 22	

Unable, because of its quarrel with the LNWR, to reach Birmingham and London via the Stour Valley line, the Shrewsbury & Birmingham sought to link up with the GWR whose line had reached Banbury. To this end they approached Shipton, an old established canal carrier based at Wolverhampton, to carry for them between Wolverhampton and Banbury and to act as collection agents in South Staffs. Shipton undertook the Banbury traffic but were precluded from performing the other function by an existing (1849) agreement with the Bridgewater Trustees by which they had become solicitors of traffic for the Trustees, having relinquished to them their heavy trade to Lancashire.

Thus it was that the Bridgewater Trustees were invited to carry out the South Staffs. boatage for the SBR, the terms being embodied in an agreement dated 15 May 1852. The railway was to provide wharves, warehouses and accommodation at Wolverhampton and Birmingham and at all intermediate places. In Birmingham, the SBR had a wharf at the Crescent[3].

At the same time, another boatage agreement to and from Victoria Basin was concluded with Geo. Price. This covered a wide area, extending to Birmingham, onto the Dudley and Stourbridge Canals and to Kidderminster.

The SBR signed another agreement in May 1852, this time with Edmund Lloyd Owen, a merchant of Bilston. Owen agreed to put 50,000 tons per annum for two years, of limestone, lime and ironstone in his own wagons on the Minera (Flintshire) Branch of the Shrewsbury & Chester Rly. for unloading to boats at Victoria Basin; and to use his influence to procure manufactured iron and other articles from the South Staffs. district for back loading.

Trade at Victoria Basin included the transfer of the light trade between Lancashire, South Staffs. and Birmingham from the Bridgewater Trustees to the railway. The Trustees withdrew their Preston Brook flyboats but put on a flyboat service between Victoria Basin and Birmingham. They were still engaged in the heavy trade to and from Lancashire and it was left to traders to choose between canal and rail. However, the iron industry had a boom period in the second half of 1852 and most of 1853 and the Trustees had to divert some of their iron trade to the SBR due to a shortage of boats.

The arrangement between the Bridgewater Trustees and the SBR was not long to survive amalgamation of the SBR and GWR in 1854. The Trustees had had an earlier (January 1853) arrangement with the GWR to collect and deliver goods in Birmingham, and a temporary transhipment station was made on the BCN near to the GWR goods station at Upper Trinity Street. The location is not known but the nearest point on the BCN would have been at Bordesley Street Basin. The Warwick & Birmingham Canal was, of course, closer to the GWR line.

This was followed by a more extensive and more binding agreement (30 April 1853) which incorporated the May 1852 agreement with the SBR. Under the terms of this, the Bridgewater was to be granted agency rights in return for suppressing the London trade of their agent, Shipton. The agreement never worked as planned, partly because the GWR had insufficient control over the" Shrewsburies" but also because the GWR looked askance at the Trustees' continuing interest in the Trent & Mersey route to South Staffs. As soon as they had made a direct railway link with the SBR (14 November 1854) the railway directors hastened to displace the Trustees from their terminal services in the Black Country, followed by those in Birmingham, offering to buy such of the Trustees stock as they wished to dispose of. Specifically, the GWR complained of the inefficient service and high charges of the Trustees and alleged that Birmingham traffic to the North which the Contract had allocated to the Railway was being diverted to the Trustees' boats, their flyboat service to the North having been reinstated. The Trustees countered with their own interpretation of the Contract and blamed the lack of facilities at Trinity Street for their alleged inefficiencies. Stevens, the GWR manager at Birmingham had written to Paddington proposing either the construction of a goods station at Hockley or sending all the Northern goods by Geo. Price. He clearly recognised that Trinity Street was not an ideal site for the GWR's main Birmingham goods depot when so much traffic relied on boatage[4].

An acrimonious correspondence about payments collected on behalf of the railway allegedly owed by the Trustees continued into 1857. Prior to this, the Trustees had been despatching their South Staffs. traffic to London by the GWR, but they immediately transferred it to the LNWR and entered into another agreement with the OWWR (then allied to the LNWR) to provide terminal services at all stations north of Droitwich. This arrangement enabled them to conduct a traffic by rail to London without stipulations regarding their canal traffic to and from Lancashire and enabled them to find a use for their boatage stock[5].

To sum up the Bridgewater's boatage activities, they provided services from Victoria Basin from 1851 to 1854/55 and from Shrubbery, Tipton Factory and Brettell Lane from 1855.

━━━━━◆━━━━━

The employee of the Bridgewater Trustees most concerned with their South Staffordshire boatage activities was Thomas Bantock. Born in Sutherland on 4 October 1823, he entered the Trustees' service in 1839 at the age of 16. In 1849 he was selected to go to Wolverhampton to look after the interests of the Trustees against the railways. Between 1854 and 1856 he represented the Bridgewater interest in a series of meetings known as the Northern Alliance Agreements which were largely concerned with boatage matters.

In this capacity he would have had the opportunity of close contacts with the OWWR and GWR representatives and this led to his being appointed Boatage and Cartage Agent to the GWR in 1857.

Puzzlingly, although William Boddington is listed as the Trustees' South Staffordshire agent in 1860, Thomas Bantock appears again and for the last time as an agent for the Trustees in 1861.

By May 1860, Bantock owned 51 boats based at eight GWR and OWWR basins and at Stourport and Pothouse Bridge[6]. This may not have been the full extent of the vessels under his control as the OWWR had built some boats in 1855 which he may have operated. The stock arrangements of some of the railway companies and their Boatage Agents were complicated, boats being bought, sold, rented or leased between the parties concerned. For instance, Bantock hired 15 boats from the GWR on 2 March 1868 and the boats of the combined fleet bore one series of numbers.

Boatage for the OWWR was also provided by Crowley and Pickford up to 1863.

LIST OF BOATS HIRED BY THE GWR TO THOMAS BANTOCK:
March 2nd 1868

NAME OF BOAT

Paddington & Wolverhampton
Birmingham
Arthur
Shrewsbury
Bristol
Basingstoke
Leamington
Albert
Saltney
Reading
Liverpool
Alberta
Wolverhampton
Oxford
Banbury

Rent £10 per month. Agent to repair and maintain. Company's name to be painted on each boat.

PRO RAIL 252 /25

During the early years of railway boatage, the Midland Railway (MR) was disadvantaged by having only one transhipment facility. Saltley Wharf was inconveniently located on the eastern outskirts of Birmingham, a five hour canal

ALLOCATION OF BOATS BELONGING TO THOMAS BANTOCK: May 1st 1860	
Stourport	3
Stourbridge	5
Bromley	5
Tipton	7
Pothouse Br.	3
Victoria	4
Shrubbery	7
Wednesbury	6
Swan Village	3
Hockley	8
Total	<u>51</u>

PRO RAIL 252/24

journey via the Tame Valley Canal to the nearest part of the iron district around Wednesbury. Nevertheless, by 1855 the MR was a competitor in the Cumberland iron ore and pig iron traffic to the Black Country and also brought Derbyshire pig iron and limestone into the area.

Throughout the 1850s and early 1860s, both Crowley and Pickford were agents for the MR. The policy of the company thereafter was to operate its own cartage and boatage services.

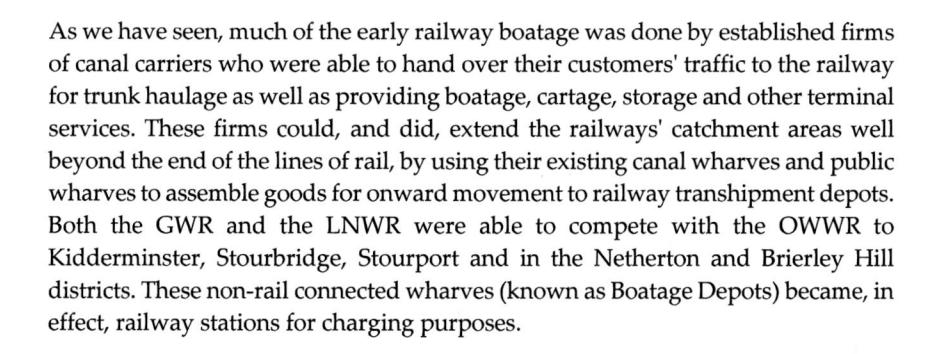

◆

As we have seen, much of the early railway boatage was done by established firms of canal carriers who were able to hand over their customers' traffic to the railway for trunk haulage as well as providing boatage, cartage, storage and other terminal services. These firms could, and did, extend the railways' catchment areas well beyond the end of the lines of rail, by using their existing canal wharves and public wharves to assemble goods for onward movement to railway transhipment depots. Both the GWR and the LNWR were able to compete with the OWWR to Kidderminster, Stourbridge, Stourport and in the Netherton and Brierley Hill districts. These non-rail connected wharves (known as Boatage Depots) became, in effect, railway stations for charging purposes.

There were two main types of rates for railway traffic, "Station to Station" and "Collected and Delivered" (C&D). If a trader, such as an ironmaster, brought or collected goods to or from a transhipment depot or a recognised Boatage Depot, he was allowed a rebate on the C&D rate which was known as a Boatage Allowance. The railway companies and the principal long distance canal carriers sought to control competition by means of various agreements between themselves but it was possible for a company to circumvent these by manipulating Boatage Allowances.

BOATAGE TABLES C&D TRAFFIC

BOATAGE OR CARTAGE ALLOWANCES—FOURTH IRON DISTRICT—*continued.*

NAME OF FIRM	NAME OF WORKS	DESCRIPTION	RESIDENCE	Bloomfield, Tipton, and Factory Basins	Bromley Basin and Nine Locks Bottom Wharf	Stourbridge Basin and Wharf	Wallows Wharf and Nine Locks Top Wharf	Bishton's and Primrose Wharves	Withymoor Wharf	Great Bridge Basin
				s. d.	s. d.	s. d.	s. d.	s. d.	s. d.	s. d.
Cookson, E., and Son	Audnam	Foundry	Stourbridge			0 6				
Cresswell, F.	Dixon's Green	Forge	Netherton	1 5				0 6	0 6	1 11
Dawes, W. H.	Withymoor	Furnaces	Netherton	1 4				0 6	0 6	1 11
Dudley, Earl of	Round Oak	Furnaces and Forge	Brierley Hill				0 6	0 11		
Evers and Martin	Park Head	Furnaces	Netherton				0 6	1 0	1 0	
Firmstone, W. and G.	The Leys	Furnaces	Brierley Hill		0 6					
Firmstone, C. E.	Leys	Foundry	Brettel Lane		0 6					
Firmstone, E.		Forge	Stourbridge			0 6				
Grazebrook, M. and W.	Netherton	Furnaces	Netherton	1 3			0 6	0 10	0 11	1 11
Hall, Henry	Old Level	Forge	Brierley Hill					1 0	1 1	
Hartshorne, G., and Co.	Primrose Hill	Chains, &c.	Netherton	1 8				0 6		2 2
Hill and Smith	Hart's Hill	Forge, &c.	Brierley Hill				0 6			

N.B.—For Allowances to Iron Merchants, see clauses 5 and 6, page 25.

BOATAGE OR CARTAGE ALLOWANCES—FOURTH IRON DISTRICT—*continued.*

NAME OF FIRM	NAME OF WORKS	DESCRIPTION	RESIDENCE	Bloomfield, Tipton, and Factory Basins	Bromley Basin and Nine Locks Bottom Wharf	Stourbridge Basin and Wharf	Wallows Wharf and Nine Locks Top Wharf	Bishton's and Primrose Wharves	Withymoor Wharf	Waterfall Lane Wharf	Great Bridge Basin
				s. d.	s. d.	s. d.	s. d.	s. d.	s. d.	s. d.	s. d.
Hingley, N., and Son	Netherton	Forge	Netherton	1 8				0 6	0 6		2 2
Hingley, N., and Son	Old Hill	Furnaces	Old Hill	1 8				0 10	0 9	0 6	2 2
Hingley, N., and Son	Netherton	Furnaces	Netherton	1 8				0 6	0 6		2 2
Hingleys and Smith	Hart's Hill	Forge	Brierley Hill				0 9				
Holcroft, James	Old Level	Furnaces	Brierley Hill					1 0	1 0		
Howard, H., and Co.	Coombs Wood	Tubes	Old Hill	2 0				1 1	1 0	0 6	2 5
Jones, John, and Sons	Dixon's Green	Furnaces	Netherton	1 6				0 7			1 11
Jones, T. P.	Powke Lane	Chains, &c.	Rowley	1 8						0 6	2 2
Lewis, S.	Withymoor	Chains, &c.	Netherton	1 7				0 6	0 6		1 11
Matthews, W.	Corbyns Hall	Furnaces	Brierley Hill			1 0					
Mountford and Homer	Marine	Chains and Anchors	Netherton	1 9				0 6	0 7		2 3
Norris, A., and Son	Woolaston	Forge	Stourbridge			0 6					

N.B.—For Allowances to Iron Merchants, see clauses 5 and 6, page 25.

To prevent this, Boatage Allowances came to be included in rates agreements. The Northern Alliance Conferences of 1854/1856 reveal a great deal of information about railway boatage at that time. The GWR, LNWR, SSR, MR, Shropshire Union and Bridgewater Trustees took part in all or some of these meetings.

If boats were detained after 24 hours, demurrage of 10s per boat per day was to be charged. Boatage Allowances (on Iron Rates) varied from 1s 3d per ton for local movements to 3s per ton for traffic between the Staffs. & Worcs. and Stourbridge Canals and Wolverhampton.

The Conference also sought to establish the prime cost of boatage, which varied from 7d per ton for one mile and under to 10d per ton for over four miles plus 3d per ton if passing Dudley Tunnel. The prime cost for the longer distance hauls to and from the iron works on the Staffordshire and Worcestershire Canal and Stourbridge Canals varied from 1s to Victoria and Shrubbery (Wolverhampton) to 1s 9d to Hockley or Monument Lane (Birmingham).

The list of "stations" to which Boatage Allowances applied (whether rail connected or not, they were given the generic term "Railway Basins") does not include Pothouse Bridge Wharf but includes Deepfields, where Crowley had a depot. Interestingly, an application by the MR to have Saltley classed as a Railway Basin (for Boatage Allowance purposes) was rejected, no reason being given[7].

―――――◆―――――

The operation of transhipment from rail to canal was not without its difficulties as we have seen at Brettell Lane, although the height of the railway above the canal at that point was taken advantage of to construct chutes for loading boats with minerals. The optimum requirement of a spacious and level site could not always be met. Wolverhampton (Mill Street) and Tipton (Watery Lane) suffered from awkward layouts and lack of space, and Monument Lane could only be accessed by wagon turntables. At Hockley, the canal was higher than the railway and hydraulic (later electric) wagon lifts were necessary to reach the basin.

At Great Bridge (SSR) the sidings were laid on falling gradients and wagons frequently demolished the stop blocks and went into the canal. A heavy stone buffer block was tried and suffered the same fate. The company then tried dispensing with stop blocks of any kind and the dangers of carelessness then became so obvious to shunters that the problem was solved.

One early traffic agreement was that of 2 May 1854 between the OWWR and the SSR which gave the OWWR the sole right to take traffic from the Wolverhampton and Dudley levels of the BCN, the LNWR and SSR to have the sole right to traffic from the Birmingham and Walsall levels[8]. Three months later, Messrs Hingley & Son, a firm of Netherton ironmasters, complained that their goods were delayed by the OWWR and they were prevented, by the agreement, from forwarding them by the SSR. This was due to a shortage of plant on the OWWR who consented for the SSR to receive Hingley's goods until the situation was remedied.

Although the main idea behind railway/canal transhipment facilities was to capture the heavy trade of the district, railway companies were not slow to use them to invade the territory of other railways. In 1860, the OWWR was complaining that the GWR was carrying butter and cheese from Wolverhampton (an important market for that produce) to Brierley Hill[9].

FOOTNOTES

1. SSR Minutes PRO RAIL 638/2
2. Stubbs Wolverhampton Directory 1861
3. An Agreement between the S&C and SBR Railways and the Trustees of the Duke of Bridgewater, 15 May 1852 PRO RAIL 252/22
4. GWR and Bridgewater Trustees working of traffic 1852/7 PRO RAIL 1057/2994
5. Mather op. cit. pp 250-254
6. List of Bantock's boats May 1860 PRO RAIL 252/24
7. Northern Alliance Agreements 1854-6 PRO RAIL 250/752
8. Note of arrangement OWWR Traffic Committee, 25 May 1854 PRC RAIL 558/12
9. OWWR Goods Agents Meetings 1859/61 PRO RAIL 558/18

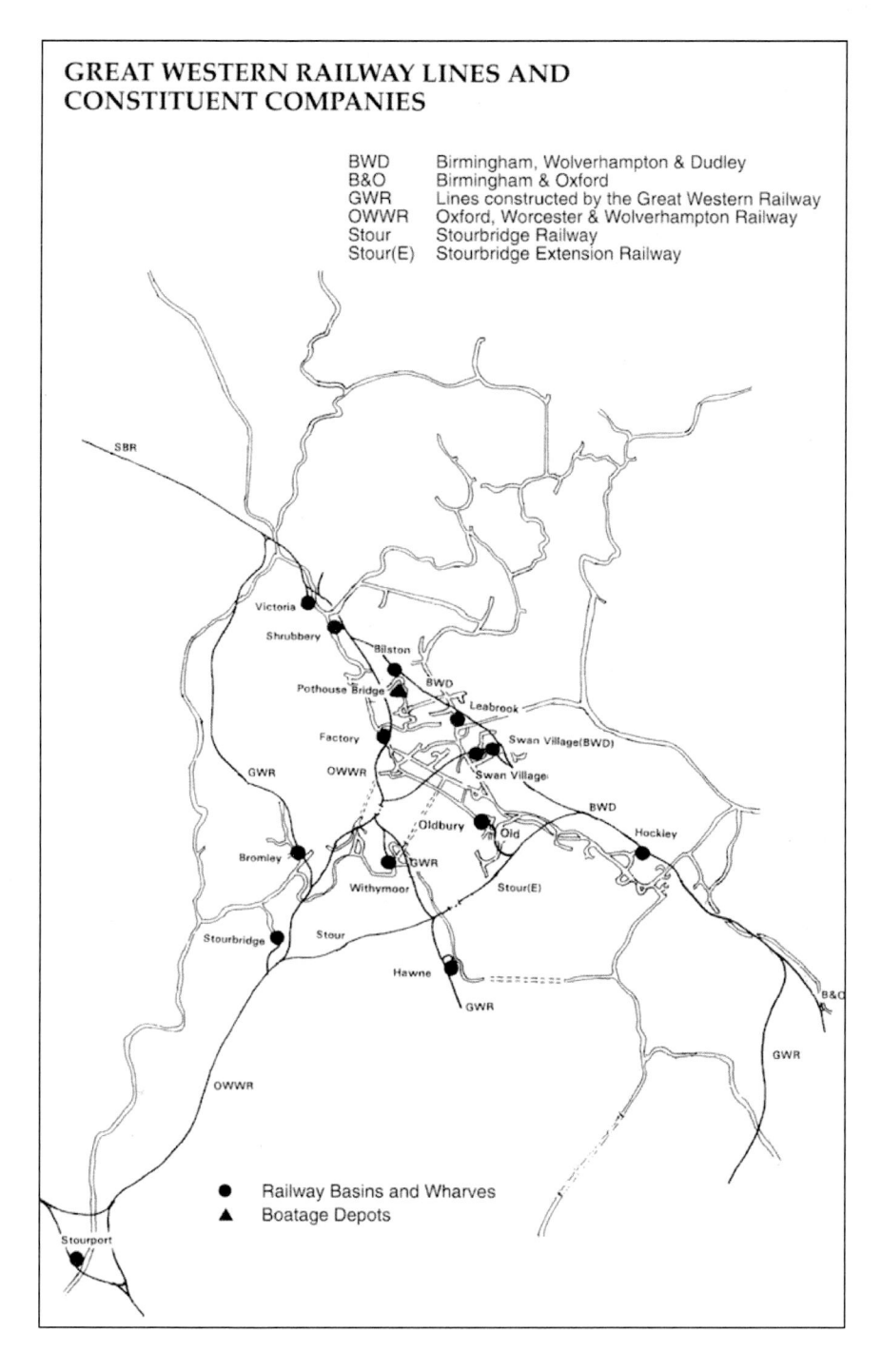

GREAT WESTERN RAILWAY LINES AND CONSTITUENT COMPANIES

BWD — Birmingham, Wolverhampton & Dudley
B&O — Birmingham & Oxford
GWR — Lines constructed by the Great Western Railway
OWWR — Oxford, Worcester & Wolverhampton Railway
Stour — Stourbridge Railway
Stour(E) — Stourbridge Extension Railway

● Railway Basins and Wharves
▲ Boatage Depots

MIDLAND RAILWAY AND CONSTITUENT COMPANIES

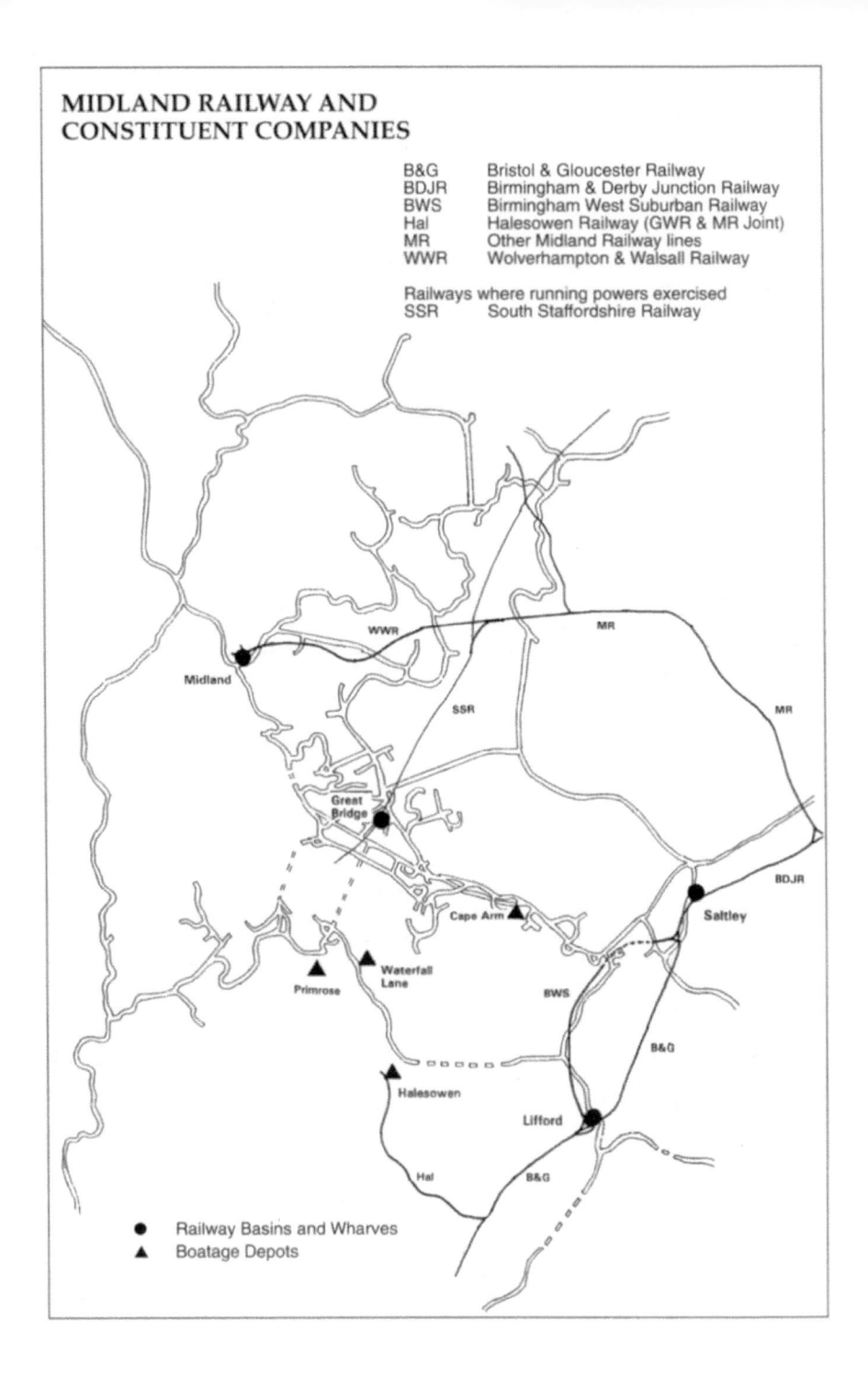

B&G	Bristol & Gloucester Railway
BDJR	Birmingham & Derby Junction Railway
BWS	Birmingham West Suburban Railway
Hal	Halesowen Railway (GWR & MR Joint)
MR	Other Midland Railway lines
WWR	Wolverhampton & Walsall Railway

Railways where running powers exercised
SSR   South Staffordshire Railway

- Railway Basins and Wharves
▲ Boatage Depots

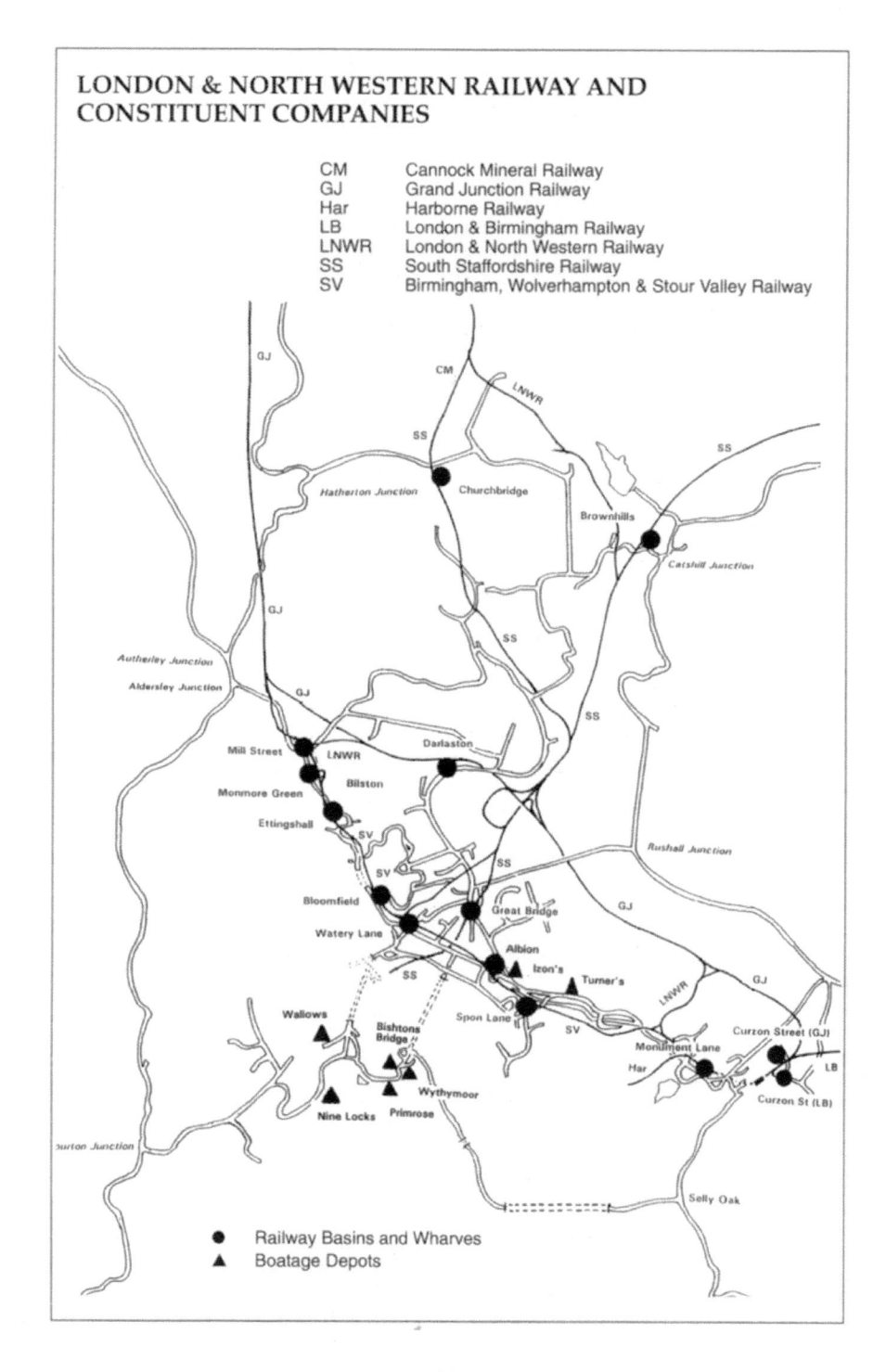

LONDON & NORTH WESTERN RAILWAY AND CONSTITUENT COMPANIES

CM	Cannock Mineral Railway
GJ	Grand Junction Railway
Har	Harborne Railway
LB	London & Birmingham Railway
LNWR	London & North Western Railway
SS	South Staffordshire Railway
SV	Birmingham, Wolverhampton & Stour Valley Railway

- ● Railway Basins and Wharves
- ▲ Boatage Depots

The High Bridge, Netherton. The SU/LNW boat is bound for Brierley Hill Boatage Depot

Dudley Libraries

CHAPTER 5

1863-1914 DEVELOPMENT AND CONSOLIDATION

By 1863 there were 19 wharves or basins in the Birmingham, South Staffs and East Worcs district where goods could be transhipped between canal and rail. There were also mineral chutes at Brettell Lane.

GWR boatage was in the hands of Thos. Bantock, although the railway was later to operate its own boatage from Hockley. Pickford and Crowley served the LNWR, while the MR had by now dispensed with agents and made its own boatage arrangements.

Non rail-connected boatage depots had been set up using, besides those belonging to the railways or their agents, various public and private wharves and basins. Agreed scales of Boatage Allowances had been negotiated.

As transport facilities had increased, so had the production of iron, the traffic with which, together with its associated raw materials and manufactures, the railway basins of the West Midlands were, at that time, overwhelmingly concerned. In 1863 the number of blast furnaces in the Black Country had reached a peak of 200, making 4,000,000 tons of pig iron. Their production had to be supplemented by imports into the district of about 3,000,000 tons per year. The Black Country still held its position as the largest producer of wrought iron with 2,116 puddling furnaces, operated by more than 100 different firms, producing 2,000,000 tons of finished iron[1].

Much of this traffic passed through railway basins as did large quantities of ironstone, iron ore and limestone brought in from other parts of the country. There was no local shortage of coal but the basins handled a certain amount inwards from other coalfields as well as metallurgical coke. In the early years of railway basins, some collieries had no railway connection and small amounts of outward coal were transhipped.

◆

As we have seen, the Midland Railway was at a disadvantage in the struggle for a share of Black Country traffic as its trains were unable to enter the district. This situation altered when the MR obtained running powers over the former SSR route to Dudley, operative from 1 September 1867. The MR then opened a station at Great Bridge which included a rail/canal interchange basin. Unfortunately the site was cramped and the basin was tiny compared with the two arms and main line canal wharfage of its big LNWR neighbour. Its small size caused operating problems which were compounded by its location. As the only MR interchange on the BCN it had to draw traffic from a wide area. Traffic from Smethwick and Netherton had to pass a flight of eight very congested locks at which a waiting time of two hours was common.

What this meant, in operating terms, was that the Midland boats had to leave the same works earlier than those of the GWR or LNWR in order for goods to be put on train the same night. In the 1890s, the train from Great Bridge (MR) left at 9.20 p.m. To catch this, boats from Smethwick had to "close" at 4 p.m. (LNWR 6.30 p.m.) and those from Netherton at 5 p.m. LNWR boats from Netherton (to Albion Railway Basin) could wait until 6.15 p.m. Goods sometimes missed the boat and had to wait until next day. Claims for damage to goods by wet were frequent because of inadequate shed accommodation.

The MR complained of being particularly disadvantaged in the inwards pig iron trade. It was customary for the senders to deliver and they liked to despatch to the station nearest the customer's works so that their contractors could do the job more cheaply than the MR agreed figure of 9d per ton.

In 1895, a total of 31 clerks and 91 men were employed at Great Bridge (MR) of whom 60 were boatmen. No less than 34 boats were based there together with 29 horses. Transhipping was done by contractors who were paid 3d per ton for loading and 2½d per ton for unloading wagons. There was no stabling, but 37 stalls and three loose boxes were hired. Whilst the MR provided its own boatmen and horses, all the boats at that time were hired. In later years, the MR were to own some boats themselves but they continued to rely on hiring to a large extent. At the turn of the century they hired boats from J. Steadman, Bilston; W.H. Tilley, Netherton; J. Wall, Old Hill and F.C. Lowe. As well as having boats based at Great Bridge they also had boats based at Netherton (Primrose MR), Lifford and Wolverhampton. Primrose (MR) was a Boatage Depot constructed c. 1900 to a modern design in order to provide the same facilities for consolidating traffic as the LNWR had enjoyed in the Netherton area for many years.

The MR owned land at Dudley Port with access to the Wolverhampton Level. To obviate the deficiencies of their Great Bridge basin, they planned to construct a transhipment basin on this site based on an existing basin next to the Grand Junction Wharf (Dudley Port) which latter was leased by the MR to Fellows, Morton and Clayton Ltd.

The cost of a connection with the LNWR South Staffs. line was estimated to be £12,000 and other work was estimated at £31,814 including £2700 for stables and £100 for an office. The new basin was planned to be 620 ft long and 24 ft wide, enabling up to 16 boats to be handled at one time.

Of the 82,124 tons dealt with at Great Bridge in 1894, only about 7,000 tons, mainly to and from the Walsall Level, would continue to go there. The 75,000 tons intended to be transferred to Dudley Port would save a mile in distance as well as the two hour delay at the eight locks giving an estimated saving in cost of at least 1d per ton. Six boats and eight boatmen would be saved and transhipping costs reduced by eliminating the intermediate men between wagons and boats, required by the layout at Great Bridge. Shorter journey times would reduce overtime paid to boatmen. Clerical costs would also come down as the offices at Dudley Port would be in one building, those at Great Bridge being scattered. In addition to economies on existing work, the MR expected Dudley Port to bring them 40,000 tons per year of new traffic.

Unfortunately, the Midland Railway's Dudley Port Interchange never materialized. There were disputes with the LNWR over the proposed connection but these were academic in view of the fact that the site was obstructed by a huge marl hole which resisted all attempts to fill it in. Although the MR Goods Manager's Office pressed hard for the new facility, Dudley Port Railway Basin was never built and, in 1902, the canal carriers Messrs Whitehouse of Smethwick applied to rent the existing basin on the site[2].

Great Bridge (MR) continued in use until 1910[3] when it was closed. 56,000 tons had been dealt with there in the previous 12 months. The site of the basin was later raised to the level of the railway and, many years later, was to become part of the British Rail Great Bridge Steel Terminal.

The MR had opened a transhipment basin at Wolverhampton in 1882, usually referred to as Midland Basin, which besides serving its local area also enabled the MR to compete for traffic to and from the Staffordshire & Worcestershire Canal.

There is no evidence to indicate that the Midland Basin gained any traffic from closure of Great Bridge (MR). Increased activity at the LNWR basins at Bloomfield, Albion, Great Bridge and Spon Lane would appear to point to the MR boatage work formerly done at Great Bridge (MR) being handled by LNWR depots[4].

The MR also had a transhipment depot at Lifford on the Worcester & Birmingham Canal. Opened in 1874, it served the isolated industrial area of Lifford, Kings

Norton and Selly Oak including a short stretch of the BCN's Dudley Canal at Selly Oak.

The Midland Railway also transhipped goods over the BCN Halesowen Wharf, sometimes known as Haywood. This was classed as a Railway Basin in the BCN statistics because it was a place where goods left their canal for the railway or vice versa[5]. There was no siding at Halesowen Wharf, goods being carted the quarter mile distance to Halesowen Station. MR traffic over this wharf was mainly in connection with the nearby Stewarts & Lloyds Tube Works at Coombswood. The Midland Railway reached Halesowen on 10 September 1883. The GWR had a station there from 1 March 1878. Even before that, there were Boatage Allowances for Halesowen Wharf in connection with the iron trade and it is also likely that, before the railway reached Halesowen, the railway companies used Halesowen Wharf for distributing "shop goods".

The earliest known MR traffic figures for Halesowen Wharf are for 1904/5 when 2959 tons of "goods" and 10,3682 tons of iron and tubes were recorded.

◆

The 1863 amalgamation of the West Midland Railway and the GWR left the latter well provided with interchanges, most of them of spacious dimensions. The most obvious gap lay in the highly industrialised area between Tipton Factory or Swan Village Basins and that at Bromley. This was not to be filled until Withymoor Railway Basin was opened on 1 March 1878, a spacious and well equipped facility which eliminated GWR boatage through the Netherton and Dudley Tunnels. GWR boatage distances were drastically shortened.

The Oldbury Railway was opened to Oldbury Goods (which incorporated a transhipment basin) on 7 November 1884. It was amalgamated with the GWR on 1 July 1894. Stourport (Mitton) Interchange on the Severn Valley line was opened in March 1885. This mainly served the iron works at Wilden and Stour Vale. On 2 April 1902, Hawne Basin, almost entirely devoted to serving the Coombswood Tube Works, was opened, in spite of which the GWR was still passing a small amount of Coombswood traffic over Halesowen Wharf in 1905.

The final GWR basin to be built was Bilston New, located on the Wednesbury Oak Loop line of the BCN. This was opened on 1 January 1908.

◆

Unlike the GWR, with its spacious Victoria and Shrubbery basins, the LNWR lacked adequate transhipment facilities in Wolverhampton. It supplemented

Wolverhampton Mill Street by opening a basin on the outskirts at Ettingshall (1881) to be followed by a basin of modern design at Monmore Green. Opened on 9 September 1902, this occupied a site formerly occupied by the Chillington Iron Company and is sometimes known as Chillington Basin. Bloomfields and Albion basins, both of which handled traffic from the Dudley and Stourbridge Canals as well as from their local districts, were extended.

In August 1873, it was proposed that the Shropshire Union Railway & Canal Co. (which was leased to the LNWR) should undertake the South Staffs. boatage, taking over Crowley's stock. This arrangement came into force on September 1,1873. On 25 February 1874 the Shropshire Union (SU) suggested that they should also take over Pickford's share of boatage, but 25 years were to pass before this happened.

In 1874, the SU started negotiations to extend the Albert (Hay) Basin siding to its depot in Broad Street, Wolverhampton. This was subsequently made but, unfortunately, no records of its use seem to have survived. It does not appear on any lists of recognised Railway Basins. In order to reach Broad Street, the line crossed the Wednesfield Road and it was stipulated that rail traffic should be hauled by horses and be confined to one wagon at a time, except where more than one was necessary for a long load.

It had been the practice of the LNWR to employ its own labour at transhipment stations but, from the beginning of 1875 it was agreed that Pickfords should unload their own traffics, the SU to handle the remainder except at Wolverhampton. By 1889, the Shropshire Union employed 88 craft in its boatage fleet[6].

Pickfords had had a long standing grievance that the LNWR did not pay a fair price for its services and that it was not given a fair chance to develop its railway business. For years it had bowed to necessity but, in the opening of the Great Central line to London in 1899, it saw a way of breaking out of the LNWR stranglehold on traffic to the north.

It was against this background that more than half a century of Pickfords railway boatage came to an end, the SU taking it over from 30 June 1901 and acquiring 24 Pickfords boats on 16 October of that year. Of these craft, five were wooden and nineteen built of iron; fifteen of the total had cabins. The cost was £1,770[7].

Thereafter the SU was the sole provider of boatage to the LNWR. To avoid confusion with its other carrying operations, boatage craft, basins, tolls and traffic were designated SU / LNW.

SHROPSHIRE UNION AGENTS IN SOUTH STAFFS (c.1900)

AGENT	BASIN AND NUMBER		STEERERS
Walter Hales	Tipton	17	Yates and Prosser
	Spon Lane	21	Bedford
	Albion	20 & 78	Yates, Prosser and Barnett
	Bloomfield	15 & 76	Wain
	Great Bridge	14	Holloway, Simpson and Prosser
J.Roycroft	Netherton	25,26,30, 31,33	Yates, Prosser
	Stourbridge	32	Yates, Prosser
	Primrose	27	Yates, Prosser
	Brierley Hill	29	Yates, Prosser
S.Bourne	S&WC & Mill Street	67	Sunday
T.P.Parkes	Brownhills	2	Barnett
	Ettingshall	10	Wain
	Darlaston	9	Nixon
	Monument La.	28	Bedford.

BW Archives, Gloucester BW / 266 /88

SHROPSHIRE UNION RAILWAY & CANAL COMPANY BOATS ENGAGED IN THE RAILWAY TRADE - JANUARY 1888

Among the Shropshire Union Railway Boatage fleet were eleven cabin boats registered at Wolverhampton. They were allocated to steerers to work traffic from the works on the Dudley Canal through Netherton Tunnel to Tipton:

32	HERCULES	330	JET
258	CHESTER	334	KODO
314	ROYAL OAK	336	(EAGLE) GILBERT
316	(THOMAS) TYNE	360	LION
317	(WASP) FLY	375	VIGILANT
323	HORNET		

Reference: Wolverhampton Sanitary Committee Minutes, Volume 12, Wolverhampton Archives

The names in brackets were carried by the boats at the time of registration.

As well as the transhipment basins, the SU / LNW operated a number of boatage depots which were shared with its non-boatage services. These were organised in groups, with an Agent in charge of each group. Although the SU / LNW owned its own boats, supplementing these by hiring when necessary, horses and boatmen were provided by "steerers", the local name for a contractor undertaking such work. Each of their wharves or basins were given a number, more than one number being used for a depot where the original facilities had been extended.

Maintenance of the SU / LNW fleet was carried out at a dock at Commercial Wharf, Horseley Fields, Wolverhampton, the premises having been taken over from Crowley.

Traffic to and from the SU / LNW boatage depots at Netherton (Withymoor, Bishton Bridge and Primrose), Brierley Hill (Nine Locks Top) and onto the Stourbridge Canal summit level was handled at the large Bloomfield and Albion Basins, both of which had been extended, and at the small basin at Tipton (Watery Lane). Stourbridge, Stourport, Kidderminster and Kinver traffic was dealt with at Wolverhampton (Mill Street). Tube traffic from Coombswood went to Great Bridge (SU / LNW). Various public and private wharves were also utilised.

———◆———

A further agreement between the main line railways and the long distance canal carriers covering the Birmingham, South Staffs. and East Worcs. district was made in 1877[8]. This was largely devoted to the control of boatage and cartage allowances but also specified boatage charges for round timber, boilers and heavy weights.

One item of particular interest was the setting of a universal rate, regardless of distance, of 1/6d per ton for any traffic charged at "Station to Station" rates to and from any works on the Staffs. & Worcs. Canal.

As regards traffic at C & D rates, the free collection and delivery area was limited. For instance there was inclusive delivery from the Great Western chutes at Brettell Lane to any works on the Stourbridge Canal summit (but not onto the Stourbridge Extension Canal), and onto the BCN as far as Woodside; and from the Netherton group of Boatage Depots (Withymoor, Bishtons Bridge and Primrose) as far as Blowers Green.

A lot of information about West Midlands Boatage at that time is to be found in the Tables of Boatage Allowances. Detailed Allowances for C&D traffic charged at Iron

Rates were listed for no less than 302 specified works on the BCN, Stourbridge and Stourbridge Extension canals and a further 16 on the Staffs. & Worcs. There was a separate list of 47 brickworks. This traffic was handled over 31 "Railway Basins" which could be railway/canal transhipment stations, boatage depots or private and public wharves.

In addition to this vast amount of activity, it has to be remembered that there were many works whose traffic was charged at other than Iron Rates. These were not individually listed as they were subject to a general maximum boatage allowance. There was no boatage allowance for mineral class traffic.

The large number of works listed highlights the problem which led the railways to develop boatage on a big scale, i.e. traffic arising from a large number of individual works, many of which produced relatively small amounts. The number of private sidings at this time, excluding those serving collieries, was 120.

Not mentioned in the 1877 Agreement are the Midland Railway's Saltley and Lifford Wharves which were located outside the boundary of the "District".

As regards wharves which were not actually owned or leased by the railways or their agents, Pothouse Bridge which we first saw mentioned in 1860 is listed as are the BCN wharves at Darlaston Green, Tipton Green, Nine Locks, Small Heath (Swan Village) and Spon Lane. Private wharves were Hadley's (Oldbury), Turners (Smethwick) and Izons (West Bromwich).

Wallows Wharf, where the Pensnett Railway had an interchange with the Pensnett Canal, was also listed. The Pensnett Railway was a mineral line owned by the Earl of Dudley who was not a party to the 1877 Agreement. Whilst we know that most of the listed non railway wharves were more or less an overflow facility for nearby transhipment depots, the way in which Wallows was actually used is open to speculation. It would have been possible to have transhipped between boats and railway wagons which could have reached the GWR at Cradley Heath over the Pensnett Railway: or, as in the case of the other non railway wharves, traders could have taken traffic to and from the Wallows in their own boats, it being later moved to a interchange in railway company boats. The latter system of operation seems to have been used to create a stockpile from which consignments could be despatched as required. It appears, at least in some instances, to have been associated with limited storage space both at works and at transhipment depots.

It is almost certain that Wallows Wharf was used by the GWR. Their transhipment depot at Withymoor had yet to be built and their boatage agent, Bantock, had no depots of their own in the area. The SU / LNW had a depot nearby at Nine Locks Top (with which Wallows Wharf is coupled in the Allowance Tables).

The Earl of Dudley was a Director of the GWR. The Midland Railway, also without facilities in this area, could also have used Wallows.

The BCN wharf at Halesowen is listed, but few firms were given a Boatage Allowance there. Its period of importance as a Railway Basin awaited the opening of the railway to Halesowen.

Halesowen was within cartage distance of the GWR station at Old Hill, but it is possible that both the SU / LNW and the Midland used Halesowen Wharf to distribute "shop goods".

———◆———

By 1898, tranships on the BCN amounted to 1,208,363 tons and several transhipment depots had yet to be built. No figures are available for tranships on the Stourbridge, Pensnett, Stourbridge Extension and Staffs. & Worcs. canals, nor for Saltley and Lifford.

Complaints from traders about high railway charges, which put the West Midlands area at a disadvantage compared to districts nearer to the ports, were growing and there was pressure to improve the canal system to provide more competition. This led to the Royal Commission on Canals, published in 1906. One of the matters which came under discussion was the system of transhipment between canal and rail.

Traders were suspicious that LNWR control of the BCN gave an unfair advantage to that railway. In reply to this, the BCN pointed out its legal obligation to be even handed in its charges and in the provision of facilities. In support of this argument, the BCN produced figures to prove that the MR and the GWR between them took far more at their basins than the LNWR. For the purposes of the BCN a Railway Basin was a point where traffic was exchanged between canal and railway. Although Boatage Depots were excluded, the non rail connected Halesowen Wharf was included (as a MR Railway Basin) although there was intermediate cartage. The GWR had 10 Basins, the LNWR had 13 and the MR had 3. Traffic between the BCN and Saltley and Lifford, substantial in the former case, was unaccounted for while traffic from other canals worked over BCN Railway Basins was included.

In 1905, out of a total of 1,108,172 tons handled over Railway Basins on the BCN, the

LNWR had 481,094 tons, the GWR 469,387 tons and the MR 157,691 tons. The average toll charged to the LNWR (4.51d) greatly exceeded that charged to the GWR and was not much less than that charged to the Midland. Average tolls in this context would seem to be meaningless. What traders wanted to know was if the same tonnage per mile was charged to all users and had they equal access to canal facilities, such as the BCN's own wharves. Despite the failure of the BCN to produce meaningful comparisons, there is, in fact, no evidence to show that the BCN discriminated between the railway companies.

The effect of Railway Basins on the income of the canal companies was also argued before the Royal Commission. The BCN was railway controlled but the privately owned Staffordshire and Worcestershire Canal and Stourbridge Canals tended to regard Railway Basins as a means by which traffic left their waters without passing over the whole length of the canal. Although it can be argued that some boatage arrangements meant that traffic actually travelled further on their canal, the point of view of the canal companies was probably generally valid although it would be difficult, if not impossible, to make an accurate overall assessment.

The railways argued in return that their greater geographical coverage and the increased competition resultant on their arrival had, by reducing rates and providing a faster and more reliable service, greatly increased the total transport market.

The canals benefited from the increased trade and not only because of the increased amount of boatage. The consumption of local minerals was stimulated and these were mostly carried by canal.

As far as the iron trade was concerned, shortages of ironstone while production of wrought iron was still rising, led to increasing imports of pig iron, much of it from South Wales between whose mining districts and the Black Country water transport was extremely inconvenient. Unless the pig could have been brought in cheaply, the entire iron based industry of the area must have suffered and with it canal tonnage and tolls.

The canals which really suffered from the transhipment of traffic off the canal near to its originating point were the trunk routes like the Shropshire Union, Trent & Mersey and Grand Junction. As far as the waterways within the Birmingham, South Staffs. & East Worcs. District were concerned it is hard to come to any conclusion other than that the inter working between these canals and the railways was not only unavoidable but beneficial.

In May 1911, the idea of a Revenue Pool (previously discussed in 1890 and 1901) was revived, the intention being to include the Birmingham, South Staffs. & E. Worcs. traffic of all three Railway Companies. A Pool between the LNW and Midland Railways was already in operation and had facilitated the closure of Great Bridge (MR) Basin[10].

It was envisaged that the volume of boatage traffic in the District would lessen through co-operation between the Railways. Specifically, the amalgamation of Albion and Swan Village; Ettingshall and Bilston New: and Spon Lane and Oldbury was suggested. The LNWR would cease to compete in the Stourbridge and Kidderminster areas.

None of these changes came about and competition between the successors of the LNWR and GWR survived six years after the 1948 Nationalisation.

FOOTNOTES

1. Gale K. THE BLACK COUNTRY IRON INDUSTRY Iron & Steel Institute 1966
2. MR Proposed Dudley Port Interchange PRO RAIL 491/796
3. BCN Tonnage Ledgers PRO RAIL 448
4. BCN Railway Basin Traffic Returns PRO RAIL 810/306
5. BCN Railway Basin Traffic Returns PRO RAIL 810/306-7
6. SU Minutes PRO RAIL 623/17
7. SU Minutes PRO RAIL 623/25
8. PRO 410/1003
9. RC on Canals Vol III 1907
10. PRO RAIL 1007/177

Midland Railway boats at Lifford. The timber may be for the nearby GKN packing case factory at Kings Norton. C.1900

Author's Collection

Shropshire Union station boat WILDEN on the Staffordshire and Worcestershire Canal c 1910

Author's Collection

SU/LNW Stourport calls at Kinver Wharf. In front of the mast are empty vinegar barrels for Stourport

C D McDougall Collection

48

A Shropshire Union station boat at Bloomfield LNWR Basin, c1910

National Waterways Museum, Gloucester

A GWR boat on the south side of Cranford Street bridge (BCN Cape Arm) in 1906. The Midland Railway Wharf was on the opposite side of the canal. GKN's London Works can be seen behind the bridge in the centre of the picture

Sandwell Libraries, Smethwick

A Shropshire Union station boat at Bloomfield LNWR Basin c1910

National Waterways Museum, Gloucester

CHAPTER 6

1914-1969 YEARS OF DECLINE

The Great War of 1914-1918 brought upheaval to the British economy in general, and to transport in particular. Among its effects were changes in the pattern of trade, labour shortages and massive rises in wages and tolls. After the war, the decline of the Black Country iron industry continued with many of the old canal-side works being closed. This accounted for much of the fall in boatage which was to continue until its complete extinction in 1969.

The other main cause was the entry into the transport market of large numbers of road hauliers, a sharp increase in railway rates in September 1920 coinciding with the disposal by the Ministry of Munitions of some 20,000 vehicles at very low prices. The effect of road haulage on boatage was more to abstract traffic from the railways rather than to replace boats by mechanised cartage. Mechanisation of railway cartage was a slow process, and horses were still in use in the 1950s. This was largely due to the small cartage areas of each station in an era of closely spaced stations. In the period between the wars we see motor cartage being introduced by the LMSR at its Brierley Hill Boatage Depot to feed horse-drawn railway boats because Brierley Hill was exempted from the normal cartage boundary arrangements, and its cartage area was larger than usual. There is evidence that traders sought to replace boatage by cartage on some longer hauls. These examples will be discussed in detail below.

The situation was that the low value traffic available to railway boats was falling due to industrial decline, while high value traffic was being lost by the railways to door to door road haulage.

After the war, the need to rationalise the railways was perceived as necessary and, with effect from 1923, nearly all the companies were grouped into four big concerns. As far as the Birmingham and Black Country area was concerned, the GWR remained unchanged but the Midland Railway was grouped with the LNWR to become part of the new London Midland & Scottish Railway (LMSR).

◆

The list of LNWR transhipment depots increased by one in 1919, but Tibbington Railway Basin enjoyed this status only for the three month period of April-June of that year, during which 48 tons were handled! Tibbington was located on the Wednesbury Oak Loop Line, not far from Bloomfield[1].

The South Staffs. boatage fleet of the SU was taken over by the LNWR in 1922 and, from October 1923, this fleet passed to the LMSR which also took over the former MR boatage activities. The LMSR continued the services to Kidderminster, Stourport, Netherton, Brierley Hill, Old Hill and Halesowen by which the LNWR and MR had penetrated GWR territory. The former SU / LNW service to Stourbridge was cut back to Nine Locks (Brierley Hill), collection and delivery from there being by road. Hence the enlarged cartage area for Brierley Hill which brought it early cartage mechanisation.

During the interwar period, iron and general goods traffic to and from Brierley Hill was boated between there and Albion Interchange Basin, the tonnage in each direction approximately balancing. Brierley Hill also operated the Firebrick traffic between the Stourbridge Canal summit or Nine Locks Wharf and Tipton (Watery Lane) and Bloomfield. In 1929, the LMSR had fitted the ANTWERP with what was intended to be a detachable outboard motor and, in May of that year, its performance was demonstrated by running from Birmingham to London in 50 hours. It proved to be far too cumbersome to be easily changed from one boat to another and was eventually fitted to the HORACE which was used on the Brierley Hill to Albion run. It was known locally as the "screw", was operated by one man and was considerably slower than the horse boats.

The Brierley Hill boatmen did one return trip per day. Going through the Netherton Tunnel, the towing line would be shortened up so that the horse was by the boat's fore-end and the boat would be allowed to run along the tunnel's towpath wall which was protected, as on much of the BCN, by a substantial iron guard. As the boat did not then need to be steered, the boatmen would take this opportunity to have their breakfast. To provide illumination in the tunnel, the boats carried a "flamer", a type of lamp which used waste oil. Among the cargoes shipped from Brierley Hill, dustbins and galvanised wheelbarrows were a common sight. One of the Brierley Hill boats, AJAX, was sunk in Parkhead Locks in 1927.

Extensive stabling, complete with sick bay was provided at Brierley Hill, the LMSR having its own veterinary surgeon, farriers and ostlers. The Goods Agent at Brierley Hill was provided with a gig, horse and driver. He would often have had dealings with the Manager of the Stourbridge Canal who was only provided with a bicycle. A Mr Gripton was the foreman here from 1911 to 1949, his son serving at Primrose Basin.

Traffic from Primrose (Netherton) Boatage Depot consisted of goods which were boated to and from Albion, the amount in each direction being approximately the same, and iron from Primrose to Bloomfield for which there was no return traffic.

BCN RAILWAY TRAFFIC

Principal gains and losses, December quarter 1929

ALBION	+ 1418	Iron and goods ex Dudley and Brierley Hill and pig iron to local foundries.
BILSTON	- 659	Iron ex J Sankey and Son.
BLOOMFIELD	- 755	Iron, Sanitary Pipes, Pitch.
BROWNHILLS	- 505	Creosote ex Brownhills Chemical Works.
ETTINGSHALL	+ 559	Iron from J.Sankey & Sons.
FACTORY	- 855	Iron & Pitch ex local works.
HALESOWEN	- 765	Tubes &c ex Coombswood Tube Works
HOCKLEY	- 1256	Billets & coal to local works.
GREAT BRIDGE	- 793	Tubes from Coombswood Tube Works, Halesowen.
MIDLAND	- 1909	Iron to Swindon & Stourvale, billets & pig to local works.
MILL STREET	- 532	Iron and other goods ex Staffordshire & Worcestershire Canal.
MONMORE GREEN	- 1130	Billets to Bayliss's.
MONUMENT LANE	- 3255	GKN traffic now dealt with at Spon Lane
NETHERTON	+ 1694	Slack, pig & limestone to Rowley Pottery and Noah Hingley's.
SHRUBBERY	+ 3759	Iron ex J. Sankey and basic slag ex Spring Vale Iron & Steelworks, Bilston
SPON LANE	- 4926	Roadstone ex Hange and Slack and Sand for Spon Lane Glass Wks. (-7000 tons). GKN traffic (+2100 tons).
VICTORIA	- 641	Grain to Norton's Mill
WATERY LANE	- 263	Brick ex Stourbridge Canal.
WEDNESBURY	- 8648	Bagnall's traffic direct to new LMS sidings at Leabrook and New Crown Works standing idle.

Birmingham Central Library Archives MS86

Primrose also had stabling which, together with the wooden goods shed, has only recently been demolished.

The only other remaining LMSR traffic on this side of the Netherton Tunnel was from Doulton's Rowley Pottery and Hingley's Old Hill Iron Works, both to Bloomfield3. Hingleys Old Hill works had closed by 1934.

The other LMS service into GWR territory operated between Wolverhampton (Mill Street) and Kidderminster and Stourport. The Kidderminster boats enjoyed a balanced traffic in each direction but the Stourport trade was mainly from that town. Carpets were an important cargo from Kidderminster and vinegar from Stourport, but a variety of other commodities were carried.

Boats called at intermediate points, such as Kinver, as required.

LMS boats also served Baldwin's ironworks at Cookley, Swindon, Stour Vale and Wilden. To reach Wilden, the boats had to navigate a short but difficult stretch of the River Stour. Both raw materials were delivered to the ironworks and finished goods (which included tinplate and stampings) collected. Some traffic from Wilden was boated up the Stour to Pratts Wharf in Baldwin's boats and loaded there to the LMS. Baldwin's station boats served Wilden from Stourport (GWR) and GWR boats served the other works but all outward cargoes from the ironworks seem to have gone to the LMS, probably because Baldwin had a distribution warehouse at Wolverhampton[4]. The ironworks trade appears to have finished by 1938 although the Kidderminster and Stourport goods boats survived until 1950.

Interestingly, between the wars, Mill Street had a non-railway traffic in iron, carried by the Midland & Coast Canal Carrying Co. from Bagnall's Leabrook Ironworks (Wednesbury). This was for a works adjacent to Mill Street Basin.

Unlike the remainder of the LMS boats, whose cargoes were only covered by a sheet, the boats used on the Staffordshire and Worcestershire Canal were fully equipped with top planks, side cloths and top cloths and looked very smart indeed in their black and white livery lined out in red.

Interchange depots were rarely formally closed in the period during which boatage services still operated. They were usually part of railway goods yards which themselves survived until the wholesale goods station closures of the 1960s onwards. In fact the sidings and shed are still in situ today (1998) at Monmore Green. What usually happened was that traffic gradually declined until it finally ceased. In some cases several years elapsed without traffic and then an isolated

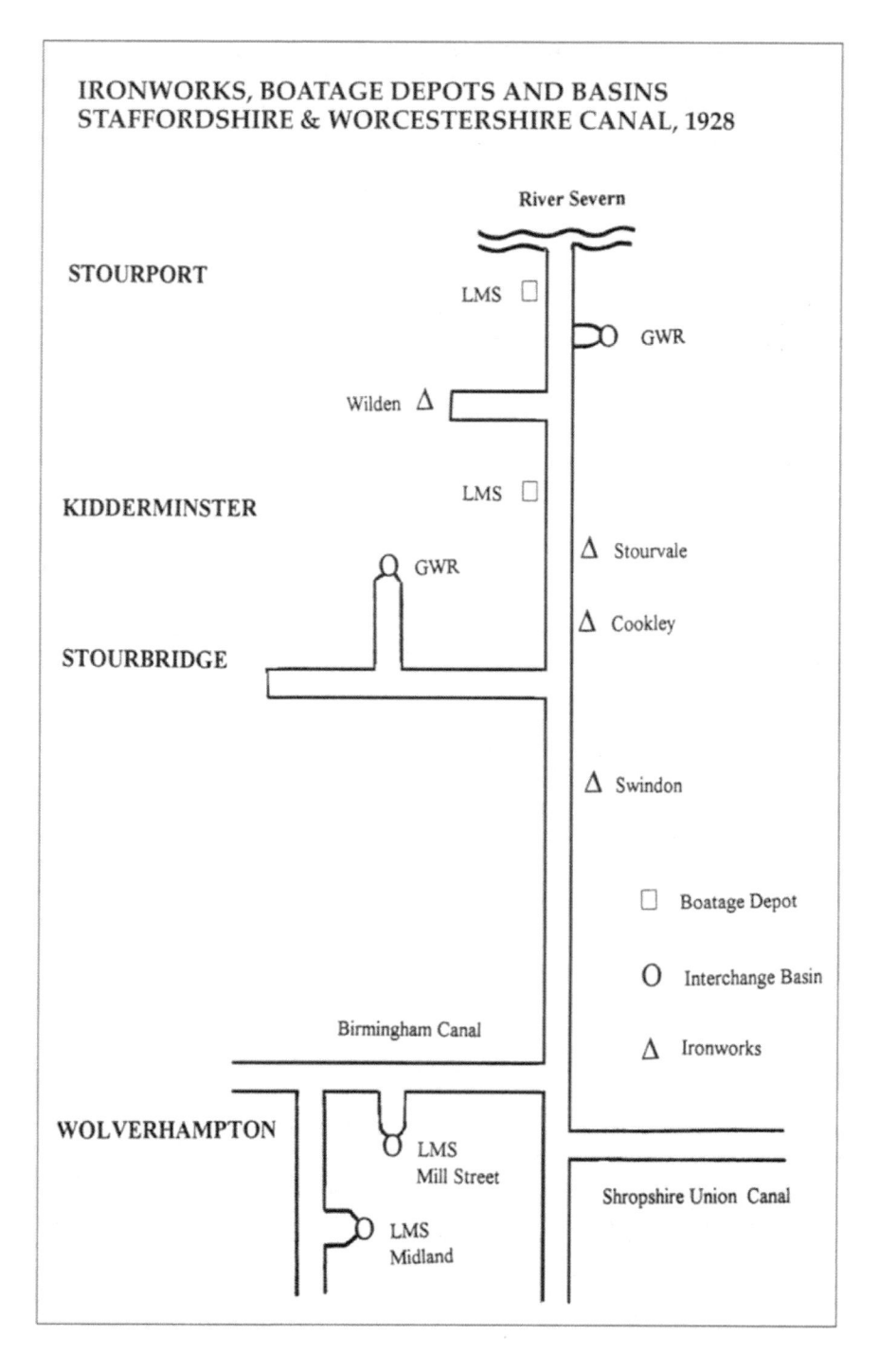

IRONWORKS, BOATAGE DEPOTS AND BASINS
STAFFORDSHIRE & WORCESTERSHIRE CANAL, 1928

River Severn

STOURPORT

LMS

GWR

Wilden △

KIDDERMINSTER

LMS

△ Stourvale

△ Cookley

GWR

STOURBRIDGE

△ Swindon

☐ Boatage Depot

O Interchange Basin

Birmingham Canal

△ Ironworks

WOLVERHAMPTON

LMS Mill Street

Shropshire Union Canal

LMS Midland

boatload or two turned up to disturb their repose. For instance, Brownhills dealt with no traffic between October 1933 and April 1936 during which month it handled 21 tons. The following month's 22 tons was the last recorded traffic here[5].

Darlaston dealt with a mere 156 tons in the 21 months before its last recorded traffic in May 1935. By 1937, Great Bridge was only handling coal for the Wellington Tube Works (only a few yards away) and was out of use by 1949, as was Churchbridge, an interchange for which there are no interwar records.

Wolverhampton (Mill St) no longer dealt with boatage traffic when the Kidderminster and Stourport boats finished in September 1950, although the basin was occasionally used after that by British Waterways, their M.B. EAGLE discharging Bentonite Clay there early in 1951.

◆

The Midland Railway's London Street Boatage Depot on the Cape Arm, which had opened in 1896, was closed in 1921[6].

Traffic over Halesowen Wharf ceased in Jan 1918 but recommenced in October 1921. In May 1928, the LMS Midland Division handled 2801 tons over Halesowen Wharf for Stewarts & Lloyds, with an additional 800 tons carried in Stewarts & Lloyds' boats to Waterfall Lane Boatage Depot and thence by Midland Division boats to Great Bridge transhipment basin. Railway traffic over Halesowen Wharf ended in June 1930.

In 1928 the Midland Basin at Wolverhampton was still dealing with traffic for Cookley, Stourvale and Swindon Ironworks on the Staffs. & Worcs. Canal and with traffic for the adjacent Swan Garden Ironworks, but it was to see its last recorded cargo in October 1938. Lifford Interchange became disused in March 1927, its remaining traffic then being handled at Monument Lane.

Waterfall Lane was still seeing tube and plate traffic in September 1934, by now going to and from Bloomfield rather than Great Bridge, but this trade had disappeared by 1949.

In September 1934, 505 tons of coal for the BCN was loaded to boat at Saltley Sidings. Figures for Saltley traffic which did not leave the Grand Union Canal are not available[7].

◆

The LMS took over 100 boats from the LNWR. It is not possible to say exactly how many came from the MR as many of that company's boats were hired, but the MR was probably using about 30 boats at the Grouping.

By 1928 the LMS fleet was showing its age and the Company embarked on a substantial replacement programme. Between 1928 and 1930, 38 steel boats were built by W.J. Yarwood of Northwich and these were supplemented by a further six in 1937/38. They were used mainly on the runs through the Netherton Tunnel to Primrose and Brierley Hill and on firebrick traffic from the Stourbridge Canal.

The older wooden boats were still favoured for certain traffics, for instance the carriage of paper from Monument Lane to Saltley and earthenware from Rowley to Bloomfield (later Albion). The Staffs. & Worcs. route required six wooden boats, reduced to three when the trade to and from Baldwin's ironworks ceased in the late 1930s. The remaining boats on the Staffs. & Worcs. work were sold in 1951. These were SYMBOL (built 1914), SATURN (built 1906) and ANTWERP (built 1915). Another boat regularly used on the Staffordshire and Worcestershire Canal was WILDEN (built 1905).

51 boats were offered for sale in April 1954 when the Primrose and Brierley Hill services were discontinued. The very last use of BR(LMR) boats was between Doulton's Rowley Pottery and Albion. Former Shropshire Union wooden boats were used on this job as the goods were light and bulky and the boats needed to carry them piled up high.

A "top" of this nature would have made the more modern boats unstable. This run was still operating in late 1954, HOGARTH (a "Trench" boat built in 1910) being the last boat to be used. "Trench" boats were built to use the small locks between Wappenshall Junction and the Shropshire Union Company's transhipment depot at the foot of the inclined plane at Trench in East Shropshire and were only 6ft 2 inches wide as against the standard narrow boat beam of 6 ft 9 inches to 7ft 2 inches.

The only LMS boats to be equipped with top planks, side and top cloths were those used on the Staffordshire and Worcestershire Canal. The remainder had open holds, the cargoes being covered by a tarpaulin. The Staffordshire and Worcestershire Canal boats had cabins as did a few of the ex-Shropshire Union boats like HOGARTH and GOVERNOR but the remainder of the LMS boatage fleet were open boats, the boatmen being completely exposed to the weather with only a fire bucket for warmth and cooking.

The fleet was maintained at Commercial Dock, Horseley Fields, Wolverhampton, which had been used for boatage craft since the days of Crowley.

The use of public and private wharves to supplement the LMS's own depots continued at least up to 1937. In October 1916, Turner's Wharf at Smethwick loaded 20 SU / LNW boats (365 tons) of glass from Chance Bros. The nearby Spon Lane Wharf unloaded 23 boats (444 tons) of grain, soda, sand and coal and loaded 14 boats (130 tons) of soap, glass, and empties. Turner's was still in use in 1934. The glass traffic had ended but there were now "goods" from Kenrick's Spon Lane Foundry.

Izons Wharf, near Albion Interchange, handled traffic from the Eagle Oil Works (Jones's) and from Barnett's Rattlechain Brickworks.

Small Heath Wharf (West Bromwich) was also used in connection with Albion, handling traffic to and from Hall End Oil Works. Tipton Green Wharf and Whimsey Bridge Wharf (Oldbury) were also used by the LMS in the interwar period[8].

———◆———

All boatage services provided by BR(LMR) ended in 1954, leaving only a little traffic in traders boats. Monument Lane, whose last traffic was the carriage of paper to Saltley, and Tipton (Watery Lane) became disused immediately. Bloomfield continued to receive a fortnightly load of firebricks for a few more years while the odd load of old rails was put on boat at Spon Lane for the District Iron & Steel Works at Smethwick. Spon Lane also handled goods from Guest, Keen and Nettlefold's works on the Cape Arm. There was a more considerable traffic in nuts and bolts from Bayliss, Jones & Bayliss in their own boats, shafted from their Victoria Works to Monmore Green Interchange.

All traffic to BR(LMR) interchange basins had ceased by 1962 except for some coal loaded to boats at Saltley which ended the following year.

———◆———

GWR boatage activities were unaffected by the 1923 Grouping and continued to be handled by the GWR at Hockley and by Thos. Bantock elsewhere. Victoria Basin saw its last traffic in March 1930. The basin was filled in and a modern goods station built on the site. It is now a builders merchant.

Bilston New, which saw its last recorded traffic in July 1935, was the next to go, followed by Oldbury in June 1936. In the case of Wednesbury, although its traffic was small and extremely intermittent during the 1930s, it was listed as handling approximately 7,000 tons per year at the time of nationalisation.

Of the remaining GWR basins, tonnage at Hawne, nearly all in connection with the Coombswood Tube Works, rose from 3,499 in September 1928 to 8,344 in September 1934, reflecting the end of LMS boatage to Halesowen Wharf. Between those dates, traffic at Hockley, Netherton, Swan Village, Shrubbery and Wednesbury, all of which had enjoyed September 1928 figures roughly comparable to Hawne, saw a massive reduction in trade.

The bulk of traffic at Netherton (Withymoor) was in connection with Noah Hingley's Netherton Ironworks, although it also handled traffic from, among others, Doulton's Rowley Pottery; Hingley's works at Old Hill; and the Hartshill Iron Co. on the Pensnett Canal.

Hockley's main customer was the Guest, Keen & Nettlefold complex served by the Cape Arm and by a nearby arm off the New Main Line. GKN outwards goods were delivered, in their own boats, on alternate weeks to the GWR at Hockley and to the LMS at Spon Lane. Part of the GKN waterside premises was designated "Great Western Wharf" with "North Western Wharf" adjacent. Hockley boats traded as far afield as Saltley (Power's), Selly Oak and Bournville.

Swan Village had a purely local trade. Interestingly, the firm of J.B. & S. Lees at Albion boated some of its products to Swan Village, despite having an LMS siding.

Shrubbery relied on only a handful of customers of which the most important was Bayliss, Jones & Bayliss, whose nearby works manufactured nuts and bolts.

Bromley was mainly concerned with Firebricks and also handled a little local chain and iron. The most important traffic at Stourbridge Interchange was steel to Swindon Iron Works on the Staffordshire and Worcestershire Canal with a traffic averaging three boats daily.

Stourport (Mitton) mainly served the Wilden and Stour Vale Ironworks. There was normally one boatload of coal from Highley Colliery to Wilden and one boatload of steel bars from Panteg in South Wales each day. The boats were iron vessels owned by Baldwin. The boatage contractors for Wilden were the Merchant family, who had the necessary local knowledge for navigating the River Stour to Wilden. Bantock operated a daily boat from Stourport Basin to Stourvale Ironworks at Kidderminster. Some sand was also transferred from the railway to the canal at the Stourport interchange[9].

The GWR continued to use various private and public wharves, often sharing them with the LMS. Izons and Small Heath Wharves operated in conjunction with Swan Village Interchange. Wallows Wharf handled traffic for Netherton.

From 1895, 116 boats were registered to the combined Thos. Bantock and GWR fleet list, but it is not possible to say how many were in service at any one time, nor how many remained in use when GWR boatage ended in 1969[10].

By 1950, carriage by railway, as opposed to traders', boats was limited to:

> Stourbridge - Swindon
> Delph - Bromley
> Hockley - Saltley
> Coombswood - Hawne
> (traffic shared with Stewarts & Lloyds boats).

It appears that only two boats were built after the First World War, No. 83 TIPTON (Registered December 1923) and No. 67 (Registered in September 1925).

◆

During the interwar period, Boatage Allowances continued to be regulated by the long established Birmingham, South Staffs. & East Worcs. Conference. For instance, in May 1923, The Hartshill Iron Works allowance to Wallows Wharf or Brierley Hill (LMS) was altered to ½d per ton.

The exemption of Brierley Hill (LMS) from the usual cartage boundary arrangements was paralleled by Great Bridge (LMS) which could collect and deliver in Wednesbury and Darlaston by cart or boat without levying the usual required extra charge on C&D traffic for movement outside the station's agreed cartage/boatage area.

In October 1933, the Conference gave some protection to boatage when it granted a special rebate between Stourport (GWR) and Wilden / Stourvale, mentioning that Baldwins had started to cart this traffic (presumably by motor vehicle as the distances were outside the usual horse cartage range). They made it clear that the special rebate was to apply to boatage only. The standard allowance would have applied to either mode[11].

◆

On 1 January 1948 the LMS and the GWR became part of the Railway Executive of the British Transport Commission. The canals came under the Docks & Inland Waterways Executive whose South Western Division proceeded to carry out a traffic survey of the BCN, Stourbridge and Staffs.& Worcs. (south of Autherley Jn.) canals. This gave the number of interchange depots remaining in use in their Division as 8 ex-LMS and 10 ex-GWR. Estimated tonnages were 82,200 and 177,000 per year respectively. The LMS wharf at Saltley Sidings was in the South Eastern Division and was thus excluded from the survey. It closed in 1963.

Of the South Western Division interchanges listed in 1948, Ettingshall, Tipton Factory, Stourport, Swan Village and Wednesbury were disused by 1950. Boatage traffic ceased at Mill Street in that year and the BR(LMR) Boatage Depots at Kidderminster and Stourport were closed. Albion, Tipton (Watery Lane) and Monument Lane went out of use in 1954, together with their associated Boatage Depots at Primrose and Brierley Hill. Stourbridge, Bromley and Hockley followed in 1958. Monmore Green and Shrubbery survived until 1962[12].

This left only Withymoor (Netherton) which succumbed in July 1965 and Hawne which closed, together with its railway, on 1 October 1969.

FOOTNOTES

1. BCN Railway Basin Traffic returns PRO RAIL 810/311
2. Birmingham Central Library Archives MS 86
3. Birmingham Central Library Archives MS 86
4. Staffs & Worcs Canal Society BROADSHEET May/June 1995
5. BCN Railway Basin Traffic Returns PRO RAIL 810/307
6. Birmingham Street Directories. The depot was in London Rd., Smethwick
7. Birmingham Central Library Archives MS 86
8. Birmingham Central Library Archives MS 86
9. Staffs & Worcs Canal Society BROADSHEET May/June 1995
10. Faulkner A. THOS. BANTOCK/GWR FLEET LIST
11. Birmingham, South Staffs & E. Worcs Conference 1923/37
12. British Waterways Traffic Survey 1962/3 BU Archives Gloucester UM 77/3

C.2594

THE RAILWAY EXECUTIVE
(WESTERN REGION)

Thomas Bantock & Co. Agents

HEAD OFFICE:
LOW LEVEL STATION.

PARTNERS { E. G. BANTOCK
M. BANTOCK.

TELEGRAPHIC ADDRESS:
"BANTOCK"
WOLVERHAMPTON.

TELEPHONE 24031/2.

Wolverhampton 18th July/52

Dear Sir,
    Stourbridge Canal Navigation.

    We are sorry to report that the level of water is down 6" all along this section of the Canal and we are having difficulty in moving our boats both in the basin and along the main Canal. Our boatmen also complain of fouling by weeds, and obstructions such as empty drums thrown into the water by children. We shall be much obliged if you can deal with the matter.

                  Yours truly,

                  Thos Bantock & Co

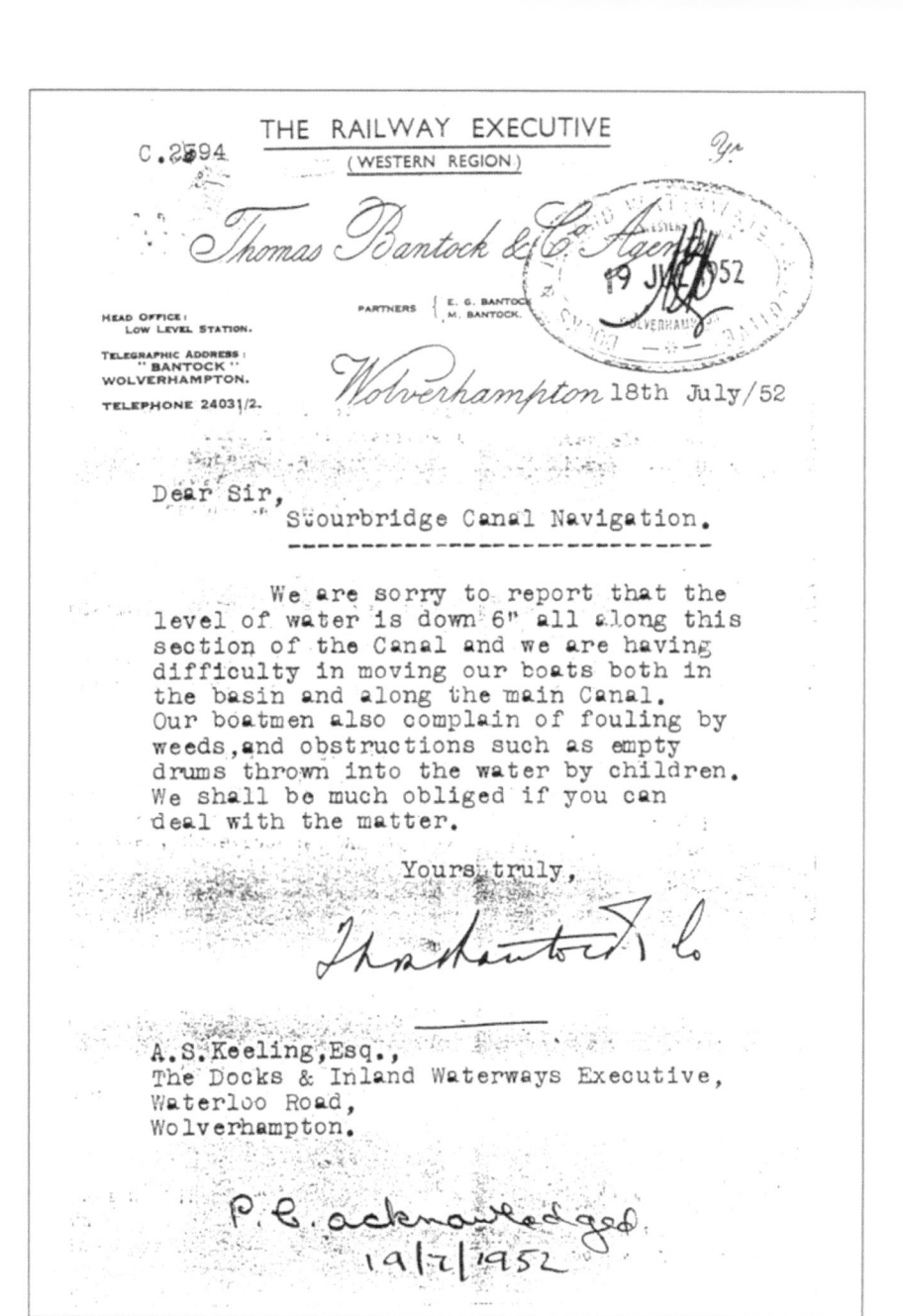

A.S. Keeling, Esq.,
The Docks & Inland Waterways Executive,
Waterloo Road,
Wolverhampton.

P.C. acknowledged
19/7/1952

The above letter from Thomas Bantock & Co to the Docks & Inland Waterways Executive in 1952 suggests that fouling weeds and rubbish in the canal were not confined to the present day
Author's collection

63

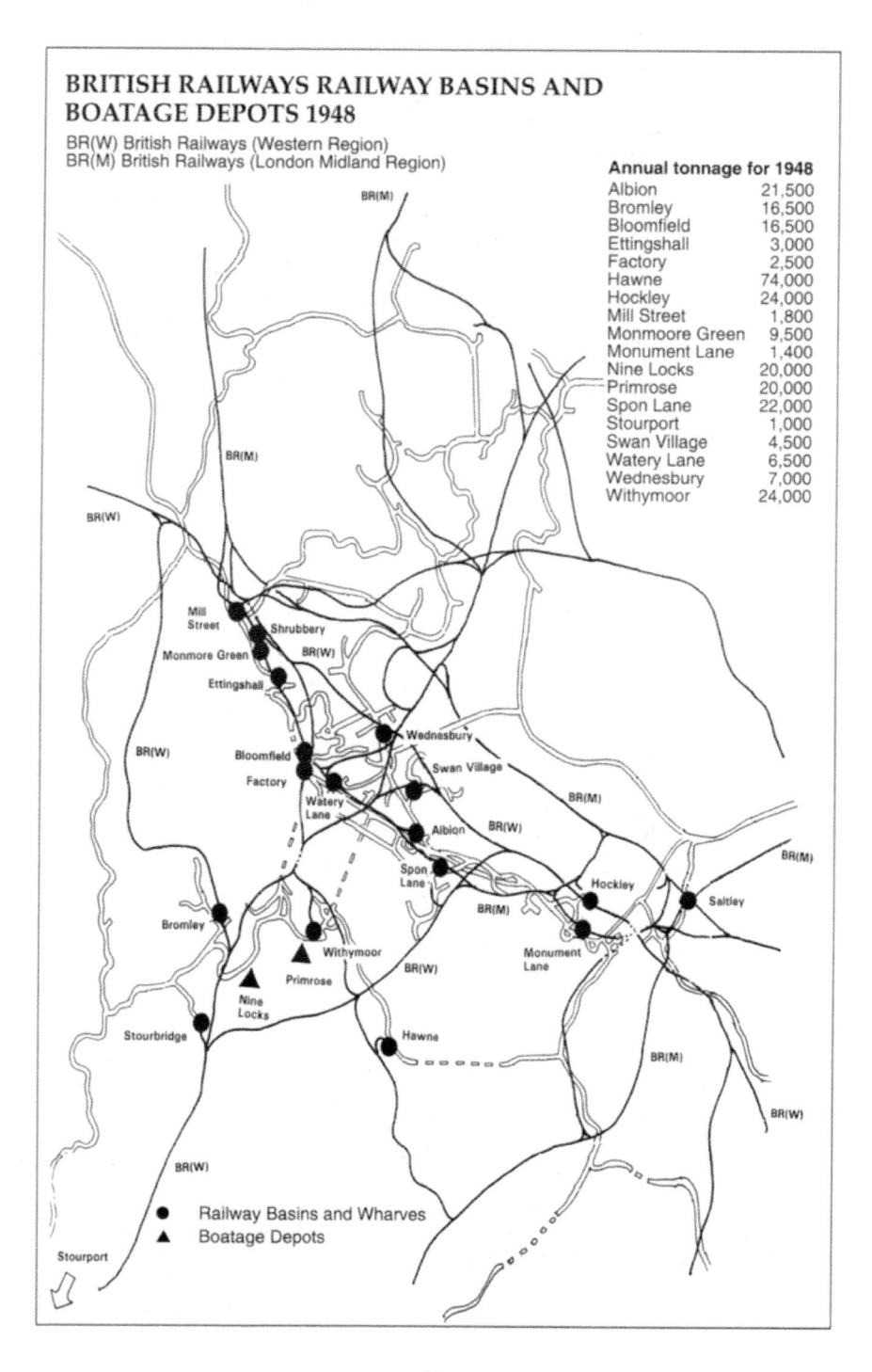

BRITISH RAILWAYS RAILWAY BASINS AND BOATAGE DEPOTS 1948

BR(W) British Railways (Western Region)
BR(M) British Railways (London Midland Region)

Annual tonnage for 1948

Albion	21,500
Bromley	16,500
Bloomfield	16,500
Ettingshall	3,000
Factory	2,500
Hawne	74,000
Hockley	24,000
Mill Street	1,800
Monmoore Green	9,500
Monument Lane	1,400
Nine Locks	20,000
Primrose	20,000
Spon Lane	22,000
Stourport	1,000
Swan Village	4,500
Watery Lane	6,500
Wednesbury	7,000
Withymoor	24,000

● Railway Basins and Wharves
▲ Boatage Depots

Kidderminster Boatage Depot. An LMS boat is loading for Wolverhampton (Mill Street) c 1947

Harry Arnold

A BR (LMR) boat leaves Brierley Hill top lock with fire bricks tfor tipton (Watery Lane) 1954

A T Smith

An LMS boat of the 1928/30 series at Groveland, Tividale. The "flamer" is ready on the fore-end
T W King (courtesy Ms Ruth Collins, Dudley Archives Centre

A station boat leaving Netherton Tunnel south end. Note the towline shortened to keep the horse close to the boat while in the tunnel
T W King (courtesy Ms Ruth Collins, Dudley Archives Centre)

Another view of boats at Groveland. Two BR(LMR) boats are stopped under Groveland Aqueduct on the Netherton Tunnel Branch. The square brick building behind the front horse had a generator that provided electricity to light the tunnel

T W King (courtesy Ms Ruth Collins, Dudley Archives Centre)

An LMS boat passes a Stewarts & Lloyds tug at the south end of Netherton tunnel

T W King (courtesy Ms Ruth Collins, Dudley Archives Centre)

Twelve BR (LMR) boats were sold to British Waterways (North Western Division) in 1954 and given cloths and cabins for long-distance carrying. This one awaits conversion at Stone dry dock
Ian L Wright

The LMS experimented with an outboard engine. ANTWERP is on her trial run to London in 1929
Stanley Holland

Railway boat BR (LMR) 48 pressed into service to install a new lock gate

Black Country Museum

BR (LMR) 22 at Brierley Hill, loaded with firebricks from the Delph to Tipton (Watery Lane)
T W King (courtesy Ms Ruth Collins, Dudley Archives Centre)

The last Shropshire Union fly-boat, SYMBOL, on dock at Chester. Built in 1914, she spent 29 years as an LMS and later BR (LMR) railway boat

Harry Arnold

Station boats loading fire bricks at the Delph for Bromley or Tipton

Author's collection

The last boat to Bromley. GWR No 9 leaves Pearson's firebrick works at the Delph (Stourbridge Canal) in 1958

A T Smith

GWR boat No 24 at Swindon, Staffordshire and Worcestershire Canal in 1954
Author's collection

Stewarts & Lloyds and Bantock boats at Hawne Basin 1956
Author's collection

GKN boat and horse at Smethwick

National Waterways Museum, Gloucester

Albion Basin. The bags may contain seeds for the LMS boatage depot at Brierley Hill

National Waterways Museum, Gloucester

Albion Basin LMSR. Almost every type of traffic was handled by railway boats. Red lead was one exception

National Waterways Museum, Gloucester

More activity at Albion Basin, 1951

National Waterways Museum, Gloucester

A heavy lift at Albion Basin, 1951. The small bags in the boat probably contain nuts and bolts
National Waterways Museum, Gloucester

Guest, Keen & Nettlefold had their own station bats. This one is unloading boxes of screws, from the GKN works on the Cape Arm, at Hockley GWR baasin
National Waterways Museum, Gloucester

CONCLUSION

The closure of the ex-GWR interchange at Hawne, by then part of the London Midland Region, brought to an end 131 years of railway boatage in the West Midlands. At Monmore Green, Hockley, Monument Lane, Swan Village, Great Bridge, Wednesbury, Netherton, Hawne, Primrose (SU) and Curzon Street the basins survived at the time of writing, mostly shorn of their sidings and buildings. At Mill Street, the goods shed and warehouse still stands. The basins there have been filled in but the rings in the wall, to which generations of Crowley, Pickford, Shropshire Union and LMS boats tied up, can still be seen off Horseley Fields, Wolverhampton, Commercial Dock, used for the maintenance of station boats since the days of Crowley and Headquarters of the SU and LMS boatage fleets can still be seen.

If you happen to visit any of these sites, pause awhile and reflect on the history of which they, together with a few surviving boats, are the only physical remains. Think of the battles for access to the canal at Wolverhampton and Brettell Lane; of rival companies' boats racing to catch the last trains; of the Midland managers chafing at the two hour delay at Riders Green and Toll End locks; of wagons ending up in the canal at Great Bridge (what a splash that must have made); of scruffy coal boats being shafted away from Saltley and gloriously smart " Stourlifters" flying along the Stour Cut.

One of these "Stourlifters", the SYMBOL, is the subject of a restoration project. She is owned by the Symbol Restoration Society Ltd., whose aim is to recreate an historically accurate working Shropshire Union Fly Boat.

Monmore Green interchange has recently been "listed". Perhaps, one day we shall once again be able to see a "Station Boat" arrive at a "Station Arm".

Generations of station boats tied up to this ring at Mill Street Basin, Wolverhampton

APPENDIX 1

TRAFFIC STATISTICS

The BCN maintained monthly traffic statistics for interchanges on their canal from 1902 onwards. Those up to 1939 are in the PRO (Rail 810/ 306-7). These give monthly or quarterly traffic amounts at each basin on the BCN, and also contain various reports of boatage interest.

There are more detailed records for September 1928, 1934 and 1937 in the Birmingham Central Library Archives (MS 86 Box 18), giving carriers, nature of cargo, originating and destination points and tonnages.

British Waterways produced estimates of railway basin traffic for its South Western Division in 1948, and again in 1962, which are in the BW Archives at Gloucester.

TRAFFIC AT BCN RAILWAY BASINS 1898 - 1962

DATE	TRAFFIC	DATE	TRAFFIC
1898	1,208,363 tons	1924	739,359 tons
1905	1,108,172 tons	1930	428,087 tons
1913	1,014,254 tons	1938	263,987 tons
1919	933,170 tons	1948	224,200 tons (estimated)
1920	1,038,519 tons	1962	91,272 tons

The period 1905-1913 was probably the busiest tor the BCN and it was during these years that the greatest amount of traffic was carried. Railway basin traffic then accounted for about a seventh of the total tonnage carried.

Statistics for Railway traffic on canals other than the BCN are hard to come by. The SU/LNW and later LMS, traffic from Stourport and Kidderminster was almost entirely handled at Mill Street, a basin which, after the opening of Ettingshall and Monmore Green, was itself almost exclusively devoted to the Staffordshire & Worcestershire Canal trade. The BCN figures for Mill Street, therefore, give a close approximation of the SU/LNW and LMS trade on the Staffordshire & Worcester Canal.

Date:	1905	1938	1948
Tons:	39,341	17,918	1,500

Traffic at GWR Basins outside the BCN were estimated in 1948 as follows:

Basin:	Bromley	Stourbridge	Stourport
Tons:	16,000	18,000	1,000

APPENDIX 2

RAILWAY TRAFFIC AT BCN WHARVES (May 1928)

FROM	TO	CARRIER	GOODS	TONS
Rattlechain	Izons Whf	Own A/C	Bricks	300
Eagle Oil Wks	Izons Whf	Own A/C	Tar	180
Izons Whf	Albion	LMS	Bricks	285
Izons Whf	Albion	LMS	Tar	135
Izons Whf	Swan Village	Bantock	Bricks	55
Spon La. Fdry	Turners Whf	Own A/C	Goods	110
Spon La. Bsn	Turners Whf	LMS	Malt	12
Turners Whf	Spon La. Malthouse	Own A/C	Malt	12
Turners Whf	Spon La. Bsn	LMS	Goods	106
Hall End Oil Works	Small Hth Whf	Own A/C	Goods	910
Small Hth Whf	Hall End Oil Works	Own A/C	Empties	65
			Pitch	360
Swan Village	Small Hth Whf	Bantock	Pitch	360
			Empties	40
Small Hth Whf	Swan Village	Bantock	Tar	340
Small Hth Whf	Albion	LMS	Goods	398
Albion	Small Hth Whf	LMS	Goods	32
Tipton Gn Whf	Bloomfield	LMS	Pitch	127
Bloomfield	Tipton Gn Whf	LMS	Pitch	193
Brades Brick Wks	Whimsey Bridge	Own A/C	Bricks	270
Whimsey Br	Oldbury GWR	Bantock	Bricks	75
Whimsey Br	Spon La. LMS	LMS	Bricks	195
Coombswood Tube Wks	Halesowen Whf	Own A/C	Tubes	11196
Halesowen Whf	Coombswood	Own A/C	Tubes	30
Coombswood	Halesowen Whf	LMS	Tubes	1125
Halesowen Whf	Coombswood	LMS	Tubes &c	480

82

APPENDIX 3

LIST OF RAILWAY BASINS
within the West Midlands

Basin	Location	Canal	Railway
ALBION	West Bromwich	Walsall	LNWR
BILSTON	Bilston	W. Oak Loop	GWR
BLOOMFIELD	Tipton	W. Oak Loop	LNWR
BROMLEY	Brierley Hill	Stourbridge Ext.	GWR
BROWNHILLS	Brownhills	W & Essington	LNWR
CHURCHBRIDGE	Cannock	Staffs & Worcs	LNWR
CURZON STREET	Birmingham	Digbeth	LNWR
DARLASTON	Darlaston	Walsall	LNWR
ETTINGSHALL	Wolverhampton	Main Line	LNWR
FACTORY	Tipton	Main Line	GWR
GREAT BRIDGE	Great Bridge	Walsall	LNWR
GREAT BRIDGE	Great Bridge	Walsall	MR
HAWNE	Halesowen	Dudley	GWR
HALESOWEN	Halesowen	Dudley	MR
HOCKLEY	Birmingham	B. Heath	GWR
LIFFORD	Kings Norton	Worcs & B'ham	MR
MIDLAND	Wolverhampton	W & Essington	MR
MILL STREET	Wolverhampton	Main Line	LNWR
MONMORE GREEN	Wolverhampton	Main Line	LNWR
MONUMENT LANE	Birmingham	Main Line	LNWR
NETHERTON	Netherton	Dudley	GWR
OLDBURY	Oldbury	Oldbury Loop	GWR
SALTLEY	Birmingham	B & Warwick Jct.	MR
SHRUBBERY	Wolverhampton	Main Line	GWR

Boatage Depots

LNW/SU	Withymoor
	Bishton Bridge
	Primrose
	Brierley Hill
	Stourbridge
	Kidderminster
	Stourport
MR	London Street Smethwick (Cape Arm)
	Primrose
	Waterfall Lane
GWR	None

Private / Public Wharves

Pothouse Bridge
Darlaston Green
Tipton Green
Small Heath (Swan Hill)
Nine Locks Bottom
Wallows
Izons
Whimsey Bridge
Turners
Spon Lane

GAZETEER OF WEST MIDLANDS INTERCHANGE BASINS AND BOATAGE DEPOTS

It is the purpose of the Industrial Canal series to examine trade on the waterways, and this volume has dealt with the traffic that was generated between canalside business and the railways.

It is clear that there was a number of interchange points that served the West Midlands and no two were the same. There were those that had a short life and others that survived through to the nationalisation of the rail industry in 1947.

The interchange points were either linear wharves or basins and boats plied the local waterways to factories, works or boatage depots. The boatage depots were canalside wharves where goods were often collected from the locality before passing onto the nearest railhead. Each railway company had its own collection of depots and was thus able to provide a collection and delivery service throughout the West Midlands.

At each railway interchange basin there was a hive of activity where goods were transferred between boats and railway wagons. Many basins were associated with a large railway goods establishment who usually supplied the personnel. The staff who worked at such sites included clerks, shunters and porters.

During the early years horse haulage was commonly employed in the sidings. Complicated track networks, often involving wagon turntables, enabled wagons to reach the wharfside. Policemen controlled movement by signals that were worked by hand. Fortunately track speeds were relatively slow. Wagons could also be moved by capstan, but gradually locomotives had a greater role in assembling and marshalling the trains.

Early working timetables show that there were a number of shunting engine movements to the different goods stations and interchange basins. The Stour Valley, for example, had three such engines (1); Monument Lane Shunt Engine, Bushbury Shunt Engine and the Stour Valley Shunt Engine that worked up and down the line spending time at sidings during different parts of the day. Freight trip engines would collect and drop off wagons also at certain times. The GWR Victoria Basin engine made a nocturnal trip each midnight to work traffic between the basin, Oxley, Priestfield and Bushbury exchange sidings as required (2).

Details of traffic and operations lie within the confines of a railway orientated book, but some details have been mentioned to indicate the destinations of some of the freight services. For those interested in the study of transport patterns a number of choices were available to canalside manufacturer. It is hoped by mentioning some of the freight services the reader might derive a better understanding of the relationship between rail and canal transport in the West Midlands. The reader should note the times these trains called at the basin. Many services called in the evening so that the station boats could make late collections from the factories and works.

The track plans that served the basins have also been included to illustrate the diversity of interchange facilities.

(1) PRO Rail 946-7 LNWR Working Timetable 1872
(2) PRO Rail 937-7 GWR Working Timetable June 1866

ALBION BASIN   LNWR, LMS & BR(M)

1863-1954

Two basins, one covered, which joined the Walsall Canal.

The branch that served the basins connected with the LNWR Stour Valley line south of Albion Station. This railway was authorised by Act of Parliament in 1862 and completed in 1863. LNWR records show that the sidings were joined to the main line during December 1863 (1).

Shunting in the sidings was performed by both locomotives and horses. Horsemen were employed on the branch from the start. Private sidings served the Roway Ironworks (Page & Son), Albion & Britannia Ironworks (J.B & S Lees), Miles & Druce, Stringer Brothers and Stones & Sons Nut and Bolt works. Traffic for all these works was handled by horses (2). The horses when not at work were kept in a stable overlooking the BCN near Albion Station.

In 1872 Albion was served by 17 freight services which included two trains from Camden to Bushbury, a Birmingham to Liverpool service and a Monument Lane to Leeds freight. There was also a North Staffordshire Railway (Stoke) freight that ran to Spon Lane and called at Albion in both directions (3).

Present situation: The basins have been filled in and part of site built upon. Odd pieces of track remain as does the covered goods shed.

(1) PRO RAIL 410 / 171 November 19th 1863 LNWR Traffic Committee refers to plan for siding connection and estimated cost of work (£402). PRO RAIL 410 / 297 December 4th 1863 states sidings at the Albion had been commissioned.
(2) There are various reference from 1863 in LNWR records to horsemen being employed Albion sidings. Two horses were killed through an accident there in 1864.
(3) PRO RAIL 946 / 7

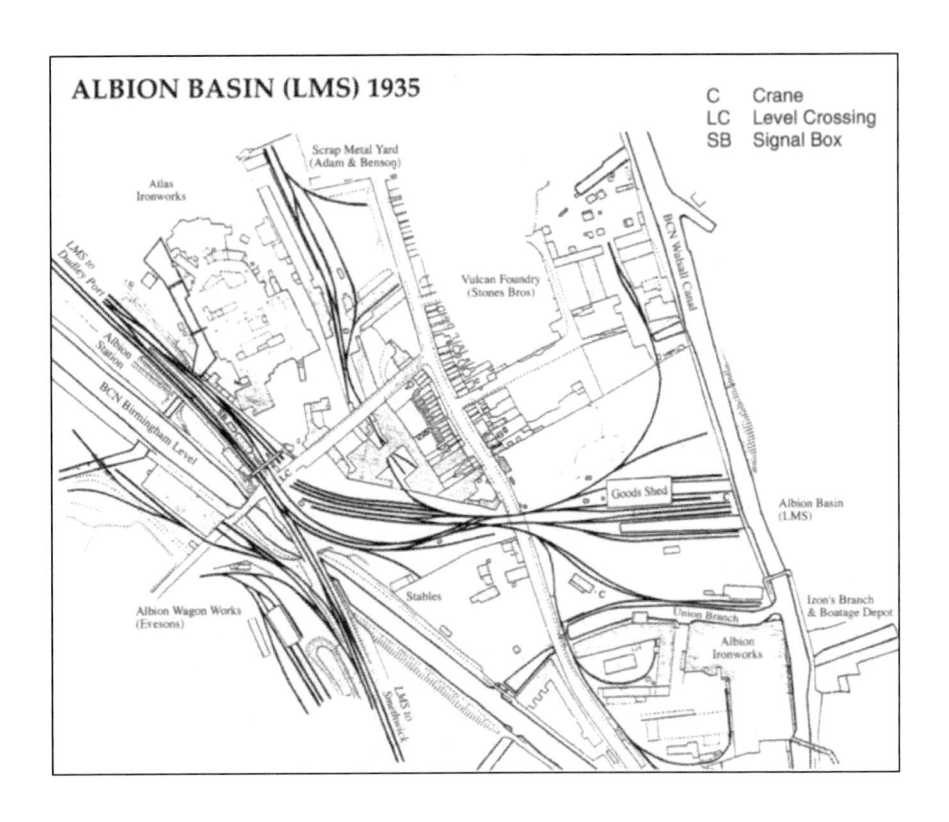

ALBION BASIN (LMS) 1935

C Crane
LC Level Crossing
SB Signal Box

BILSTON BASIN   GWR

1908-1935

One basin with covered shed that joined the Bradley Loop north of Pothouse Bridge.

The railway sidings connected with the lines to Bilston Goods, south of Bilston station. Traffic was generally tripped through to Oxley sidings, Wolverhampton. But there were five afternoon services that deserve mention:

GWR Working Time Table 1909 (1)

		Bilston	
		Arrive	Depart
6.55pm	Didcot - Oxley	3.00am	3.10am
8.05pm	Victoria Basin - Paddington	8.30pm	9.00pm
4.20pm	Crewe – Bordesley	10.50pm	11.10pm
11.20pm	Oxley - Exeter	11.45pm	11.55pm
11.30pm	Oxley - Swindon	11.55pm	12.08am

Present situation: The basin has been filled in and track removed. Site however remains undeveloped.

(1)   PRO Rail 937 / 100

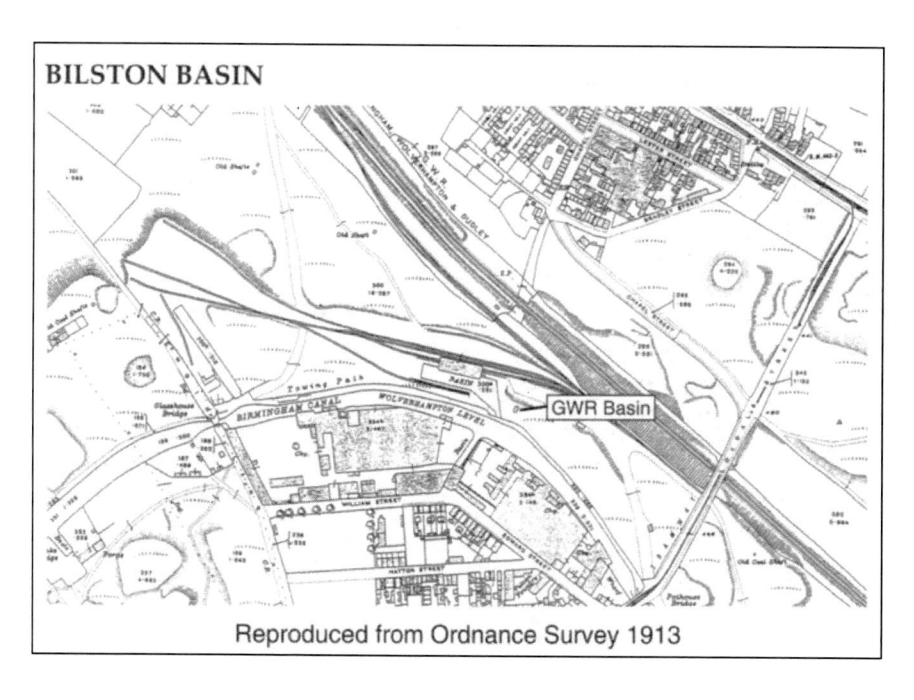

BILSTON BASIN

Reproduced from Ordnance Survey 1913

The interior of Bilston Basin. Note the corrugated sheets being loaded into the wagon. Bilston and Wolverhampton had a number of canalside works that manufactures sheet iron

Ned Williams

BISHTON'S BRIDGE

LNWR / SUC Dudley Wood Boatage Depot

This wharf was situated on the towpath side of the Dudley (No.2) Canal 160 links west of Bishton's Bridge (1). It was placed between the BCN Dudley Wood Wharf and Kendall's Chain Works.

(1)   BCN Distance Tables c.1911.

BLOOMFIELD BASIN   LNWR, LMS, BR(M)

1852-1954

There were three basins that joined the Bradley and Wednesbury Oak Loop near Bloomfield Junction.

The railway sidings connected with the LNWR Stour Valley Line north of Tipton Station. This basin was first planned by the SVR to accommodate 4 boats and was referred in their minutes to as The basin above the locks at Tipton. Plans were later modified and three basins instead of one were made. One basin was adapted from the old route of the canal. There were a number of wagon turntables used here that permitted access to the canal wharfs from a number of angles. Additional sidings were put down from time to time as traffic increased (1).

The 1872 working timetable shows that Bloomfield was served by 17 weekday freights which were the same as Albion. However there was also a footnote that is worth reproduction:

To meet the extra traffic at Spring Vale, Bloomfield and stations between Dudley Port and Bushbury, the Stour Valley shunting engine leaving Bushbury at 6am for Albion will return to Bloomfield at 9.10am thence to Deepfield and Spring Vale. After dinner the same engine to revisit the same stations for shunting and marshalling leaving Spon Lane at 5.50pm for Bushbury.

Present situation: The site is covered by a firm that renders down brick for aggregate. Track and turntables were discovered when the firm set up here and these probably still remain.

(1)   PRO RAIL 410 / 172 April 14th 1864 refers to the making of an additional siding at Bloomfield Basin. In May 1864 this siding, for Mr Brogden's traffic, was said to have cost £92.

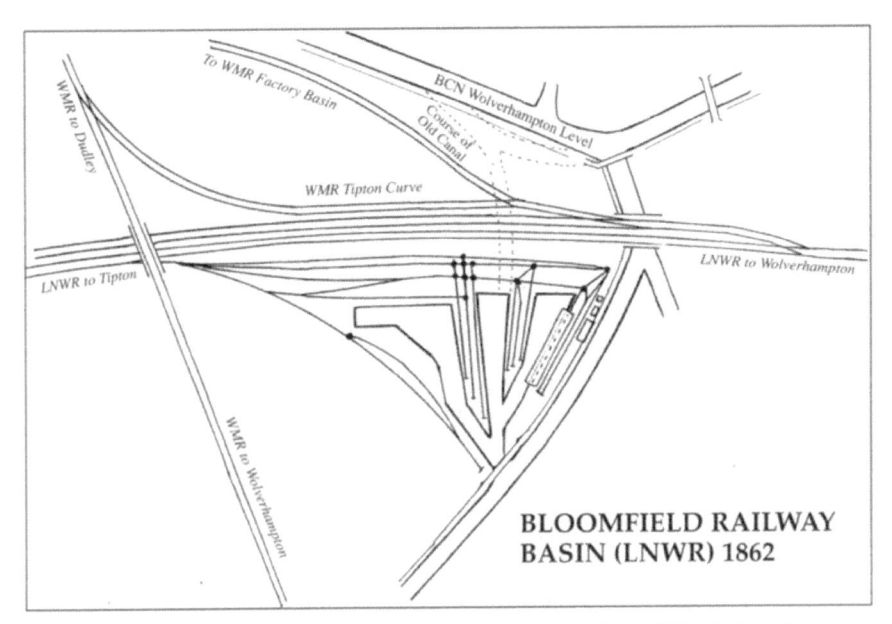

A sketch plan of Bloomfield Basin which shows the original course of the old Birmingham Canal (Wednesbury Oak Loop)

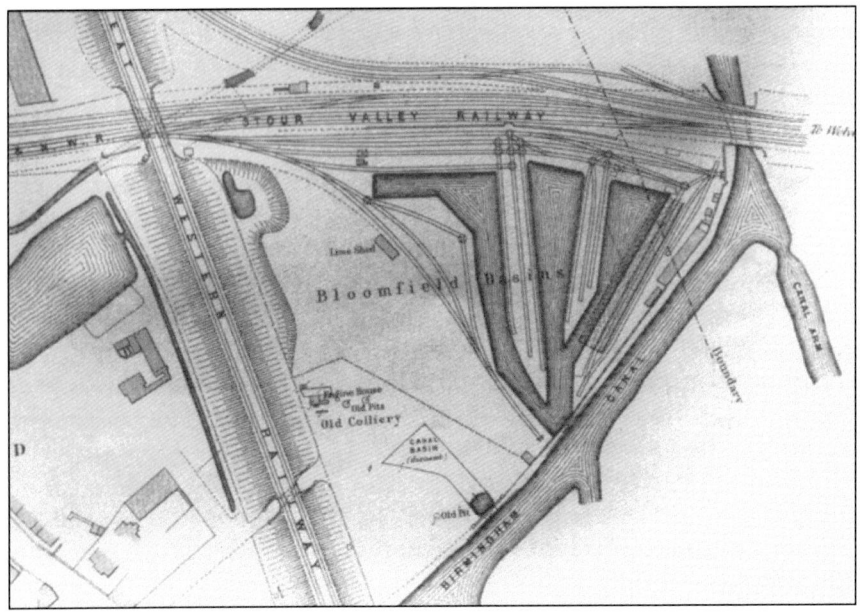

The above plan of Bloomfield Basin shows the additional land the LNWR wanted to take for Bloomfield Basin in 1893　　　　　　　　　　　　　　　　　　　　　　　　*Author's collection*

BRETTELL LANE   OWWR, GWR

There were chutes placed beside the Stourbridge Canal at Brettell Lane for the transhipment of minerals from rail to boats. The siding that served these chutes ran from a wagon turntable which in turn connected with a siding from the goods shed.

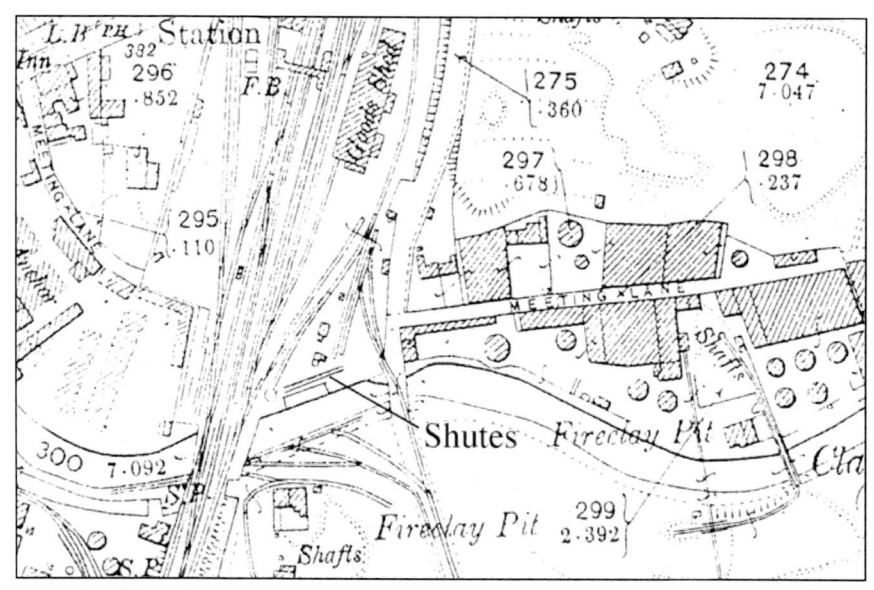

Reproduced from the Ordnance Survey 1901

BROMLEY WHARF   OWWR, GWR, BR(W)

1858-1958

A *linear wharf that was placed beside the Stourbridge Extension Canal near the junction with the Fens Branch.*

Sidings connected with the Kingwinsford Branch.

Bromley Basin, in 1909, was served by three weekday trips to and from Kingswinsford Junction. The departures from Bromley were at 2.00pm, 6.45pm and 9.00pm respectively (1).

Present situation: One railway track and the wharf remain, albeit overgrown. This end of the canal is still in water, although there is an uncertain future if the bridge across the junction is removed.

(1)   GWR Working Timetable, PRO Rail 937/100

BROMLEY WHARF (GWR) 1901

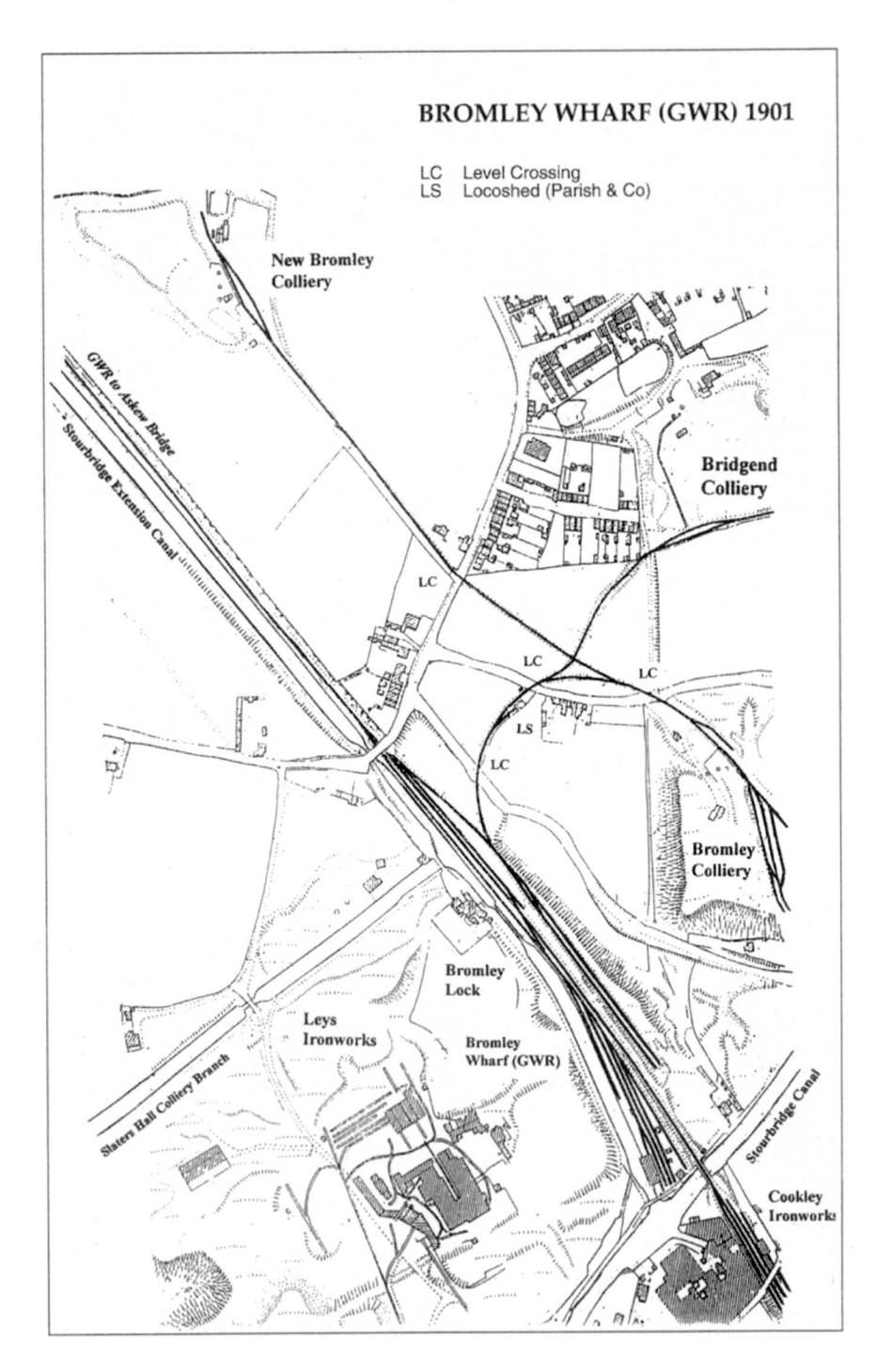

LC Level Crossing
LS Locoshed (Parish & Co)

New Bromley Colliery

Bridgend Colliery

GWR to Askew Bridge

Stourbridge Extension Canal

LC
LC
LC
LS
LC

Bromley Colliery

Bromley Lock

Leys Ironworks

Slaters Hall Colliery Branch

Bromley Wharf (GWR)

Stourbridge Canal

Cookley Ironworks

93

Behind the guillotine stop lock on the Stourbridge Extension Canal is Bromley Basin (GWR)

Michael Hale

The shed at Bromley Basin (1968)

Michael Hale

BROWNHILLS BASIN   SSR, LNWR, LMS
1856 - 1936

Two basins, one covered, joined the Wyrley & Essington Canal at Brownhills.

The sidings connected with the South Staffordshire Railway south of Brownhills Station.

The 1872 Working timetable refers two freights each way between Dudley and Wichnor Junction and one each way between Birmingham and Wichnor. There were also three trains that arrived from the Norton Branch, the last (6.40pm arrival) left coal at the basin.

Present situation: Site is partly occupied by a supermarket, although the basins remain intact.

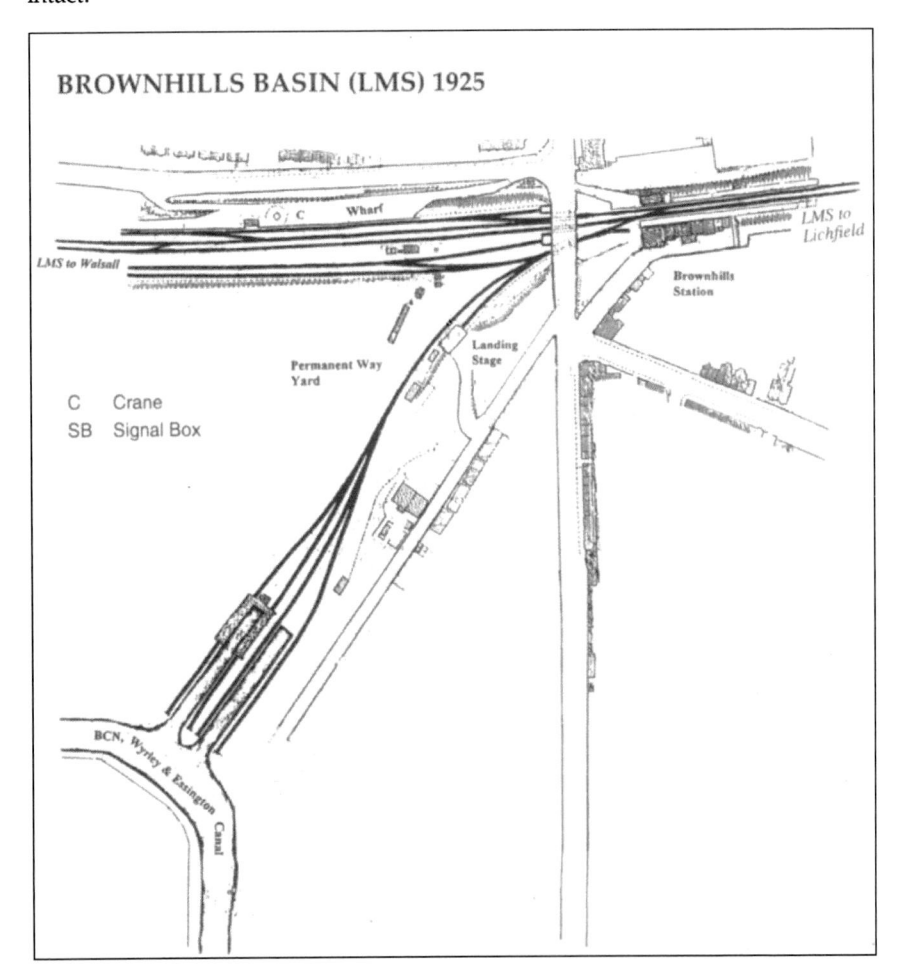

BROWNHILLS BASIN (LMS) 1925

C   Crane
SB   Signal Box

CAPE ARM   MR

The Cape Arm was part of the original BCN that became a loop when Telford's line was constructed. It served a number of factories including the GKN London and Nettlefold's Screw Works.

BCN Distance Tables for 1885 (1) refer to the arm by two titles. In addition to Cape Arm, it was also known as the Smethwick Grove Branch. This piece of canal was separated from the main line by the embankment that carried the feeder from Rotten Park through to the Engine Arm. The entrance to the arm passed through a tunnel under the feeder embankment. It then curved round to serve the London Works and Nettlefold's Screw Factory. Mapplebeck's Tube Works were at the Abberley Street end. The Cape Basin joined the Cape Arm opposite Nettlefold's Works. This long basin served a number of works including the Grove Foundry, The Cape Sheet Ironworks and the Regent Grove Ironworks.

The Midland Railway had a wharf (A) that was on the corner of London Street and Cranford Street. The GWR and LNWR are believed to have used a wharf (B) which was next to the Nettlefold's Screw Works. It is also understood that there were no railway staff, clerical or manual, employed at the Nettlefold's wharf (2).

(1)   PRO Rail 810 / 305
(2)   Information from Frank Popplewell, a former GWR employee at Hockley.

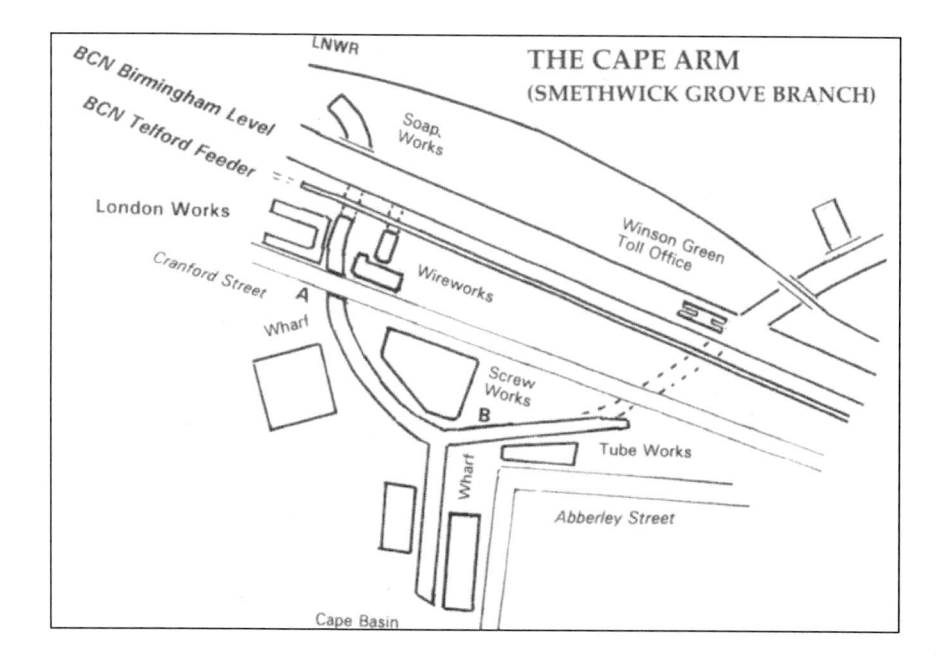

CHURCHBRIDGE BASIN   SSR, LNWR, LMS

1860-

One basin, complete with covered shed, joined with the BCN Churchbridge Branch at the junction with the Hatherton Canal (Staffordshire & Worcester Canal)

Railway sidings connected with the LNWR Cannock and Rugeley line south of Churchbridge Station. Standard gauge private sidings to Gilpin's Edge Tool Works joined with the basin sidings. Traffic in the basin siding was generally horse worked. But locomotives also worked along the branch to Hawkins (Old Coppice) Colliery Exchange sidings, constructed in 1900. Gilpin also had a 2 ft gauge tramway that ran from their works to Great Wyrley Colliery.

The LMSR working timetable for 1929 (1) states that the service to Churchbridge Basin had been suspended. This statement is assumed to refer to time-tabled traffic and is perhaps an indication that basin traffic had ceased. Trips, as required, continued to be made to the colliery and Gilpin & Co's sidings. Rail traffic on the branch ceased after the colliery closed in 1960.

Present situation: All track removed and basin filled in. The canal has been abandoned and completely removed north of the A5. There is shallow water near the basin site and a base of an old wharfside crane remains hidden amongst the undergrowth.

(1)   PRO RAIL 957/ 127

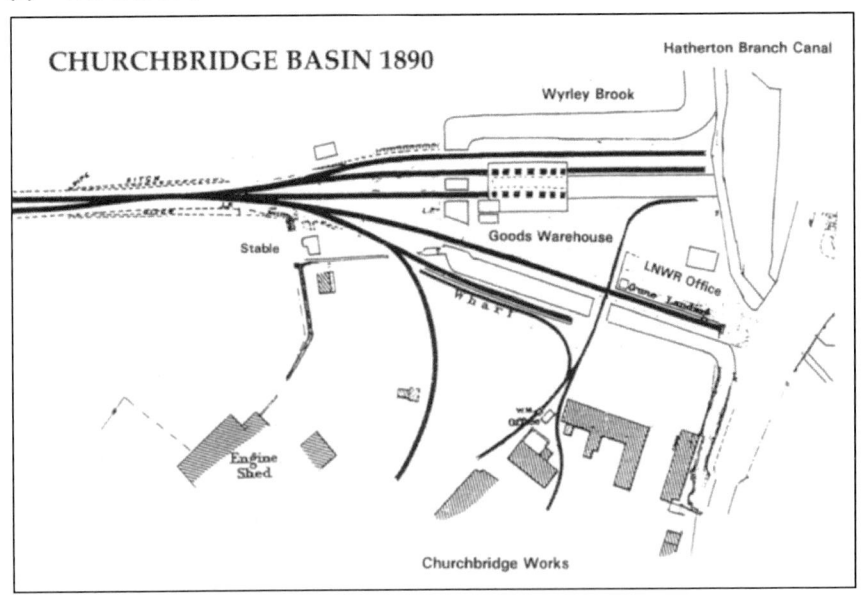

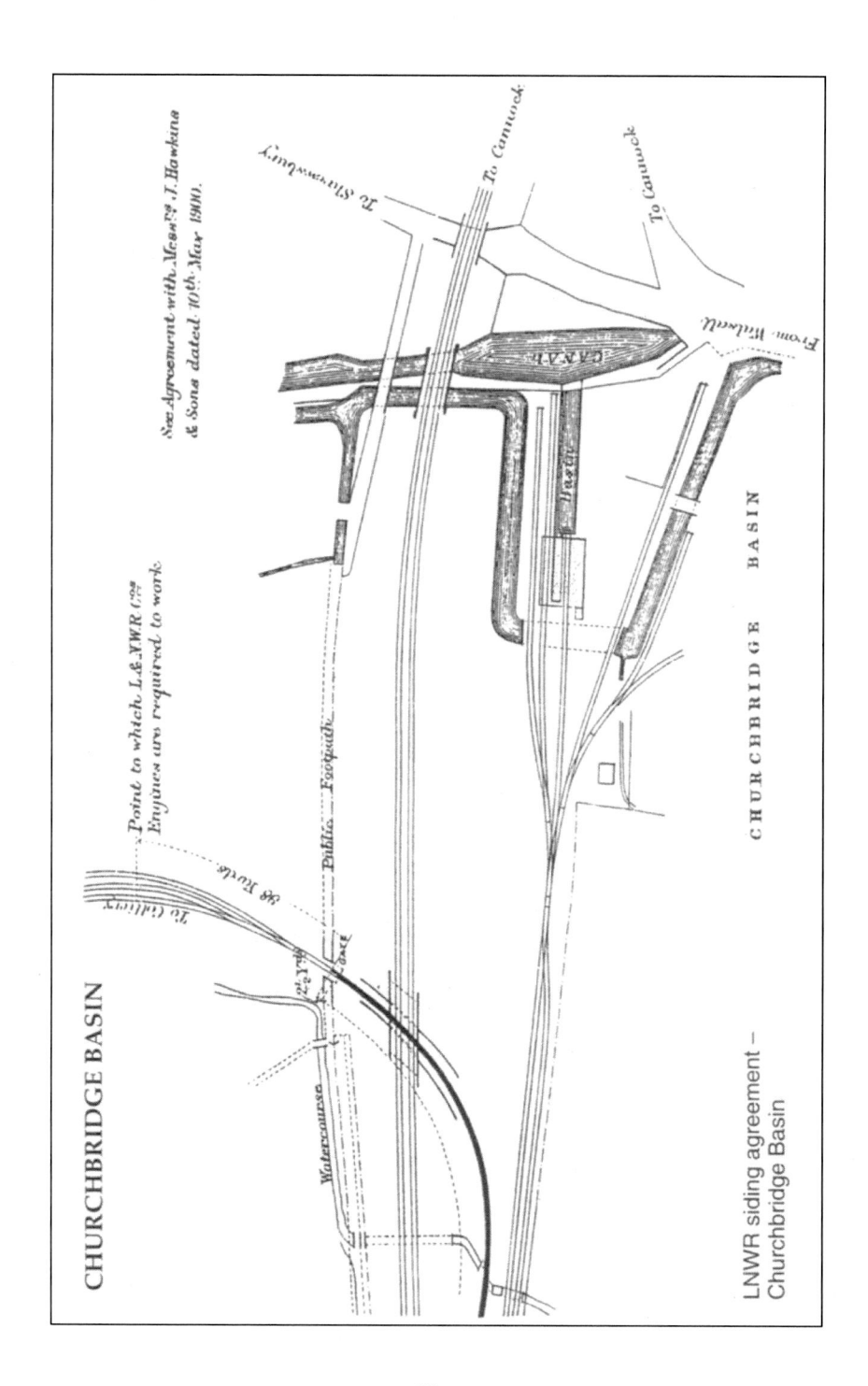

CHURCHBRIDGE BASIN

LNWR siding agreement –
Churchbridge Basin

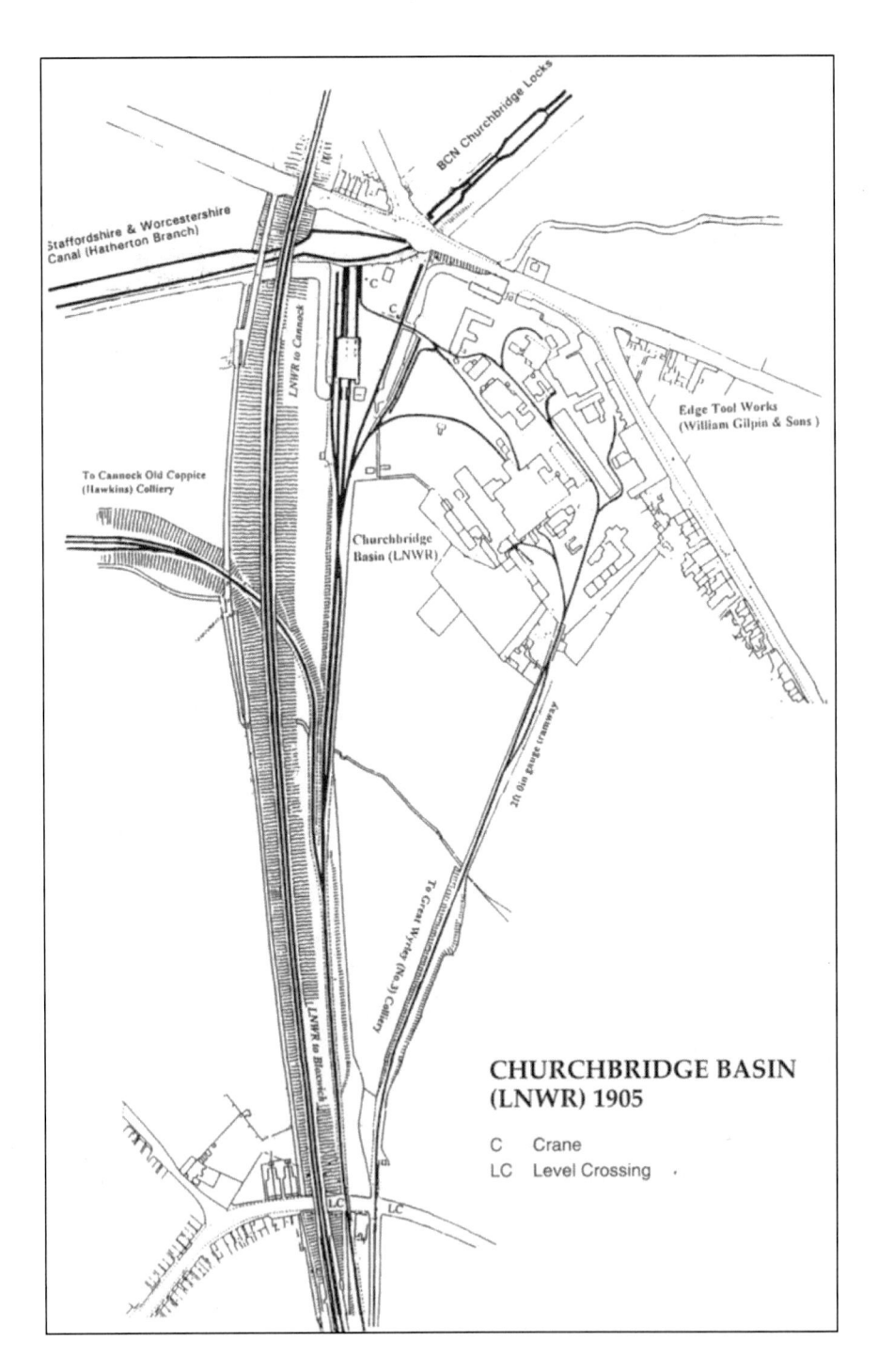

CHURCHBRIDGE BASIN (LNWR) 1905

C   Crane
LC Level Crossing

CURZON STREET BASIN   GJR

1838-

One basin, with covered shed, joined the Digbeth Branch.

This basin would probably hold only one boat at a time and was adapted from the lock side pound of the 6th, or bottom, lock of the Ashted Flight.

A single track ran down to the basin. The basin ceased to be used prior to 1880 and the siding was removed.

Present situation: The lock pound remains and was dredged in 1997. Curzon Street was an important goods depot until 1960, when it was converted to a Parcels Concentration Depot. The sidings that served this depot was then drastically altered and all trace of the track that served the old wharf disappeared about that time.

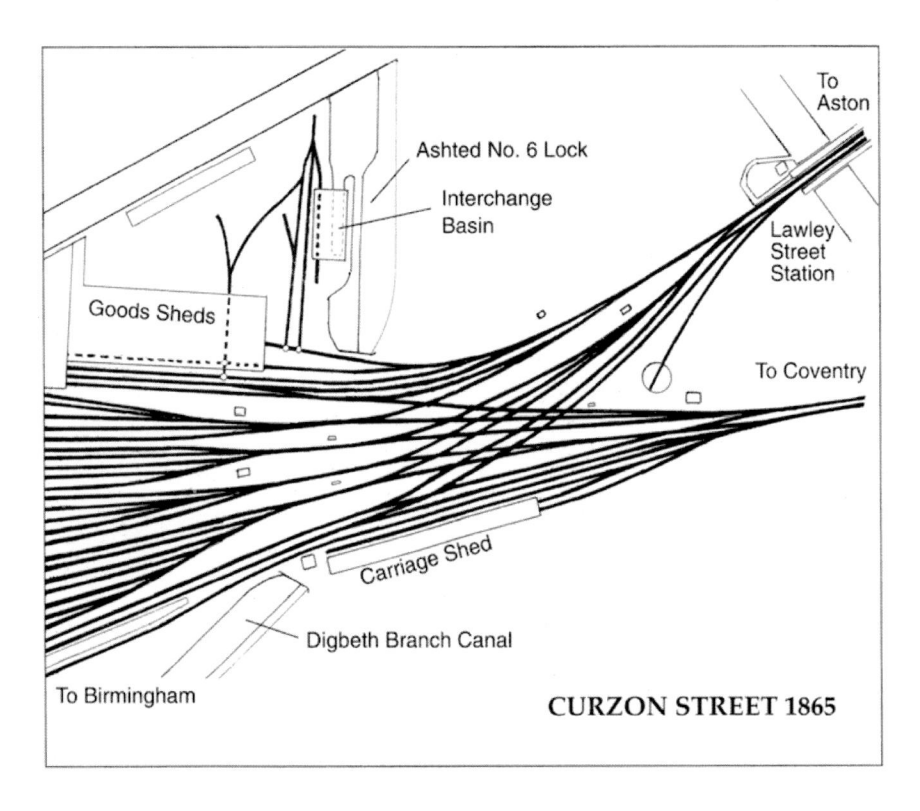

CURZON STREET 1865

CURZON STREET WHARF   LBR

1839-1848

A linear wharf and covered shed placed beside the Digbeth Branch below the 6th Lock

This wharf had a relatively short existence. It was served by a siding from main station that dropped down to canal level by a wide and curved route. All traffic to the canal, it is believed, was worked by horses.

The construction of the Birmingham Extension Railway that commenced in 1849 obliterated most, if not, all traces of the wharf. Later railway extensions by the Midland Railway have covered over the rest.

DARLASTON BASIN   GJR, LNWR, LMS

1845-1935

One basin, with covered shed, which joined the Walsall Canal near Darlaston.

An early railway interchange basin whose sidings connected with the GJR. Darlaston was one of four interchange basins in the West Midlands that had been adapted from earlier basins. Bilston, the MR Basin at Great Bridge and Monmore Green had previous uses for colliery or ironworks traffic.

Darlaston Basin had previously been used by the Birmingham Coal Company who also operated the Toll End Furnaces. The Darlaston mines produced principally ironstone for their furnaces.

The GJR line cut across the surface of the Coal Company colliery. Property adjoining the basin and a strip of land were acquired to make, in 1845, the short branch from the GJR. Sidings were constructed at the junction which became known as Darlaston Green Sidings. A single track ran down to the basin but opened out into a number of sidings for the shed and wharfside. Contemporary railway maps refer to the basin as Darlaston Green Goods Station.

Traffic may well also been handled for Jesse Tidesley (Crescent Ironworks) and the London & North Western Bolt and Nut works.

The 1872 LNWR working timetable states that Darlaston Green Sidings were served by 12 down and 10 up trains.

Present situation: The basin remains although clogged with reeds.

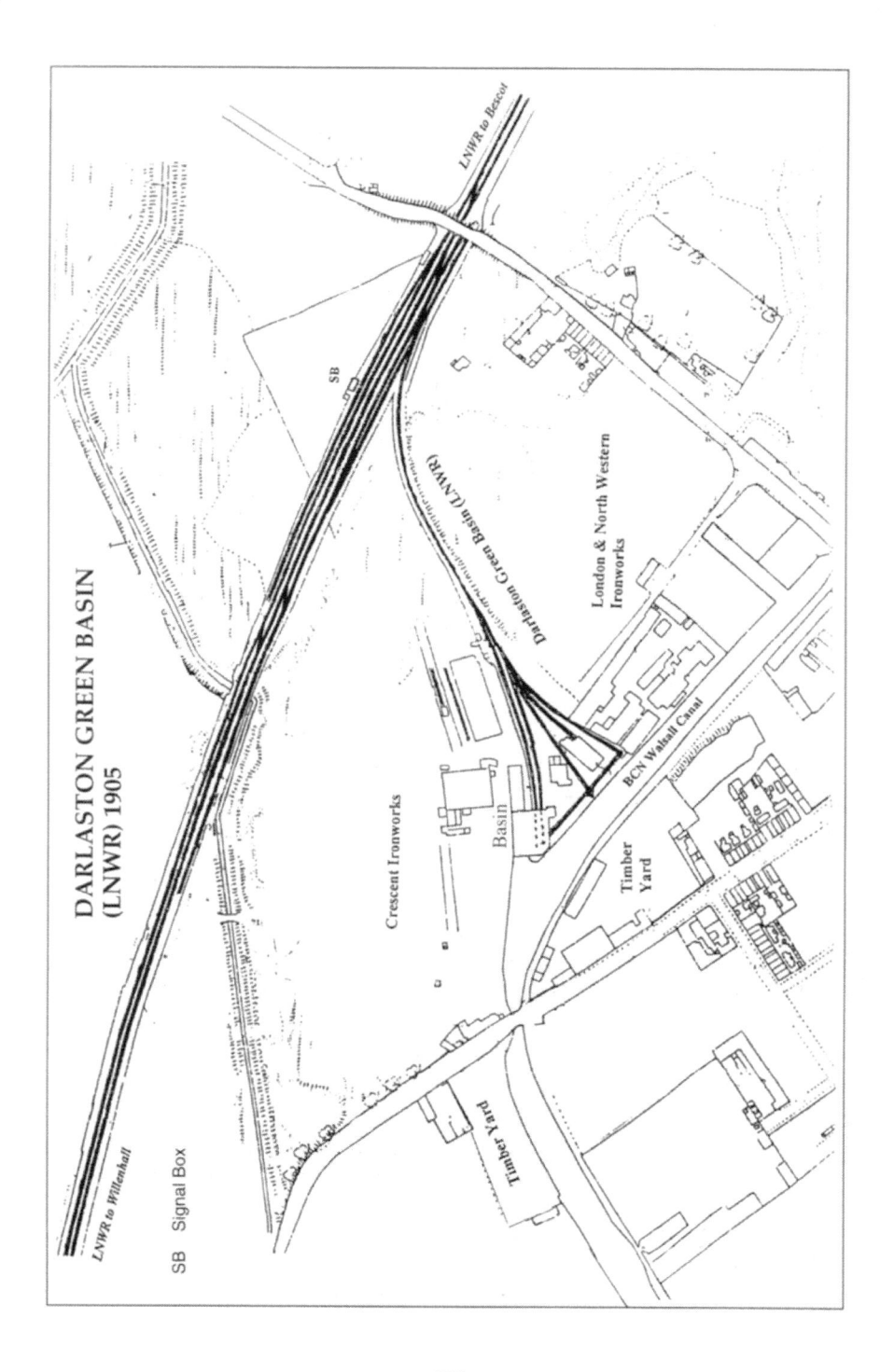

DARLASTON GREEN BASIN (LNWR) 1905

SB Signal Box

102

ETTINGSHALL WHARF   LNWR, LMS

1881- 1950

The wharf and covered shed were situated beside the Birmingham Canal close to Roundshill Stop.

The sidings were an extension of the lines within Ettingshall Goods. In 1929 (1) Ettingshall Goods Station was served by 22 freight trains. These included:

	Ettingshall Arrive	Depart
1.30am Monument Lane - Bushbury	5.30am	5.40am
5.49am Ettingshall - Bescot		
11.15am Bushbury - Wednesbury	11.54am	12.02pm
1.58pm Stechford - Ettingshall(SX)	5.23pm	
7.00pm Monmore Green - Soho	7.05pm	7.23pm
5.10pm Monument Lane - Bushbury	8.00pm	8.08pm
9.05pm Monument Lane - Crewe	12.22am	12.32am

Present situation: There are factory units on the site and the bank has been built up from the old level.

(1)   LMSR Working Timetable PRO Rail 957 / 127

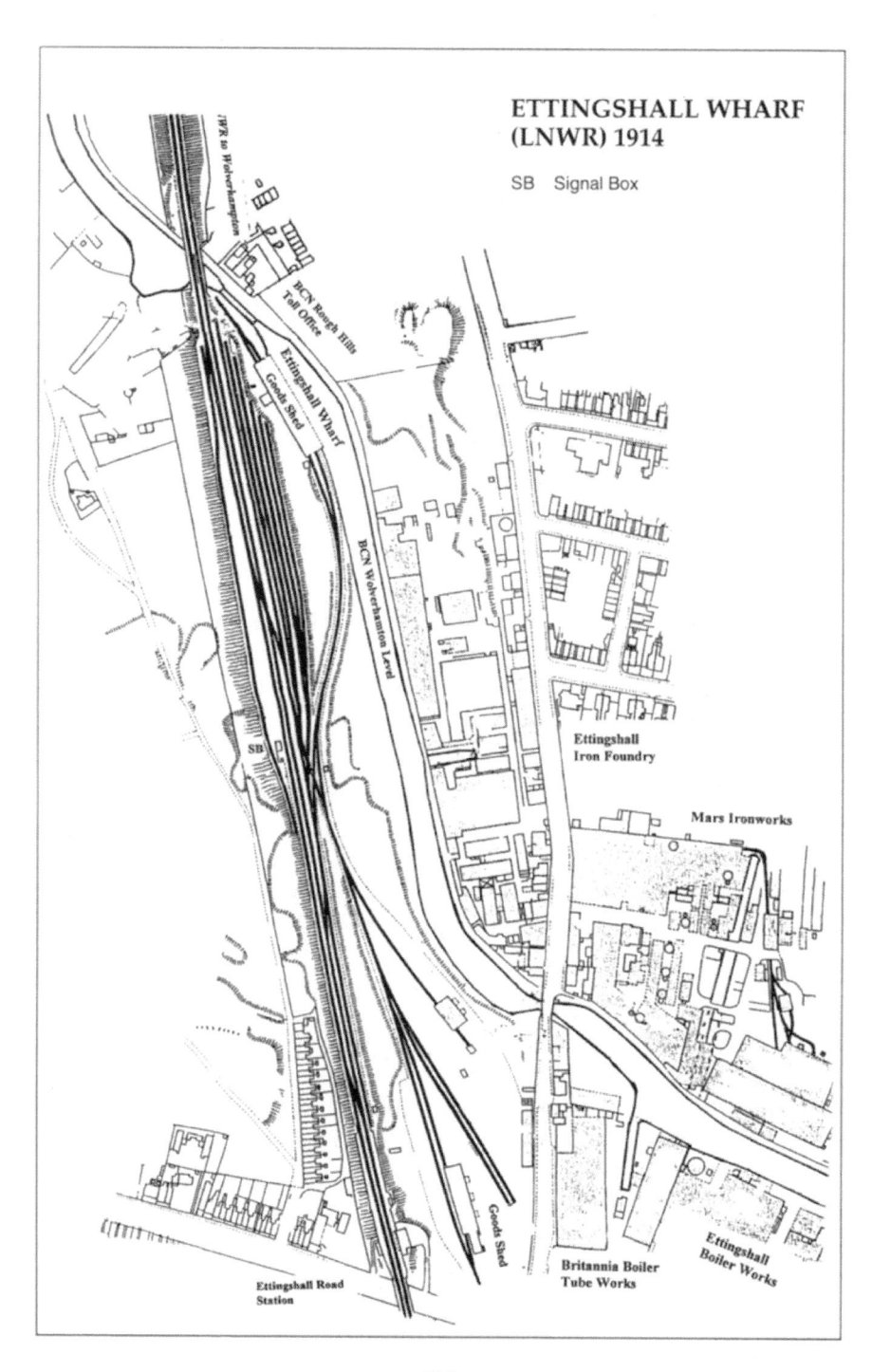

ETTINGSHALL WHARF (LNWR) 1914

SB   Signal Box

FACTORY   OWWR, WMR, GWR, BR(W)

1855-1949

Two basins that joined the BCN near Factory Bridge.

When the canal was completed through Tipton in the year 1771 there was a water mill on the site. The Bloomsmythy Mill was probably one of the earliest ironworking sites in the district. At this location, iron smelting was carried out as early as the thirteenth century (1). The mill remained on the site and iron manufacture was continued through to the eighteenth century.

The premises were acquired by James Keir and Alexander Blair who rebuilt and enlarged them to make a soap factory. Here they made alkali which they converted into soap, white lead and red lead. A canal basin was constructed into the site. This basin which handled the chemical traffic for the soap works was in place by 1791. In later years the factory was under the proprietorship of John Stevenson. These works were for sale in 1836 and shortly afterwards had ceased production. The premises then became a brass foundry and were later purchased by the OWWR to make way for their new railway to Wolverhampton. The OWWR decided to make a railway interchange basin here.

Railway sidings connected with the spur line, Tipton Junction to Bloomfield Junction, which was completed in 1854 to join the OWWR with the SVR. The connection was severed at the Bloomfield end after 1866. The spur line thereafter only handled traffic for the basin line. Standard gauge sidings also served the Tipton Proof House whose buildings were constructed, c1869, adjacent to the canal basin. A feature of Factory Basin was a lift bridge across the two canal channels. This bridge has survived and can be seen at the Black Country Museum.

The 1909 Working Timetable (2) refers to 8 freights that served the basin. These included 3.40 pm from Oxley to Withymoor Basin, the 6.30pm from Victoria Basin to Pontypool and the 8.40pm Cannock Road Junction (Wolverhampton) to Reading.

Present State; The side bridge across the entrance to the basin has survived, but all trace of the basin has been buried under new factory units.

(1)   D. Dilworth, The Tame Mills of Staffordshire.
(2)   PRO Rail 937 / 100

TIPTON GWR AND LNWR BASINS 1900

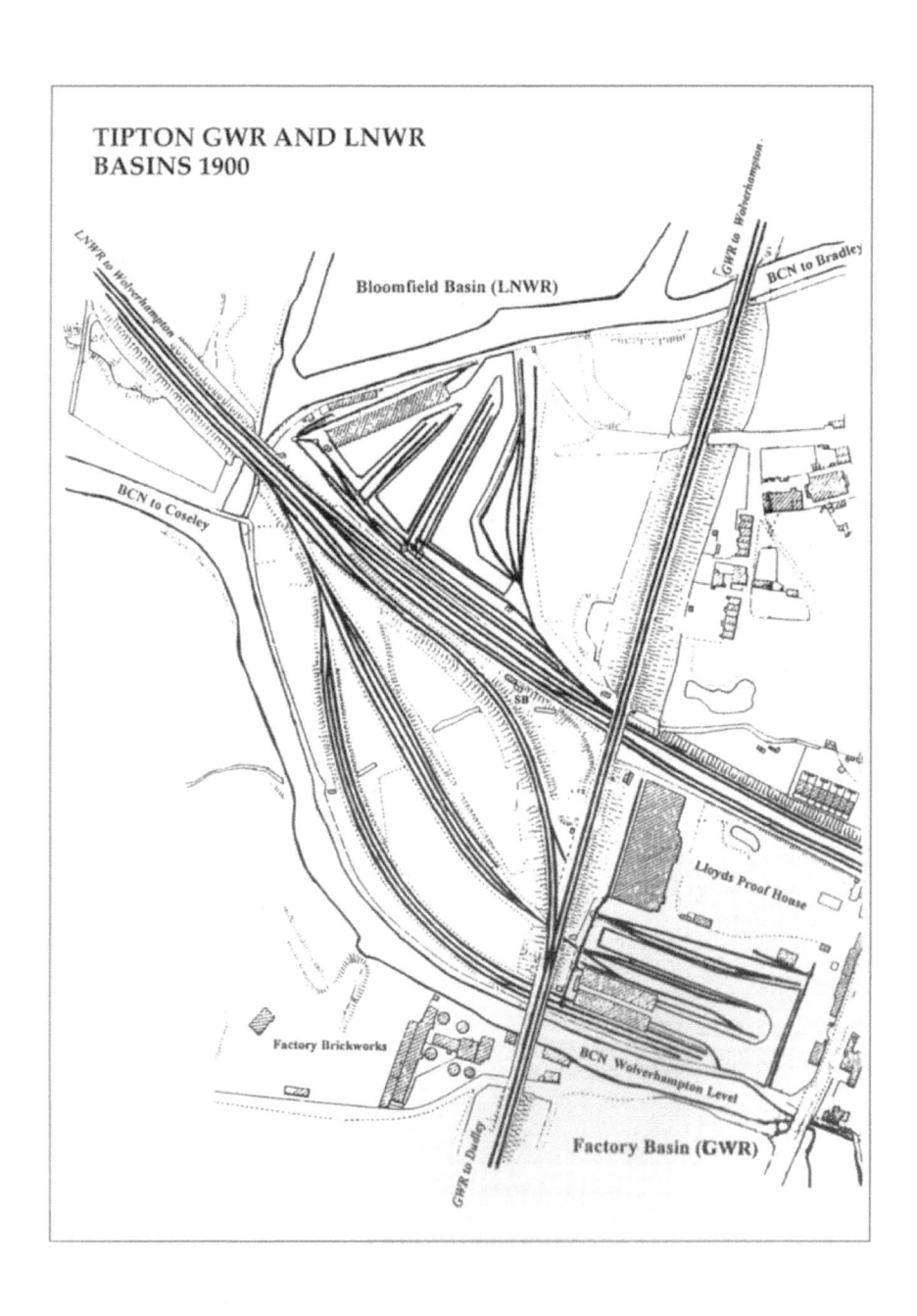

Tipton Factory and Bloomfield Basins from the air, 1949

Aerofilms Ltd

The GWR installed a lift bridge across Factory Basin. This bridge is now at the Black Country Living Museum

National Waterways Museum, Gloucester

GREAT BRIDGE   SSR, LNWR & MR, LMS, BR(M)
1850-1949

Two basins joined with the Walsall Canal near the bottom of Ryders Green Locks. A third, and separate, basin was located on the towpath side opposite the other two. This single basin was exclusively used by the Midland Railway (from 1867) for their traffic.

The first interchange basin at Great Bridge was adapted from an earlier basin. It was previously used to carry away coal and ironstone from nearby mines. The second pair of basins were purpose built for the South Staffordshire Railway. These second set handled important interchange traffic during the early 1850s.

Railway sidings connected with the South Staffordshire Railway north of Great Bridge (SSR) Station. These sidings were once the headquarters of the SSR goods manager. G.P Neale has described these early years:

> *Served by the line between Wednesbury and Greatbridge were a large number of Ironworks and Furnaces and by sidings and connections with the Canal the whole of the busy "black country" could be reached. So highly important were the business developments in this respect that it was, shortly after the opening, decided to have a local traffic manager on the spot, and an old comrade of Mr Payne's, Mr John Brown, was ultimately engaged as goods manager of the line with his head quarters at Greatbridge; he had previously been with the Midland Company at their Gloucester Station. Under his charge the traffic had largely developed, and Greatbridge became a busy centre. The water carriers, Messr Crowley & Company, as well as Pickfords Agents, Messr Howson & Ketley, were frequent visitors; Messr Eborall & Soar for the L & N. W and Walklate for the Midland kept in touch with the work in the interests of their respective companies.*
>
> *The sidings adjoining the Canal basin gave us a lesson in Station Yard working. They were laid unavoidably on falling gradients, and in spite of warnings and cautionary notices, again and again, the wooden stop blocks at the end were broken up and wagons went into the Canal. A heavy stone buffer block suffered the same fate, and Mr McClean's resident Engineer, Mr Walker, determined to try the effect of dispensing with buffer stops of any kind; the danger of careless running of wagons was patent to the shunters, and there followed a perfect immunity from such occurrences- the danger ensured the safety! (1)*

Operation of the South Staffordshire Railway passed to the LNWR who took over the working of the interchange basins.

The single basin was taken over by the Midland Railway who used it for their interchange traffic. The Midland possessed a fleet of boats which were based here.

These boats collected and delivered to goods to a number of regular customers.

In 1872 (2) 26 LNWR freights served Great Bridge, most of which ran between Dudley and Bescot or Wichnor Junction. Shunting engines were stabled here for most of the day (6am -10.00pm).

In 1909 (3) six freights called at Great Bridge for Midland Traffic. These included the 8.20pm and 10.15 Dudley - Derby trains. The site was small and cramped. Sidings that served the basin were associated with the other sidings that served the main goods depot. In LMS days, and presumably MR days, there were two stable blocks placed nearby where the shunting and boat horses would be kept.

The last interchange traffic ceased before 1949, but the sidings were retained for the goods station and later steel terminal. The old Midland Basin was filled in during the 1960s, but the former LNWR basin remained. The covered shed was taken down about 1968 and one canal siding survived until the late 1970s.

Present State; Great Bridge (LNWR) Basin remains in water. Timbers from the old shed are dumped in the basin together with at least one sunken boat.

(1)   Railway Reminiscences, G.P Neale, 1904.
(2)   PRO Rail 946 / 7
(3)   PRO Rail 963 / 95

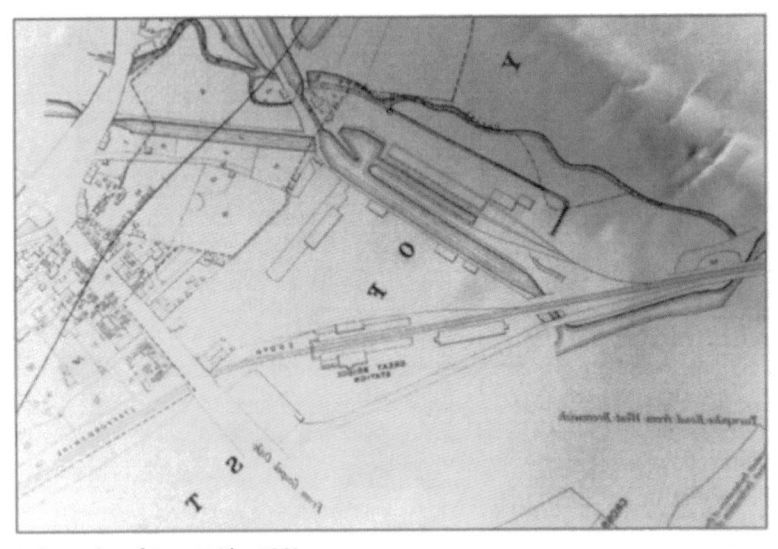

Railway plan of Great Bridge 1862

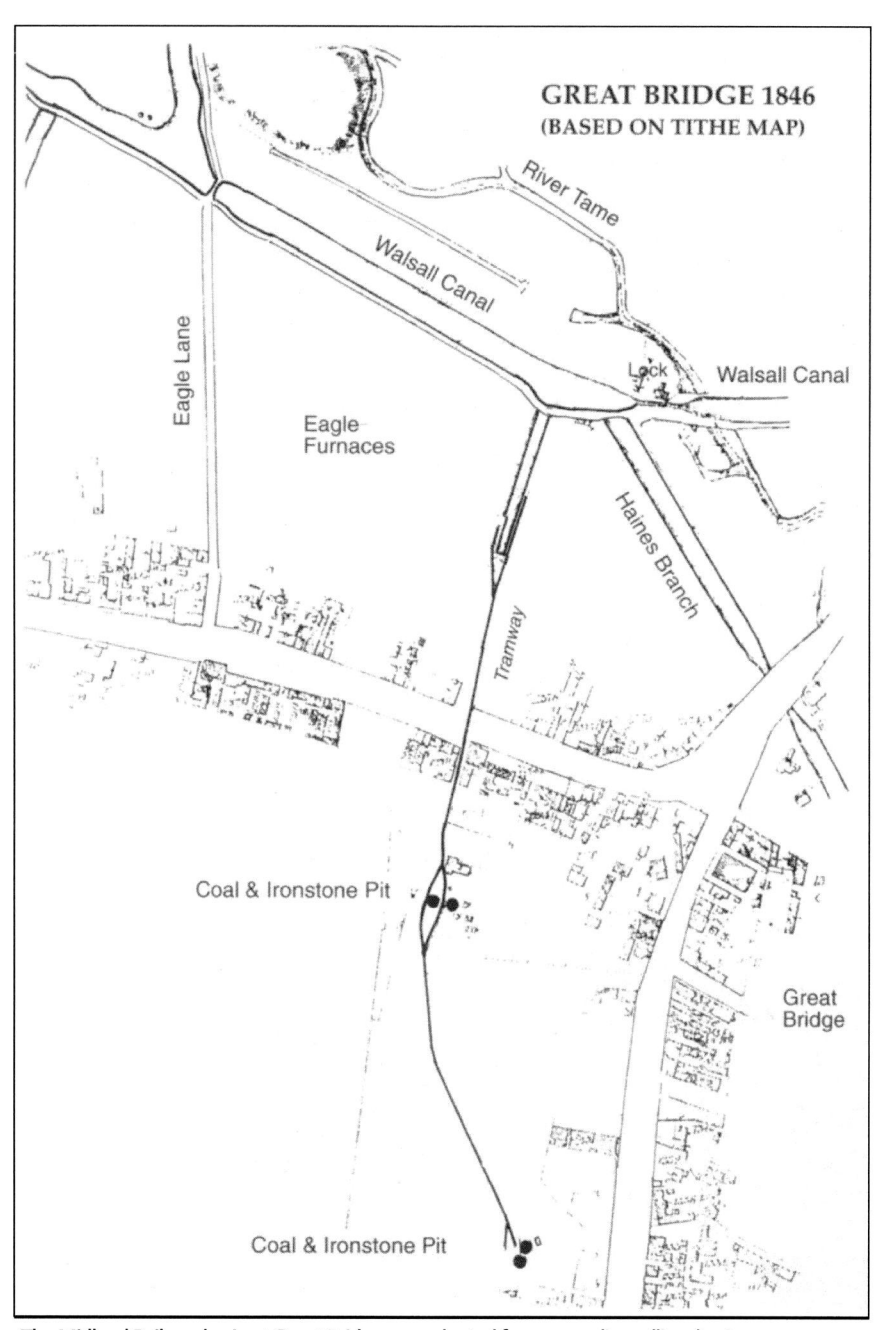

The Midland Railway basin at Great Bridge was adapted from an earlier colliery basin

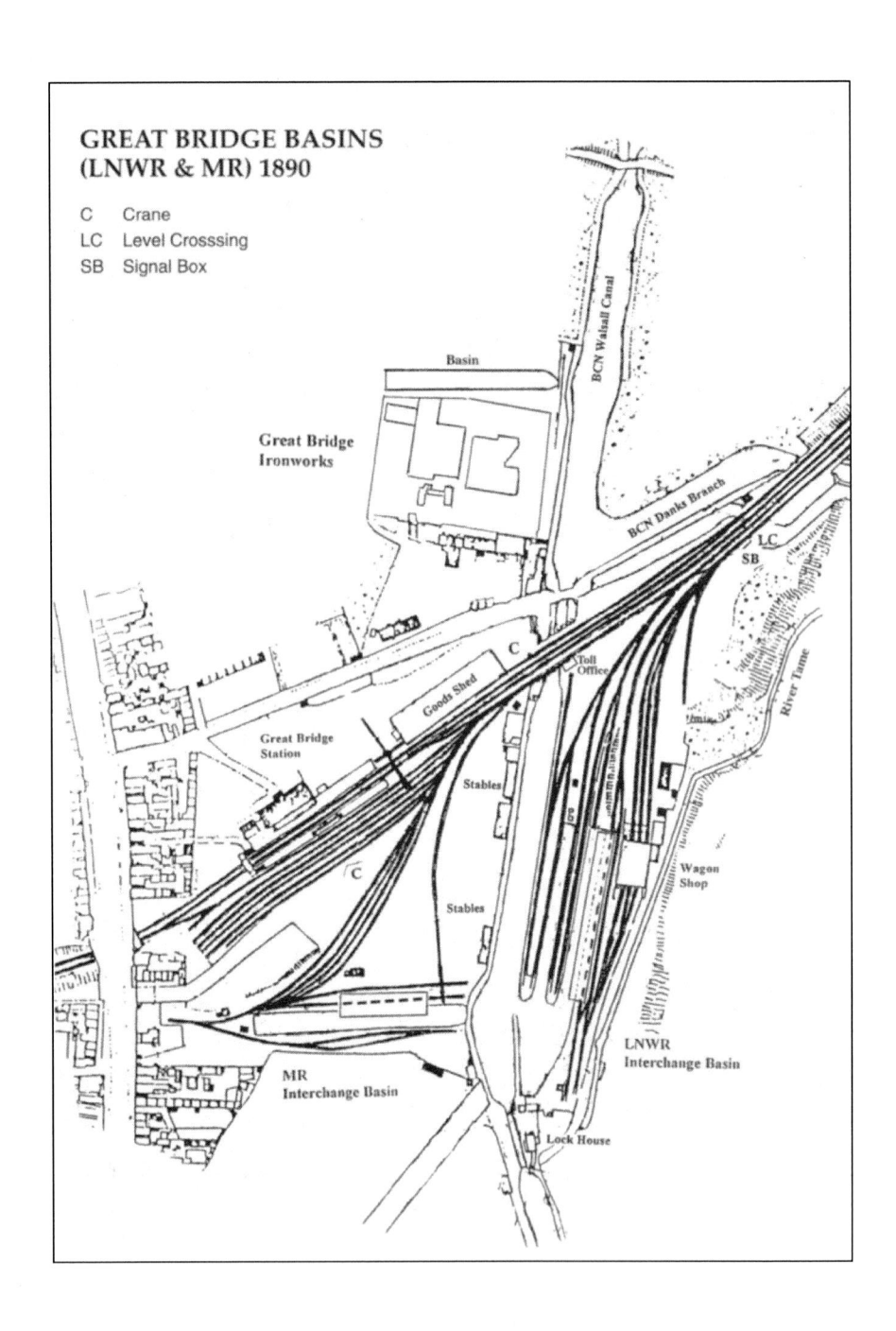

GREAT BRIDGE BASINS
(LNWR & MR) 1890

C   Crane
LC Level Crosssing
SB Signal Box

Basin

Great Bridge Ironworks

BCN Walsall Canal

BCN Danks Branch

LC
SB

Toll Office

Goods Shed

Great Bridge Station

Stables

River Tame

C

Stables

Wagon Shop

LNWR Interchange Basin

MR Interchange Basin

Lock House

The interior of Great Bridge LNWR Basin before overall roof removed

Alan Price

A view of Great Bridge Basin in 1969 after the shed roof had been taken down. Note the entrance to Midland Basin on left side of picture is still in water

National Waterways Museum

HALESOWEN (HEYWOOD) WHARF   BCN
1798-1930

Halesowen (Heywood) Wharf was established by the Dudley Canal Company as a wharf and coal merchants yard. It passed to the BCN who maintained the wharf for public trade. Distance tables for 1885 state that there was a warehouse and crane here (1). Both the GWR and MR used Halesowen for interchange traffic carting by road to Halesowen Goods Station.

Midland Railway Working Timetables (2) record a number of freights that passed along the Halesowen Branch to Halesowen Goods.

6.15 am Kings Norton - Halesowen (7.15 am arrive)
9.40 am Kings Norton - Halesowen (11.12 am arrive)
1.15 pm Washwood Heath - Halesowen (4.55 pm arrive)
7.42 pm Kings Norton - Halesowen (8.10 pm arrive) Mixed Goods
11.40 am Halesowen - Kings Norton (2.10 pm arrive)
5.40 pm Halesowen - Lawley Street
8.25 pm Halesowen - Birmingham

With the 5.40 and 8.25 departure from Halesowen, the Guard was to wire Birmingham if conveying shipment traffic.

(1) PRO Rail 810/305
(2) PRO Rail 963 / 95

Plan c.1890 Halesowen Wharf

HAWNE   GWR, BR(W), BR(M)
1902-1969

One basin and covered shed that joined the Dudley No.2 Canal near Halesowen.

Hawne basin was adapted from an earlier basin which had been constructed for the Hawne Colliery. A tramway from Hawne Colliery ran to the wharfside so that the coal could be loaded into boats.

The basin was later purchased by the GWR who used it chiefly to capture the trade from the nearby tubeworks. A railway branch was constructed from the GWR Old Hill to Halesowen Railway and sidings laid out beside the basin.

These sidings were enlarged and improved as traffic increased. Sidings also served Walter Somers and Coombswood Colliery. An important traffic was tubes from Stewarts & Lloyds at Coombswood. In later years additional private sidings were provided for Stewarts & Lloyds' tube trade.

In 1909 there were nine trains that worked down to the basin. A number were short workings between the Junction Sidings (Old Hill Branch) and the Basin.

    5.35am Old Hill - Basin (arrive 6.05am)
    6.00pm Halesowen - Basin (arrive 6.35pm)
    7.35pm Junction Sidings - Basin (arrive 7.45pm)
    9.15pm Junction Sidings - Basin (arrive 9.30)
    7.15pm Basin - Junction Sidings (North traffic for 7.25 ex Halesowen)
    8.50pm Basin - Junction Sidings
    9.00pm Basin - Old Hill
    10.00pm Basin - Junction Sidings (Clear all traffic for 9.00 ex Halesowen)

Hawne remained the last interchange basin to be used for canal interchange traffic.

The basin was later taken over by the Coombswood Canal Trust who use the basin for residential moorings. The basin shed was declared unsafe by British Railways and pulled down.

Present State: The basin remains in water and has regular boaters traffic to and from the Dudley No 2 Canal. The distinctive entrance bridge has also survived and is now called Burton's Bridge after the restorer Chris Burton.

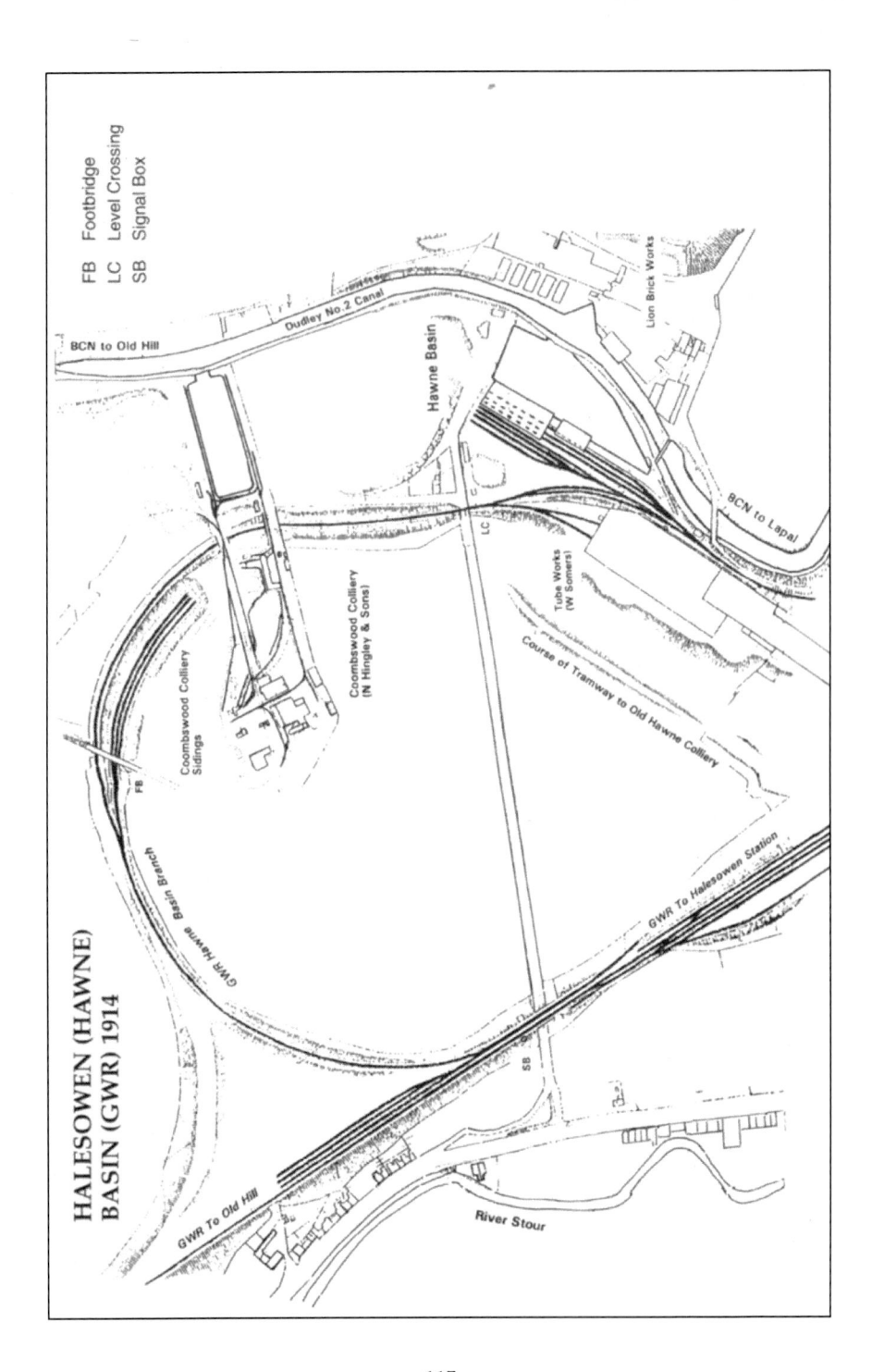

HALESOWEN (HAWNE) BASIN (GWR) 1914

FB Footbridge
LC Level Crossing
SB Signal Box

Tubes being transhipped at Hawne GWR Basin

National Waterways Museum Gloucester

HAY (ALBERT)   SBR

1850-1851

Hay Basin has had a complicated history. It was constructed by the BCN for the Shrewsbury & Birmingham Railway and sidings were laid to the basin. The connection was taken up some time after 1852 when the BCN decided to let the basin as a public wharf. The LNWR then made various attempts to relay sidings to it and the basin across the Wednesfield Road. Each time the proposals were opposed by Wolverhampton Borough Council who insisted on bridges should replace level crossings on their streets. By February 1864 work had started on a new siding but it was stopped after a disagreement concerning the widening of the bridge over Littles Lane. Sidings were eventually put down during the 1870s, but traffic was restricted.

HAY BASIN (LNWR) 1900

FB   Footbridge
LC   Level Crossing
SB   Signal Box

HOCKLEY   GWR, BR(W)
1855-1958

Two basins, one covered, which joined the Birmingham Heath Branch.

Sidings connected with the railways which served Hockley Goods. The lines passed under All Saints Road to the base of a wagon lift which raised the wagons to the basin level. This lift was hydraulic powered until replaced by a new electric lift in 1939. Hockley was the largest GWR goods station in Birmingham. The Working Timetable (1) for 1909 mention frequent trips to and from Bordesley and Oxley. Many through freights called here including;

12.35am Bordesley - Birkenhead
12.50am Basingstoke - Oxley
 6.55am Swindon - Oxley
11.40pm Handsworth - Paddington

The sidings that led to the basin once handled important traffic and were at the end of the main branch that passed through the goods depot. A description published in the Great Western Magazine provides a good illustration of the types of traffic handled:

> *The depot is in direct communication with the Birmingham Canal Navigation, and fleet of Barges, owned by the Company convey merchandise to and from firms having waterside premises. Commodities so delivered and collected include coils of wire, cases and bags of screws, slab copper, steel strip. iron, electric cable, tea etc; the distance involved in some instances amounts to between five and six miles (2).*

The GWR decided in 1935 to remodel the Goods Depot at an estimated cost of a quarter of a million pounds. Work commenced in 1938 and was finished in 1943. Part of the alterations included new trackwork. The basin roads now came off a turntable at the end of one of the yard roads.

From 1945 work carried on as before, the basin remained busy. Christopher Burton, the last Chief Clerk at Hockley describes the operation of this link in the post war years:

> *To get to the basin wagons had first to be shunted out to the north end of one of the yard roads. It was noticeable that, when doing this the shunters used to take a wicked delight in shunting them out rather fast for the pleasure of watching "Monty", the capstan man, who was no athlete and had long legs, to run after them to put the break down. Then under Monty's guidance and with much squeaking of capstan ropes, they were worked, one at a time over two turntables and passed through a cavernous arch under All Saint's Street to the electric wagon lift. The lift took them up one at a time to the high level of the basin yard.(3)*

The basin yard had stables, road motor garage and a few coal merchants. By 1958 the traffic into the basin had dwindled to between one and two boats per day. Their contents were enough to make 3 outwards wagons; one to Bristol, Cardiff and London(Paddington).

General basin traffic ceased in 1958, but some rubbish traffic was continued for a number of years later (4). Hockley Goods closed in 1967 and was later demolished. The Basin Yard remained and was used by the British Rail Millwrights until 1977.

Many of the old buildings survived and the site was renovated in 1983 and it became the Hockley Port Centre. The canal wharves and the remaining piece of the Birmingham Heath Branch have been adapted as residential moorings.

(1) PRO Rail 937 / 100
(2) The Great Western Railway Magazine, March 1939
(3) Behind the Lines, Christopher Burton 1979
(4) Recollections of John Greenham, Shunter at Hockley

A view of the tunnels under All Saints Street through which wagons passed to base of wagon lift
Heartland Press collection

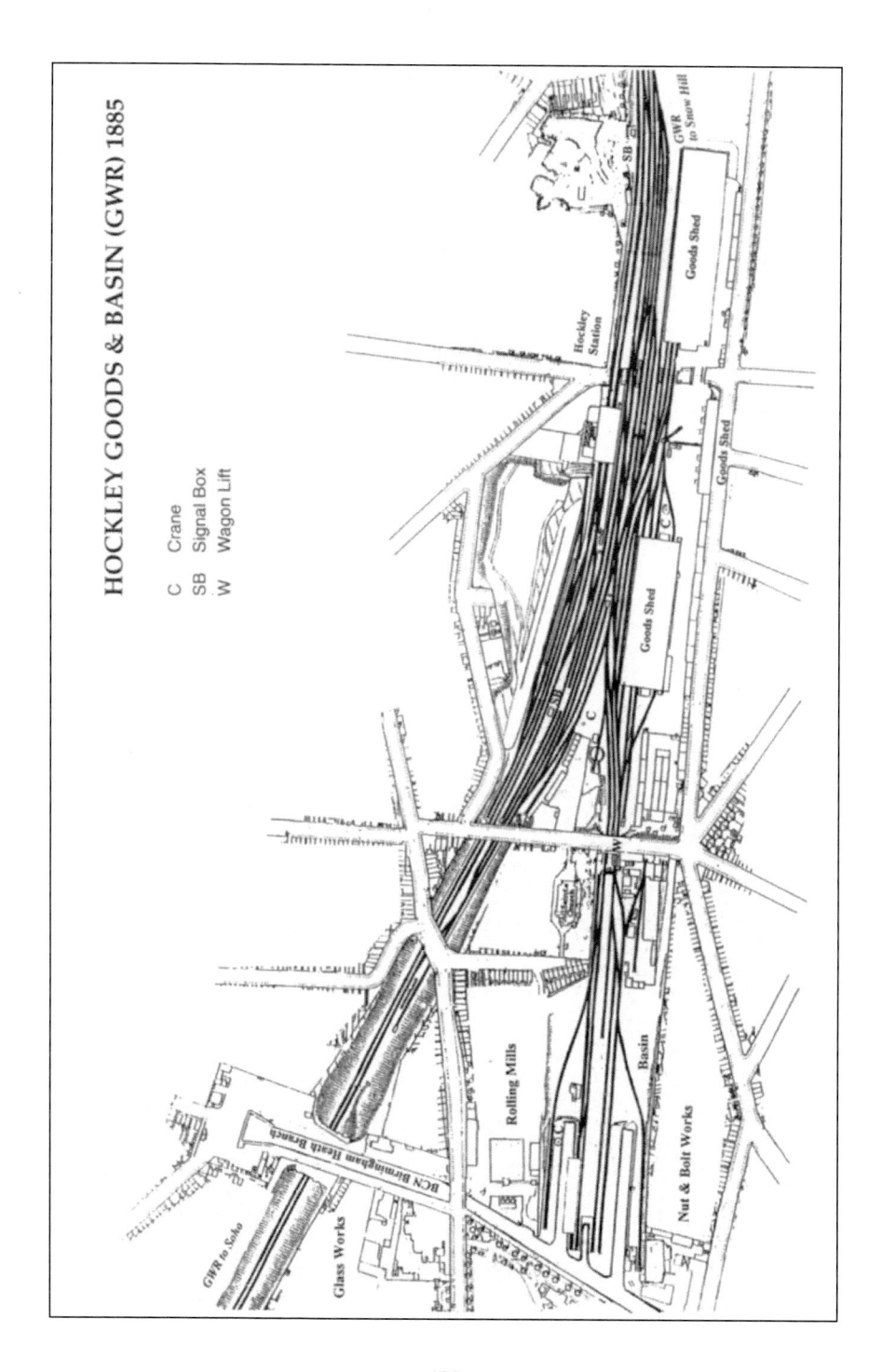

HOCKLEY GOODS & BASIN (GWR) 1885

C   Crane
SB Signal Box
W Wagon Lift

Two views of Hockley Goods, from All Saints Street. These pictures were take before work started on the rebuild of the depot

Heartland Press Collection

Hockley Basin (GWR) was at a higher level than Hockley goods yard. The original water lift was replaced by this new electric lift in 1939
Heartland Press Collection

Although the basin sheds have been removed, the two basins at Hockley remain. They now form part of Hockley Port, which provides residential moorings for boaters

Ray Shill

Hockley Wharf stable blocks

Ray Shill

IZONS BRANCH   LNWR

The Izons branch was a short piece of canal that joined the Walsall Canal near the Albion. It was built by the BCN and was the terminus of a colliery tramway. Wood & Ivery's brickworks was erected on property adjacent. The LNWR used the branch as a boatage depot.

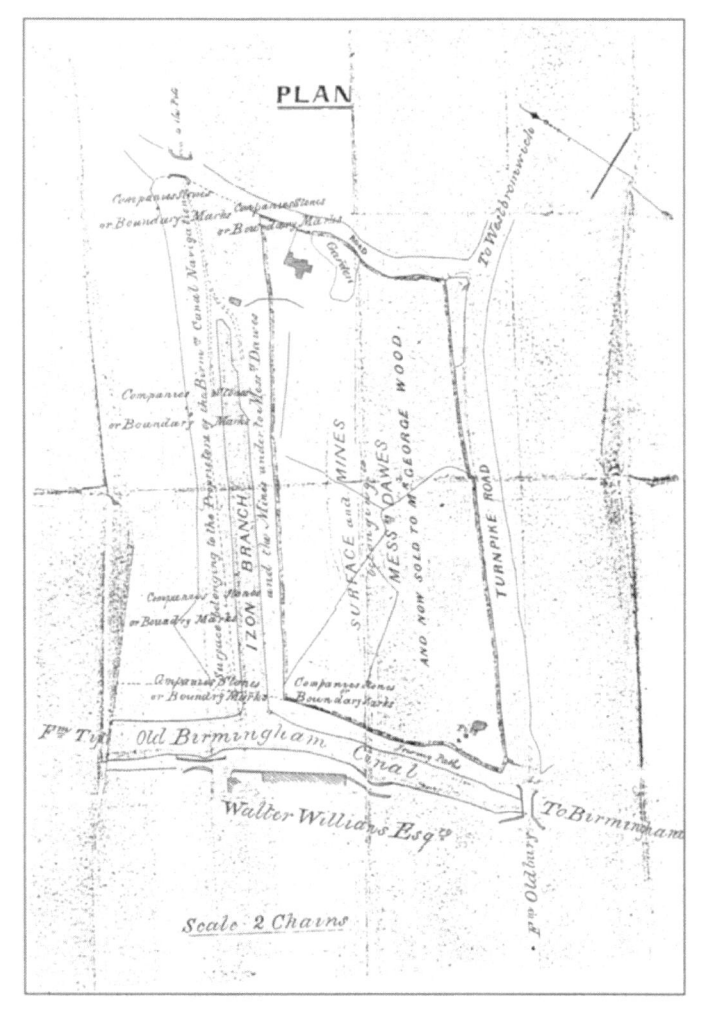

Plan dated 1861 which shows the Izons Branch and the land taken by George Wood for his Albion Brickworks. The extent of BCN property which includes the whole of the basin is indicated by the placement of boundary posts around the site. The tramway served Cutlers End Colliery, then worked by Williams & Smith.

LIFFORD   MR, LMS

1874-1927

A linear wharf, with covered shed, which stood beside the Worcester & Birmingham Canal at Lifford.

The sidings that served it joined the Birmingham & West Suburban Railway from Kings Norton to Granville Street. When this line was improved by the Midland Railway (1883-1885) the former BWS lines at Lifford were became part of the goods station.

According to the 1909 Working Timetable (1), Lifford was served by two goods each way that ran between Lawley Street (Birmingham) and Gloucester.

(1)   PRO RAIL 963 / 95

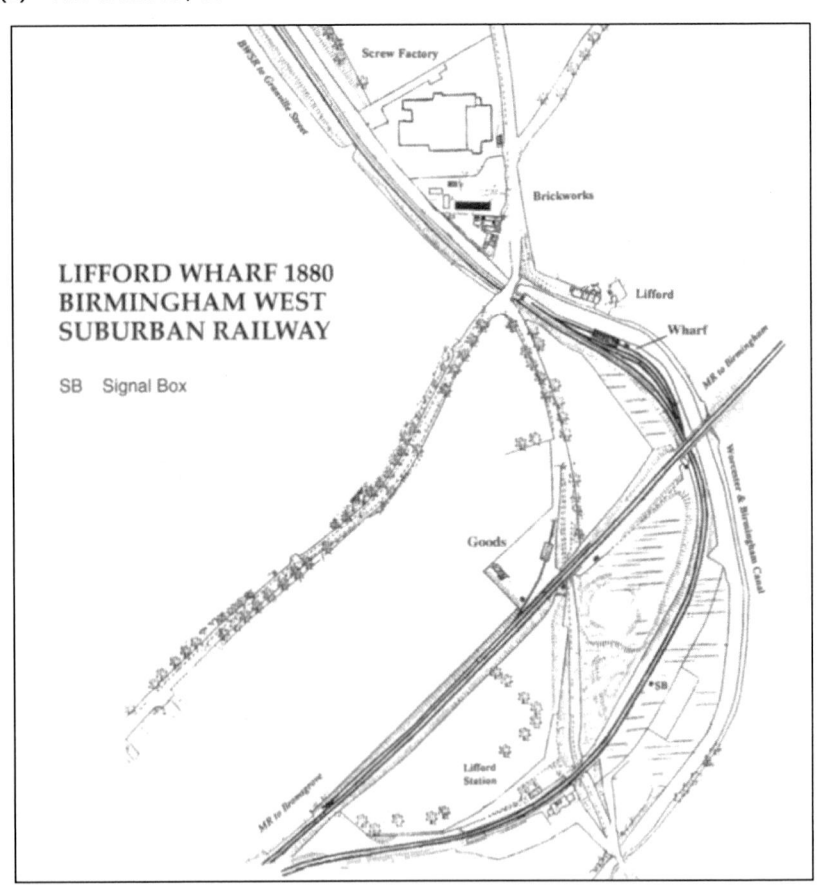

LIFFORD WHARF 1880
BIRMINGHAM WEST
SUBURBAN RAILWAY

SB   Signal Box

MIDLAND   MR, LMS
1882-1938

A basin, complete with covered shed, which joined the Wyrley & Essington Canal at Wolverhampton.

Sidings connected with the Midland Railway at Heath Town. The Midland Railway reached Wolverhampton by way of the Wolverhampton & Walsall Railway through Wednesfield. Trains worked from Washwood Heath and Water Orton via Walsall to Wolverhampton (Wednesfield Road) Goods.

The 1909 working timetable (1) mentions the following services:

9.45am Wolverhampton - Walsall makes a trip to and from the canal basin as required.
10.30am Water Orton - Wolverhampton arrived at 12.20pm and then shunted Midland Basin and Mill Street(LNWR) as required.
10.20pm Wolverhampton to Washwood Heath. The engine makes a trip to and from the canal basin as required before starting train.

Special Goods to Wolverhampton also worked trips to basin as and when required.

(1)   PRO RAIL 963 / 95

Midland Basin, Wolverhampton, as seen from the canal side bridge

Author's collection

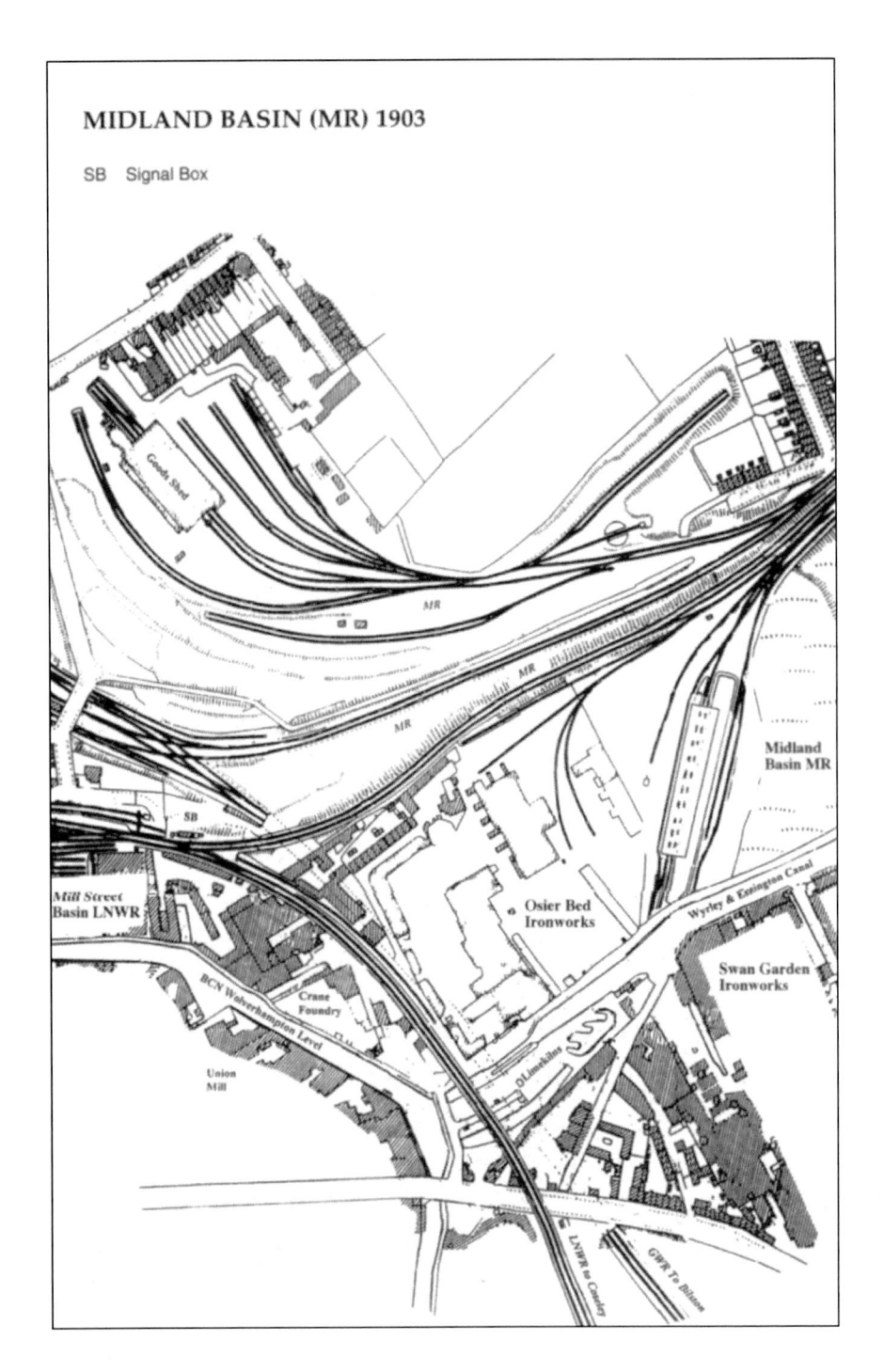

MIDLAND BASIN (MR) 1903

SB   Signal Box

Another view of the Midland Basin looking towards the Wyrley & Essington Canal. Note the faded lettering: LMS Railway Canal Depot
Collection Ned Williams

MILL STREET   LNWR, LMS, BR(LM)
1851-1950

Two covered basins connected with the main BCN canal at Wolverhampton.

The basin adjoined Mill Street Goods Station, but they were on different levels. The Goods Station was at the same level as the Stour Valley Railway which approached Wolverhampton by a long multi-arched viaduct. The canal basins were located below and lifts provided the means of moving goods between the two levels.

Standard gauge sidings reached the basin from a short branch that descended on the opposite side of the viaduct. This branch was extended as a private siding to serve the Crane Foundry and Sparrow's Tin Plate Works (1). Wagon turntables on the branch connected with a siding to the basin. This siding, in turn, joined three other lines that ran the length of the basins.

According to the 1872 Working Timetable, a number of trains were designated Mill Street Goods which ran to and from Bushbury Sidings. On weekdays there were 6 trains from Bushbury and 7 trains from Mill Street.

(1)   LNWR Siding Agreement 1854
(2)   PRO RAIL 946 / 7

London & North Western Railway Mill Street Goods Depot

Wolverhampton Public Libraries

130

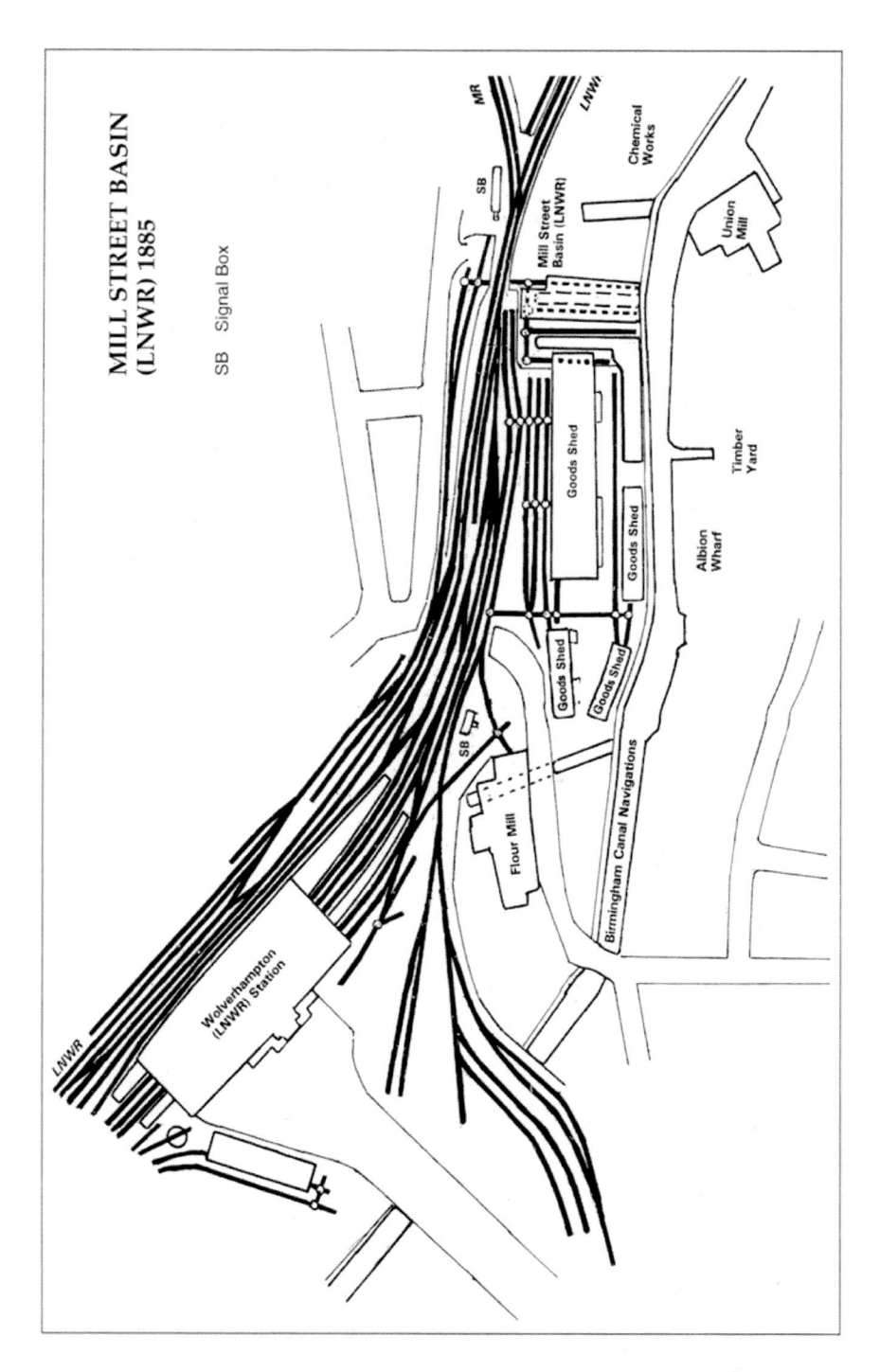

Inside Mill Street LMS Basin today. The arms have been filled in

Ray Shill

The two side bridges admitting boats to Mill Street Basin, Wolverhampton, have been removed. The warehouse and goods shed (centre) remain

Ray Shill

MONMORE GREEN   LNWR, BR(M)

1901-1963

Two basins, later reduced to one, joined the main line of the Birmingham Canal at Monmore Green.

The Basins were served by a branch railway that was constructed between 1899 and 1901 from the Stour Valley Railway south of Monmore Green Station (1). The new line included a bridge over the Bilston Road.

The Basins were formerly the property of the Chillington Iron Company. They were linked by a 2ft 6in tramway to the ironworks and furnaces. Both ironworks and railway were constructed the designs of J.U. Raistrick in 1829. There was originally one basin which was later enlarged into two as trade on the canal increased. This new arrangement comprised one long and one short basin. A boat yard was located at the end of the long basin where the company boats were maintained. These improvements were carried out about 1848. The metalwork of side bridge over the basin still carries the legend Thomas Perry, Highfields Foundry 1848.

Chillington Iron Company went into receivership in 1885 and their extensive estate was sold off in 1885 and 1886. Only the edge tool works remained. The LNWR acquired the basin property and applied to Parliament in 1893 to develop it for railway use. In 1898 a further application was made to Parliament. Powers were sought to widen the bridge over Cable Street and erect a bridge across Bilston Street and the Wolverhampton Tramways lines. When these powers were granted work went ahead to construct the sidings and branch railway.

A new basin with two arms of equal length replaced the earlier Chillington Basin, but the entrance and side bridge were retained. The one arm of the basin was removed in the 1930s by the LMS who installed a Babcox & Wilcox overhead crane on the site.

The LMS working timetable for 1929 shows a variety of destinations were served from Monmore Green (2):

	Monmore Green arrive	depart
5.15am Bushbury - Ettingshall	5.57am	6.07am
11.15am Bushbury - Wednesbury	11.30am	11.49am
12.06am Wolverhampton - Monmore Green	12.12pm	
4.30pm(S0) Wolverhampton - Stechford	4.35pm	4.40pm
7.00pm Monmore Green - Soho		
6 10am Stechford - Bushbury	10.19am	10.25am
1.55pm Monmore Green - Bushbur.		
8.50pm Ettingshall- Bushbury	8.55pm	9.05pm

General interchange traffic remained until 1963, but the odd boat continued to use the basin thereafter. There was occasional brake block traffic from a local foundry, for example (3).

The sidings that served Monmore Green and Walsall Street goods were connected in 1967 and the depots merged to form Wolverhampton Steel Terminal.

Present state; The basin shed and siding are presently used by English, Welsh & Scottish Railways as part of the Wolverhampton Steel Terminal. The canal basin remains in water although the entrance is blocked with weeds.

(1) PRO Rail 410 / 321 December 14, 1898. R Finnegan, Contractor, Northampton was awarded the contract to construct new goods basin (£14,774-8-0d)
(2) PRO Rail 957/ 127
(3) Recollections of a Wolverhampton Goods Clerk.

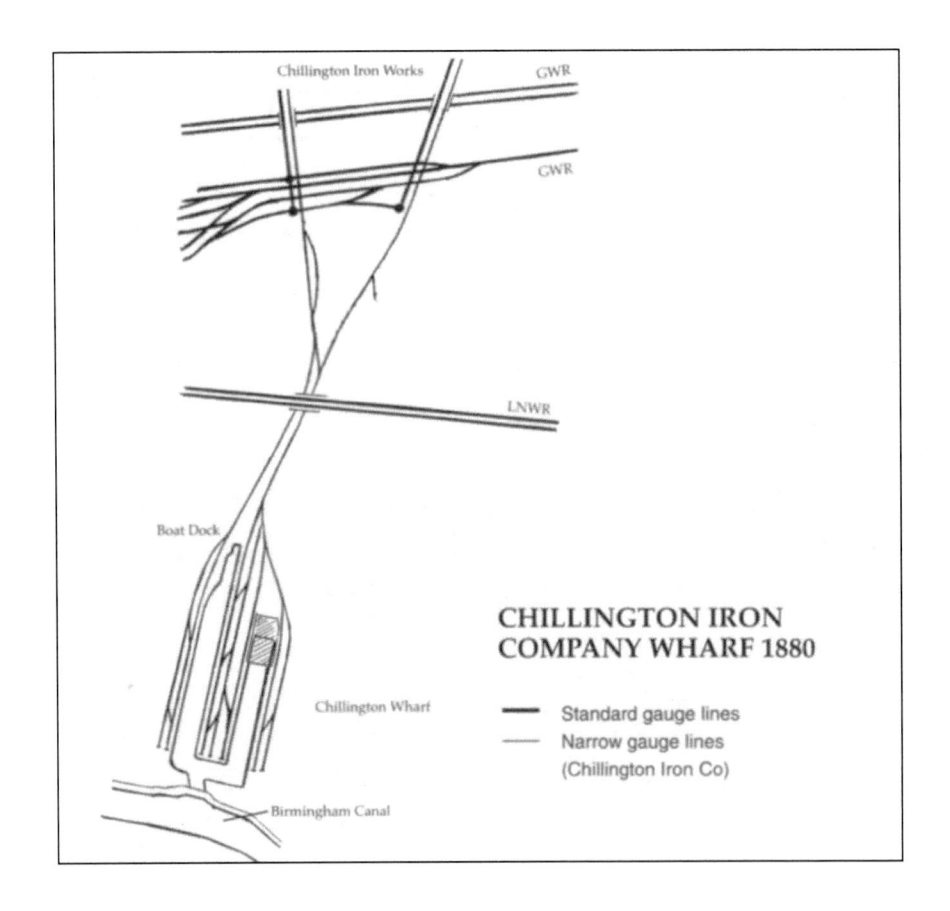

CHILLINGTON IRON COMPANY WHARF 1880

— Standard gauge lines
--- Narrow gauge lines
(Chillington Iron Co)

MONMORE GREEN (LNWR) & SHRUBBERY BASIN (GWR) 1903

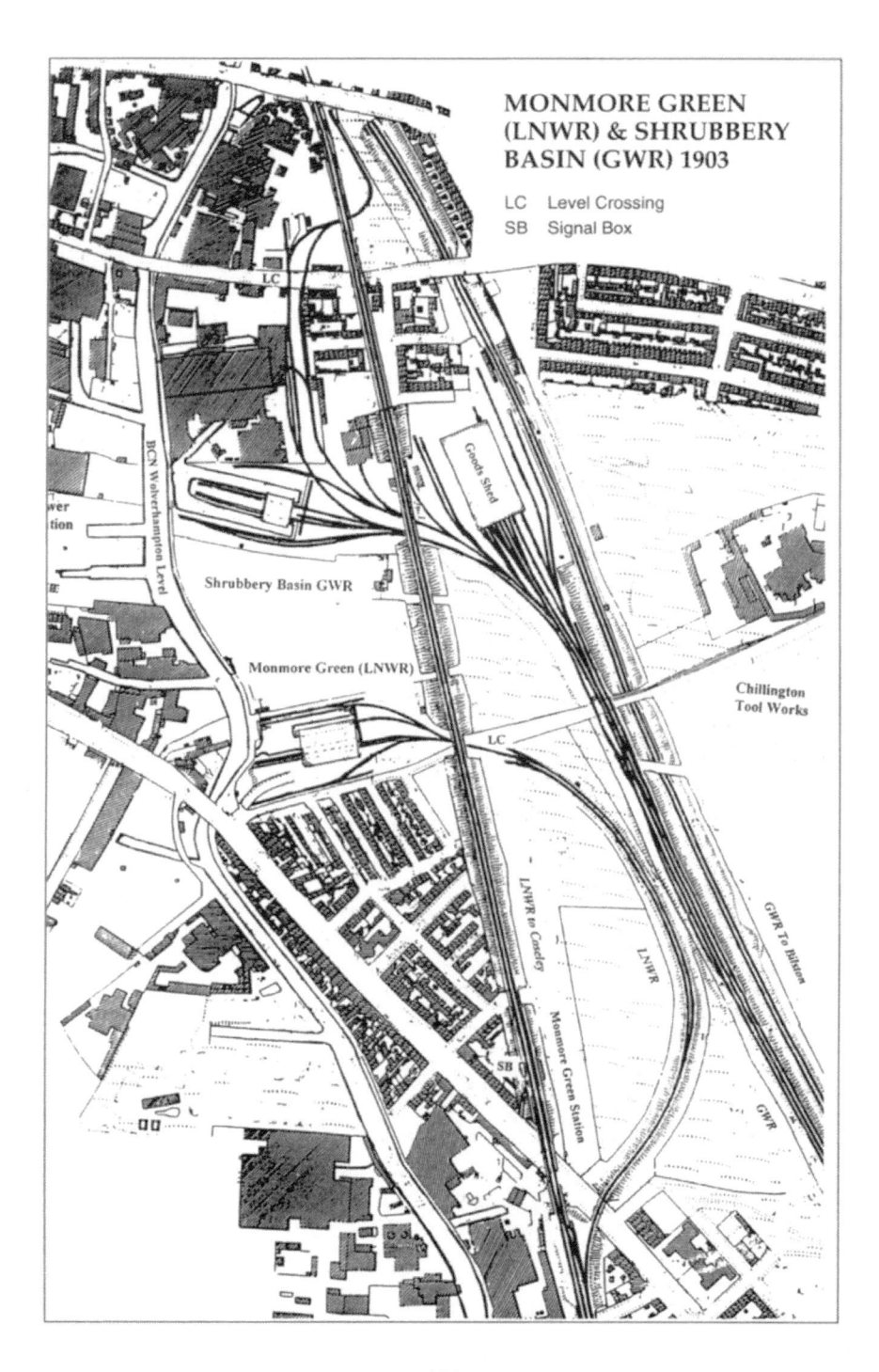

LC Level Crossing
SB Signal Box

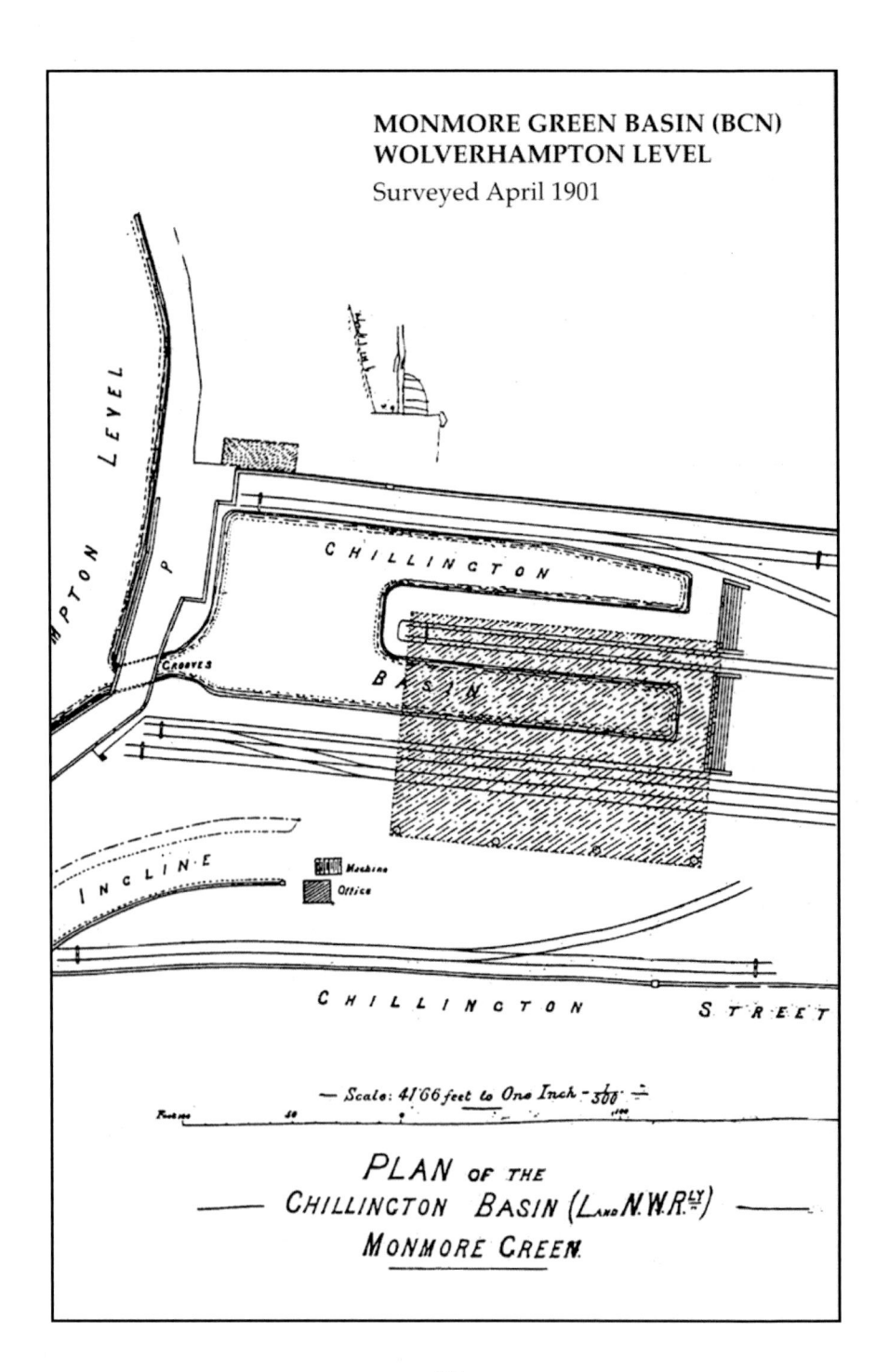

MONMORE GREEN BASIN (BCN)
WOLVERHAMPTON LEVEL
Surveyed April 1901

PLAN OF THE
CHILLINGTON BASIN (L AND N.W.R.LY)
MONMORE GREEN

The shed at Monmore Green Basin, 1973, now a listed building

Ray Shill

The entrance to Monmore Green LMS Basin, Wolverhampton

Ray Shill

MONUMENT LANE   LNWR, LMS, BR(M)
1852-1954

One basin that joined the main Birmingham Canal near Monument Lane Bridge.

Sidings connected with the main goods shed railways. A collection of turntables enabled wagons to run alongside the basin.

The first references to Monument Lane appear in SVR minutes as the basin at Sheepcote Lane. Work seems to be underway by 1852 as tenders for shed roofs and wagon turntables were accepted(1).

According to the 1872 working timetable (2) twenty five freights called, originated or terminated at Monument Lane. These included the

12.35am Camden - Bushbury
2.30pm Monument Lane - Wichnor Junction
3.30pm Monument Lane – Leeds
6.40pm Monument Lane - Leeds
10.00pm Monument Lane - Curzon Street Goods and Vauxhall Empties

The 10.10am train (No.22 Stour Valley Goods) was changed to make a trip from Dudley Port to Monument Lane instead of Spon Lane Only.

Monument Lane Goods was a collection of goods sheds and coal merchants sidings. The coal yard was served by a number of wagon turntables that were lined up in line on the canal side of the depot. A private siding served the Midland Flour Mills. The track plan was altered after 1910 when all the coal merchants wagon turntables were removed (3).

Monument Lane Goods Station was demolished after 1967.

Present State; Houses now occupy the site of Monument Lane Goods but the basin remains complete with side bridge across the entrance.

(1)   PRO RAIL 45 / 2 Various reference 1852. They included tenders for roofs at Tipton Bloomfield and Stewards Aqueduct. In May 1852 Fox Henderson tendered for 30 turntables for Monument Lane, Stewards Aqueduct and Bloomfield Goods.
(2)   PRO Rail 946 / 7.
(3)   LNWR Sidings Agreement.

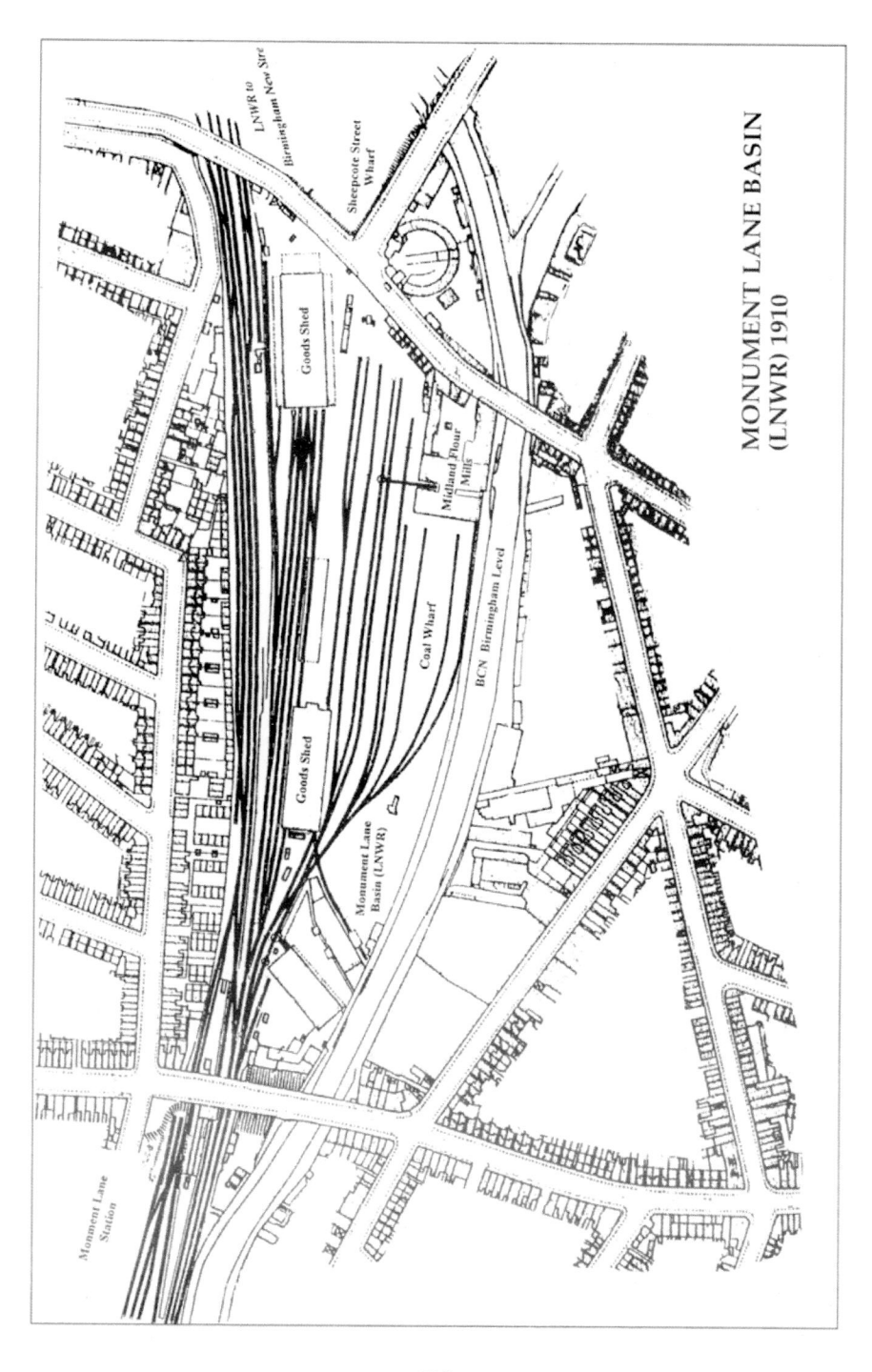

MONUMENT LANE BASIN (LNWR) 1910

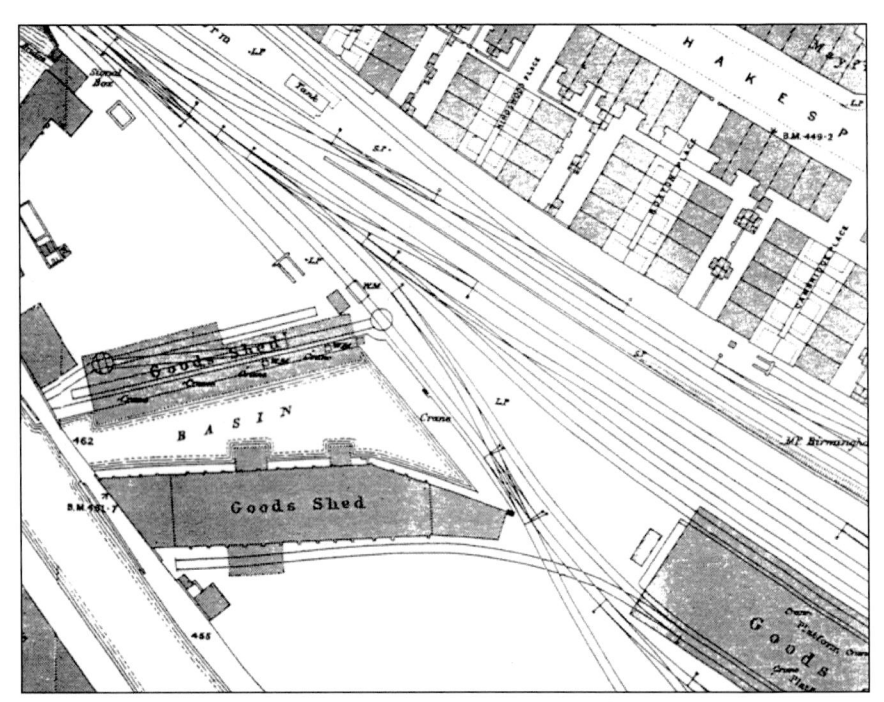

Plan of Monument Lane Basin, reproduced from Ordnance Survey 1901

Monument Lane Basin in more recent times, On this occasion it was being used to store dredgings from the Gas Street Clean-up *Ray Shill*

NINE LOCKS   BCN

This wharf was used for railway boatage purposes. It was located on the towpath side above the top lock between the Ticket Office and the Shropshire Union Wharf (q.v.).

NINE LOCKS (BLACK DELPH)   BCN

This wharf and basin, appears to have also been used for railway boatage purposes. It was located beside the bottom lock with a frontage onto Delph Road. This basin is still in water although no longer used as a wharf.

NINE LOCKS   LNWR / SUC

1877-1954

A boatage depot complete with basin was established above the Delph Locks on the Dudley No 1 Canal. During the early years traffic appears to have been conducted from the adjacent BCN wharf. By 1910 a separate basin and loading shed had been constructed.

Present state: The basin has been filled in and the site now forms part of the Link 51 factory.

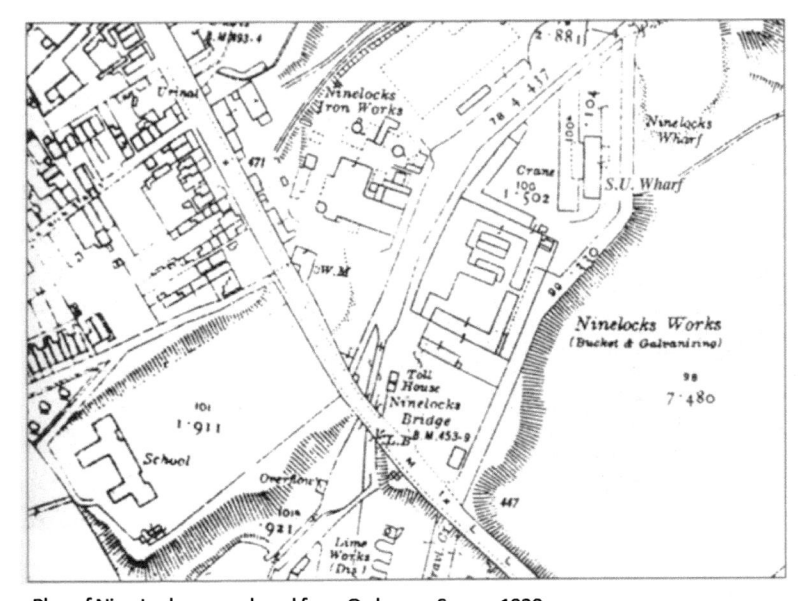

Plan of Nine Locks, reproduced from Ordnance Survey 1920

140

OLDBURY   GWR
1884-1936

Two basins joined the Oldbury Loop opposite Dank's Boiler Factory.

The railway branch that served this basin was constructed for the Oldbury Railway Company, but was worked by the GWR from the start. This railway commenced at Langley Green and was carried through to the terminus beside the canal basin principally by embankments.

A number of freights commenced and terminated at Oldbury Goods which were supplemented by additional trips to and from Langley Green. The traffic in 1909 (1) was as follows:

  4.50am Bordesley - Oldbury (arrive 7.25am)
  5.20am Oxley - Oldbury
10.35am Bordesley - Oldbury (arrive 2.30pm)
  4.25pm Stourbridge Junction - Oldbury (arrive 6.10pm)
  5.40pm Brettell Lane - Oldbury (arrive 10.05pm)
11.00am Oldbury - Oxley
  3.40pm Oldbury - Bordesley
  6.55pm Oldbury - Oxley (for Hull & North Traffic)
11.10pm Oldbury - Stourbridge Junction (Pontypool traffic to be put off at Langley Green)

Present State: The canal has been filled in and the basin site is generally wasteland.

The staff are obviously posing for this photo of Oldbury GWR Basin which shows the extent to which station traffic was handled by private traders *Author's collection*

Oldbury GWR Basin as viewed from the air in 1934
Aerofilms Ltd

OLDBURY BASIN
(GWR) 1902

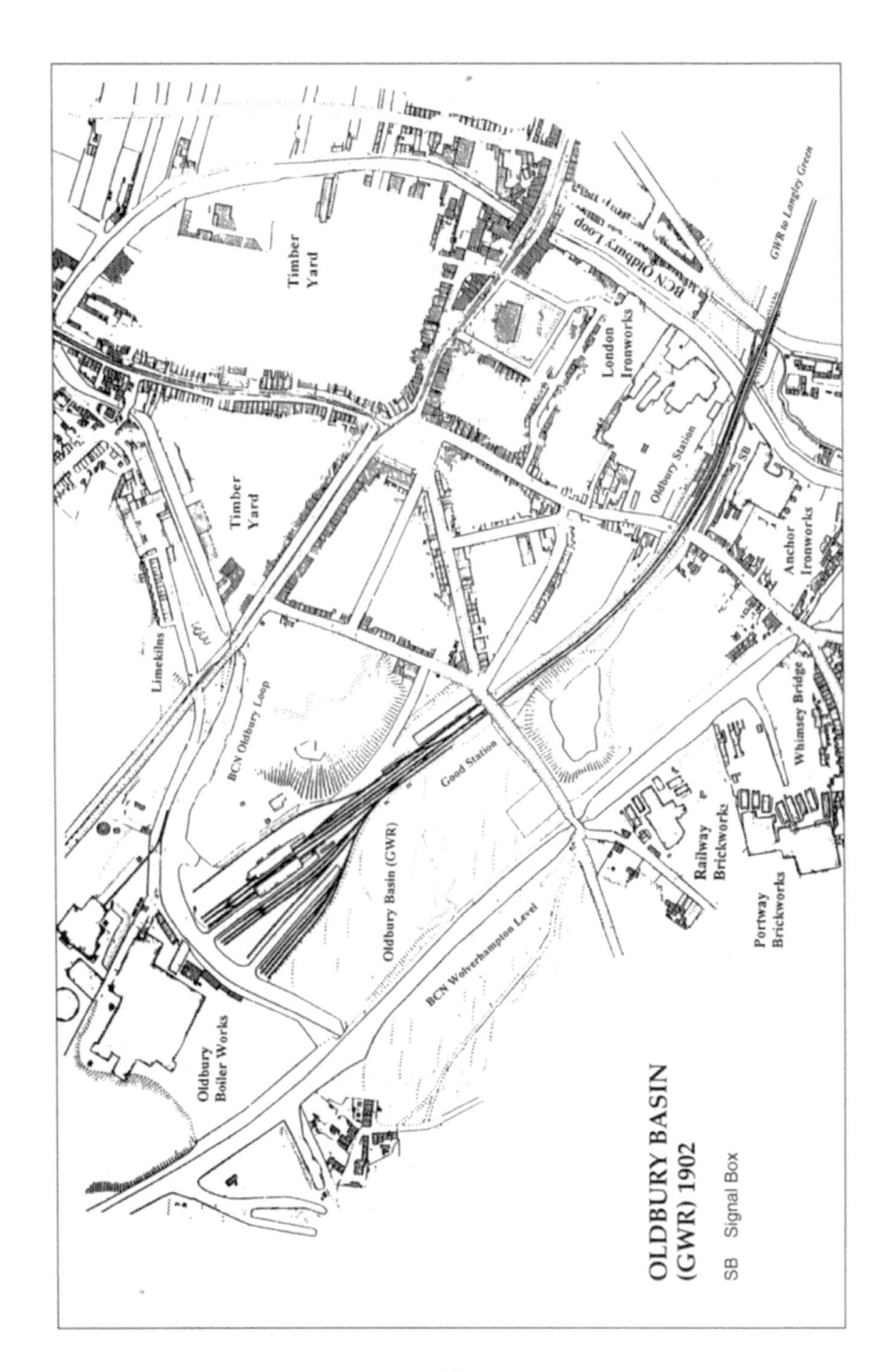

SB   Signal Box

POTHOUSE BRIDGE   BCN

This was a BCN wharf placed beside the Bradley Loop at Bilston. The wharf was located on the towpath side a few yards south of the Bradley Bridge. It was used by the GWR as a boatage depot.

When the railway first opened, there were plans to construct a railway link to the canal (1), but this did not happen. Industry was congested on both sides of the waterway and the sidings were not built. It was not until 1908 that vacant land was purchased to make a rail served basin.

(1)   PRO RAIL 44 / 4 BWD Minute August 13, 1852.

PRIMROSE BASIN   LNWR/SUR, LMS, BR
1865-1954

The Shropshire Union Railway & Canal Company took a lease of land at Primrose Hill Wharf in 1865 (1). Their property was adjacent to the Testing Machine Company's premises. Later, a basin was constructed opposite on the towpath side of the canal. The wooden wharf buildings and stables survived complete until 1990. Both have since been taken down and the site is presently occupied by a builders merchants. The basin remains in water and is used for private moorings.

(1)   PRO Rail 810 / 18 BCN Proprietors Minutes February 24th 1865

Miles from that company's rails, the LMS made sure passers-by knew who owned Primrose Basin (Ex SU/LNW). This lettering appeared on the rear of the now demolished stable block

Author's collection

The shed at Primrose Basin SU/LNWR, with stables on the right

Ray Shill

Primrose Basin SU/LNWR, LMS, BR (LMR)

Ray Shill

PRIMROSE BASIN MR
c1900-

Primrose Basin (MR) was located on the east side of Primrose Bridge. No trace of this basin remains.

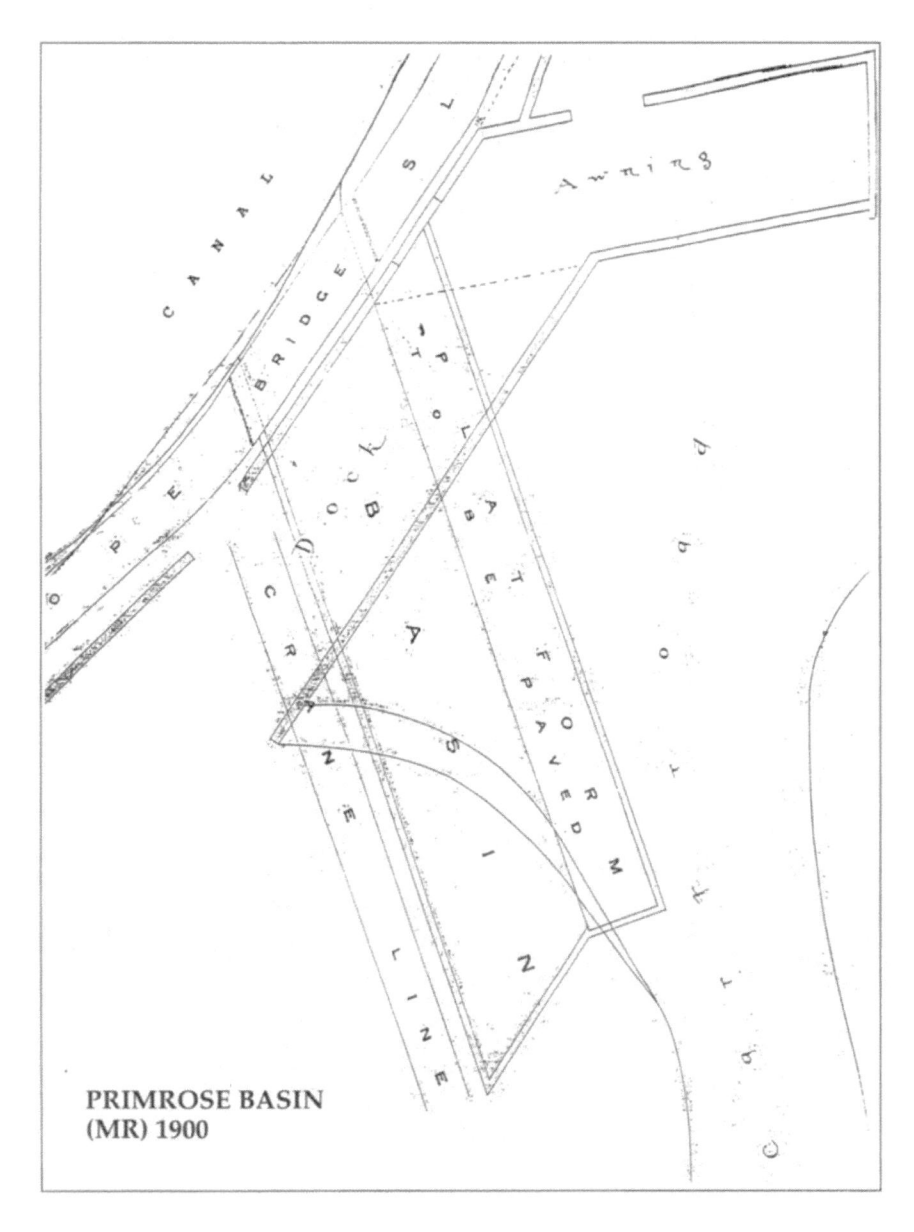

PRIMROSE BASIN (MR) 1900

SALTLEY   BDJR & B&G Joint Committee, MR,LMS, BR(M)

c1844-1963

A *linear wharf located beside the Warwick & Birmingham Canal adjacent to the canal reservoir.*

This wharf seems to have opened at the same time as the canal and was one of the earliest interchange points on midland waterways.

Traffic was tripped from Washwood Heath. Coal was a particularly important trade. It was shovelled out by hand from wagon to boat and taken along the canal. One example includes E.H. Walker's coal traffic from Saltley Sidings to the Perfecta Seamless Steel Tubeworks, Plume Street and Smith Stone & Knight Paper Mills at Cheston Road (1)

After the wharf closed, the basin and reservoir were used to store boats which may well still remain. The land was levelled and basin filled in during 1996 for the construction of a new road.

(1)   Birmingham Library MS86 BCN Traffic May 1928.

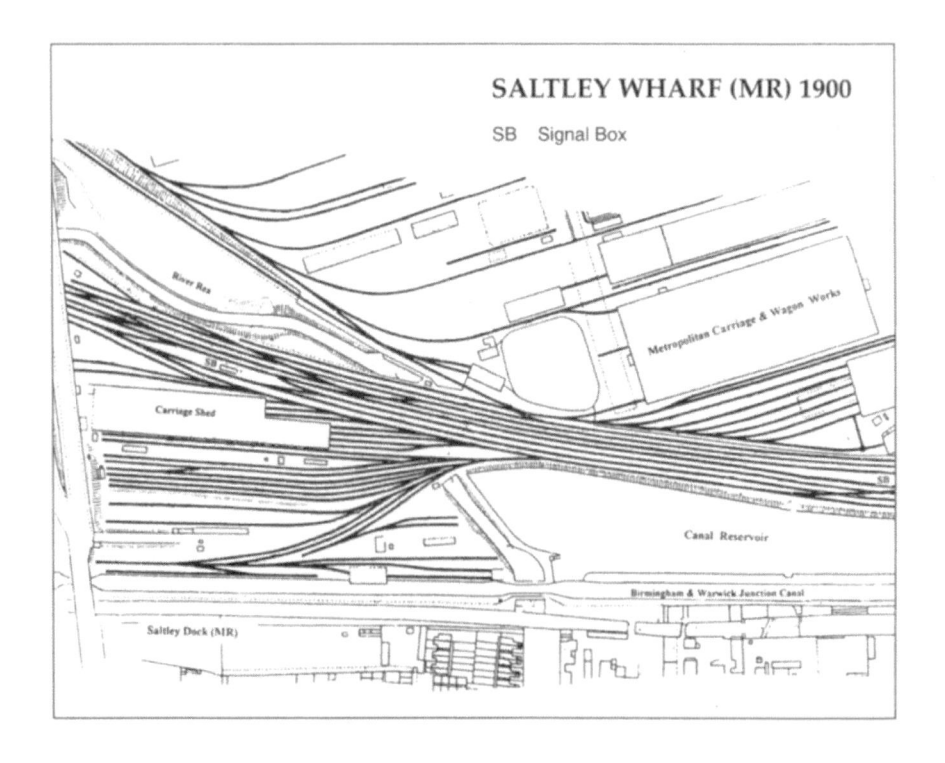

SALTLEY WHARF (MR) 1900

SB   Signal Box

SHROPSHIRE UNION (WOLVERHAMPTON)

The Shropshire Union Wharf at Wolverhampton was the second depot they had there. The first being placed beside the Cannock Road. The new depot used part of the old line of the canal to form a basin. A siding was constructed across the Wednesfield Road, but traffic was only worked by horses.

Present State: The offices and warehouse a presently occupied by a nightclub. The basin remains in water and is still used by British Waterways. A length of track survives in the yard.

SHRUBBERY   OWWR, WMR, GWR, BR(W)

1855-1963

The canal arm that served Shrubbery Basin joined with the BCN main line south of Walsall Street Bridge, Wolverhampton. There were two basins for the interchange traffic and a third that was used by the Shrubbery Ironworks.

A standard gauge railway to Walsall Street Goods and Shrubbery Basin was completed in 1855 by the contractors, Peto & Co. The railway that served the basin also had sidings into Hickman's Saw Mills and the Shrubbery Ironworks.

Shrubbery Ironworks originally belonged to Thorneycroft's but were later taken over by the Wolverhampton Corrugated Iron Company. When the latter company transferred their operations to Ellesmere Port, Knowles Oxygen acquired the property.

According to the GWR 1909 working timetable (1), traffic was tripped to Priestfield by the Walsall Street shunting engine. Morning engine brought in traffic from Priestfield (Depart 09.30) on its way from shed. The last traffic to Priestfield to arrive at 9.30pm for 10.05pm ex Oxley.

Present State; The basins have been filled in and now form part of the British Oxygen site.

(1)   PRO Rail 937 / 100

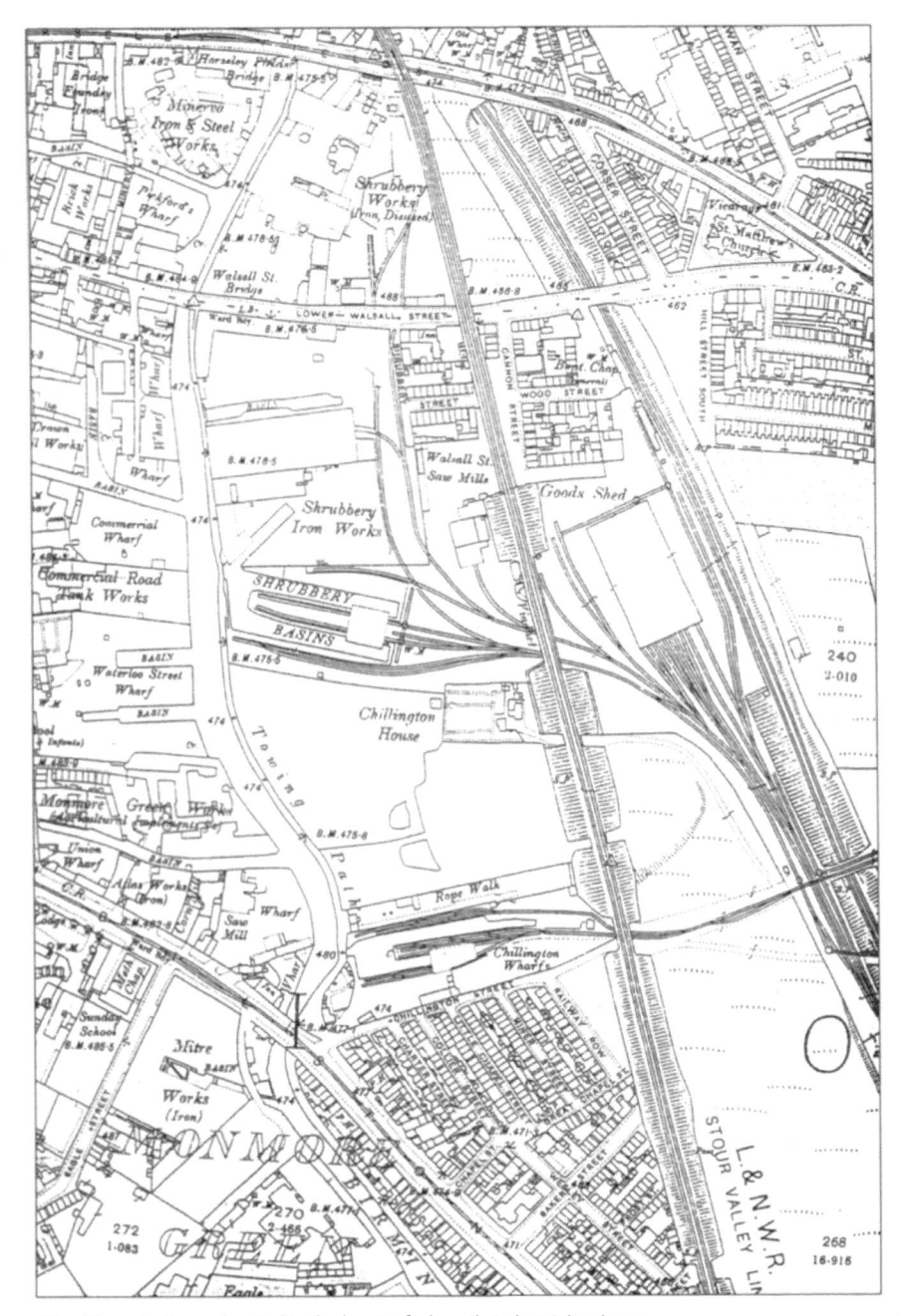

Shrubbery Basin was located in the heart of a heavily industrialised area
Reproduced from Ordnance Survey 1884

SPON LANE   LNWR, LMS, BR(M)
1852 - c1960

One basin joined with the BCN old main line west of Steward's Aqueduct.

Railway sidings connected the SVR north of Spon Lane Station. The basin sidings were separate from Spon Lane Goods and worked by another signal box. These sidings also served the private lines that belonged to the Oldbury Carriage & Wagon Company.

A basin was first suggested to be made here in 1851 when estimates were prepared for its construction (1). Early references call it the basin at Steward's Aqueduct.

At first, water was taken from the canal for the horses, but this practice was discontinued in 1860 when the water was discovered to be polluted! (2)

All wagons labelled Spon Lane containing Pig Iron, Mine, Ironstone, Timber and Railway wheels must be left at Spon Lane Basin (3)

20 freights served Spon Lane Basin in 1872 (3). These included

10.15pm Camden- Bushbury (arrive 5.25am)
12.15am Birmingham- Liverpool (arrive 1.15am)
 2.35pm Stafford - Spon Lane (Stoke Mineral, North Staffs Rly) (arrive 4.40 pm)
 3.30pm Monument Lane - Leeds (arrive 4.18pm)
 5.20pm Spon Lane Basin - Stoke (North Staffordshire Railway)
 6.40pm Monument Lane - Leeds (arrive 7.15pm)

Spon Lane Basin remained in water until the electrification of the Stour Valley Railway was completed in 1967.

Present state: The basin has been filled in and sidings removed. The roving bridge across across the main line of the canal by the basin remains, although the entrance has been bricked up.

(1)   RAIL 45 / 2 Minutes of the Birmingham, Wolverhampton & Stour Valley Railway September 2nd 1851.
(2)   LNWR General Stores and Locomotive Expenditure Committee , PRO Rail 410 / 357
(3)   PRO Rail 946 / 7, LNWR Working T/ T 1872

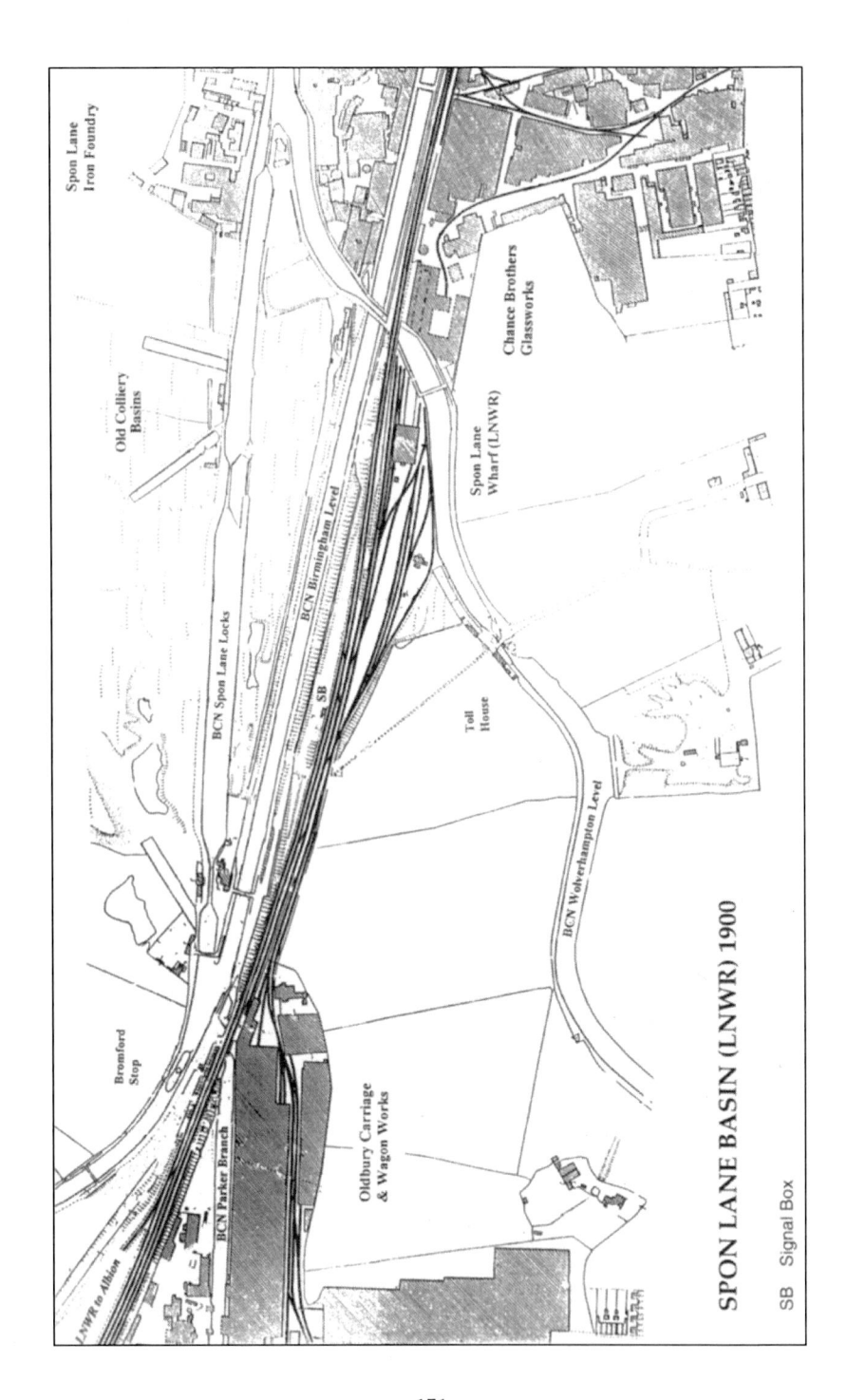

SPON LANE BASIN (LNWR) 1900

SB Signal Box

Side view of Spon Lane Basin shed in 1962

Heartland Press Collection

View of Spon Lane Basin shed in 1966

Heartland Press Collection

SPON LANE BASIN 1966

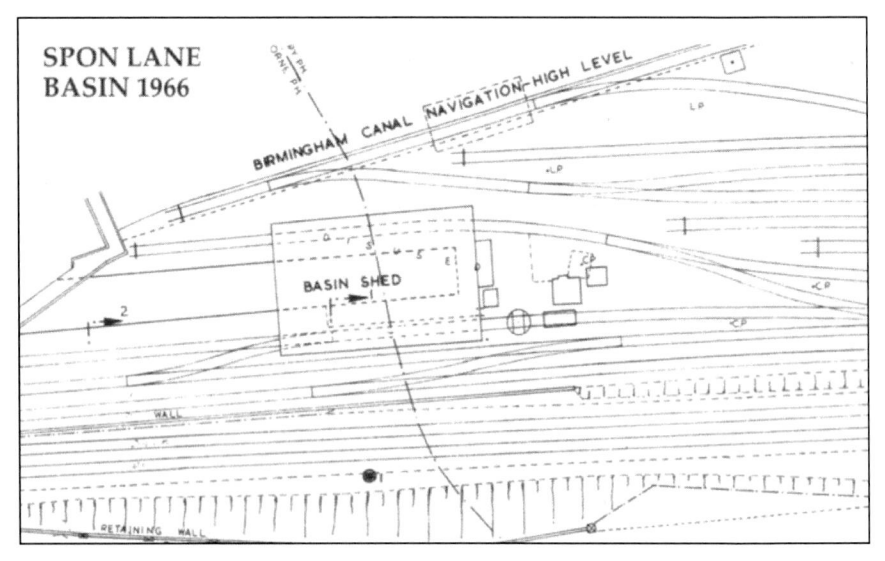

STOURBRIDGE   OWWR, WMR, GWR, BR(W)
1858 - 1956

One long basin constructed on railway company land in 1858 that joined the end of the Stourbridge Town Arm.

Railway accommodation was first provided by sidings that were connected by an incline to the OWWR. This was replaced by a direct railway connection from Stourbridge Junction (1st Station) in 1879.

Sidings fanned out across the basin land, some of which had been reclaimed from the Stour. In addition to the basin sidings there were tracks into the Gasworks and a Leather Works. Another two lines were extended across the main road into John Bradley's Ironworks.

An important traffic from Stourbridge was the Glass Trade. A number of glassworks were located alongside the Stourbridge Canal. The GWR prided itself on carrying the raw materials as well as the finished article.

In 1909 (1) there were six trips each way from Stourbridge Junction to the Basin. The last three carried specific traffic:
   8.20pm Basin - Stourbridge Junction   London & North traffic
   9.50pm Basin - Stourbridge Junction   Reading & West traffic
   10.30pm Basin - Stourbridge Junction   Clear remaining traffic

Rail traffic ceased during the 1960s and the basin has now been filled in.

(1)   PRO Rail 937/ 100

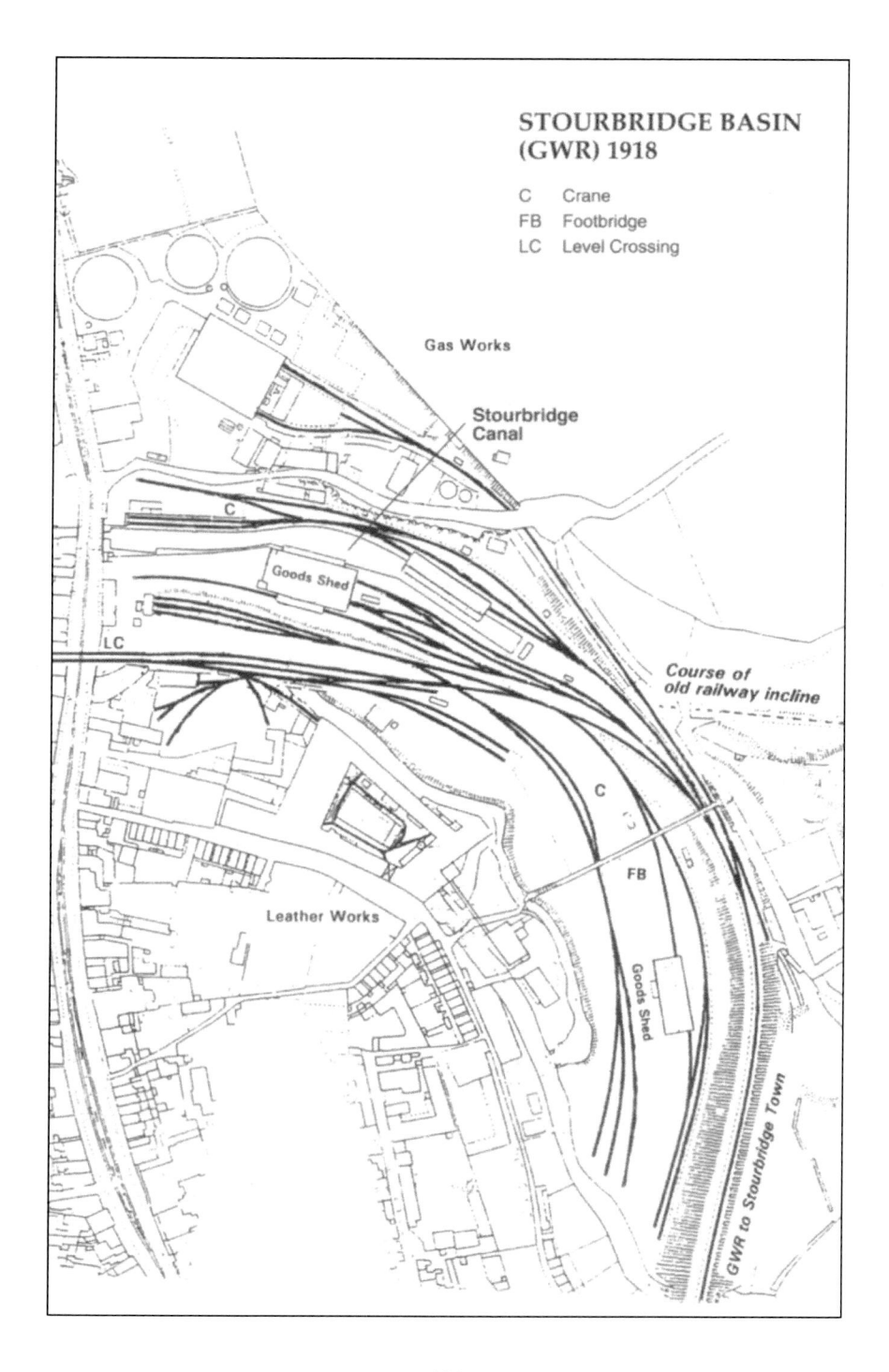

STOURBRIDGE BASIN (GWR) 1918

C   Crane
FB Footbridge
LC Level Crossing

Gas Works

Stourbridge Canal

Goods Shed

LC

Course of old railway incline

Leather Works

C

FB

Goods Shed

GWR to Stourbridge Town

Ex-GWR pannier tank on train of wagons at Stourbridge Basin

John Dew

STOURPORT   GWR, BR(W)
1885-1950

One basin which joins the Staffordshire & Worcestershire Canal north of Stourport.

Railway sidings connected with the GWR Hartlebury - Bewdley Branch (Severn Valley Railway). In 1909 (1) fourteen weekday freights called, originated or terminated from Stourport. These include:

9.10am Worcester - Shrewsbury
1.15pm Stourbridge Junction - Shrewsbury
7.00am Shrewsbury - Worcester
1.35pm Shrewsbury - Stourbridge Junction

Present state; Houses have been built across the railway tracks, but the basin remains in water.

(1)   PRO Rail 937/ 100

SWAN VILLAGE   GWR
1856-1874

A basin joined the Balls Hills Branch at the junction with the Ridgacre Branch.

Broad Gauge and Standard Gauge sidings were made down to the canal, but were converted to standard in 1869.

The basin ceased to be used as an interchange point after 1874. The site is now occupied by the Ridgacre Pub.

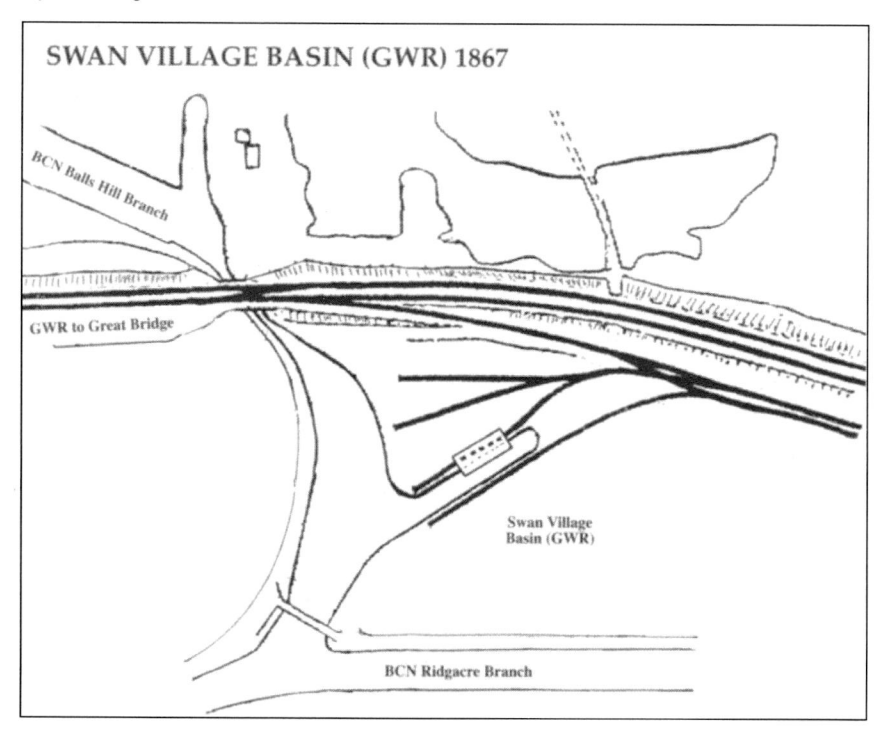

SWAN VILLAGE BASIN (GWR) 1867

SWAN VILLAGE   GWR, BR(W)
1874-1950

One long basin joined the Balls Hill Branch Canal.

Railway sidings connected with the GWR Swan Village to Great Bridge line.
In 1909 (1) seven freights served Swan Village Basin:
3.20am. Swan Village Basin - Oxley
5.55am Cannock Road Junction - Swan Village Basin (6.35am, LNWR traffic)

4.00am Victoria Basin - West Bromwich (7.10am / 7.45am) 11.45am West Bromwich -
Oxley (1.30pm/ 2.00pm)
2.25pm Cannock Road Junction - Swan Village Basin (5.00pm, LNWR traffic)
8.40pm Swan Village Basin - Oxley
10.10pm Swan Village Basin - Bordesley

After the basin closed the tracks were used for wagon storage.

Present State; The basin remains in water although its connection with the rest of the canal network was severed when the Spine Road was constructed.

(1)   PRO Rail 937/100

Swan Village Interchange Basin and shed 1952. The sidings on the extreme right led down to the original railway wharf

Michael Hale collection

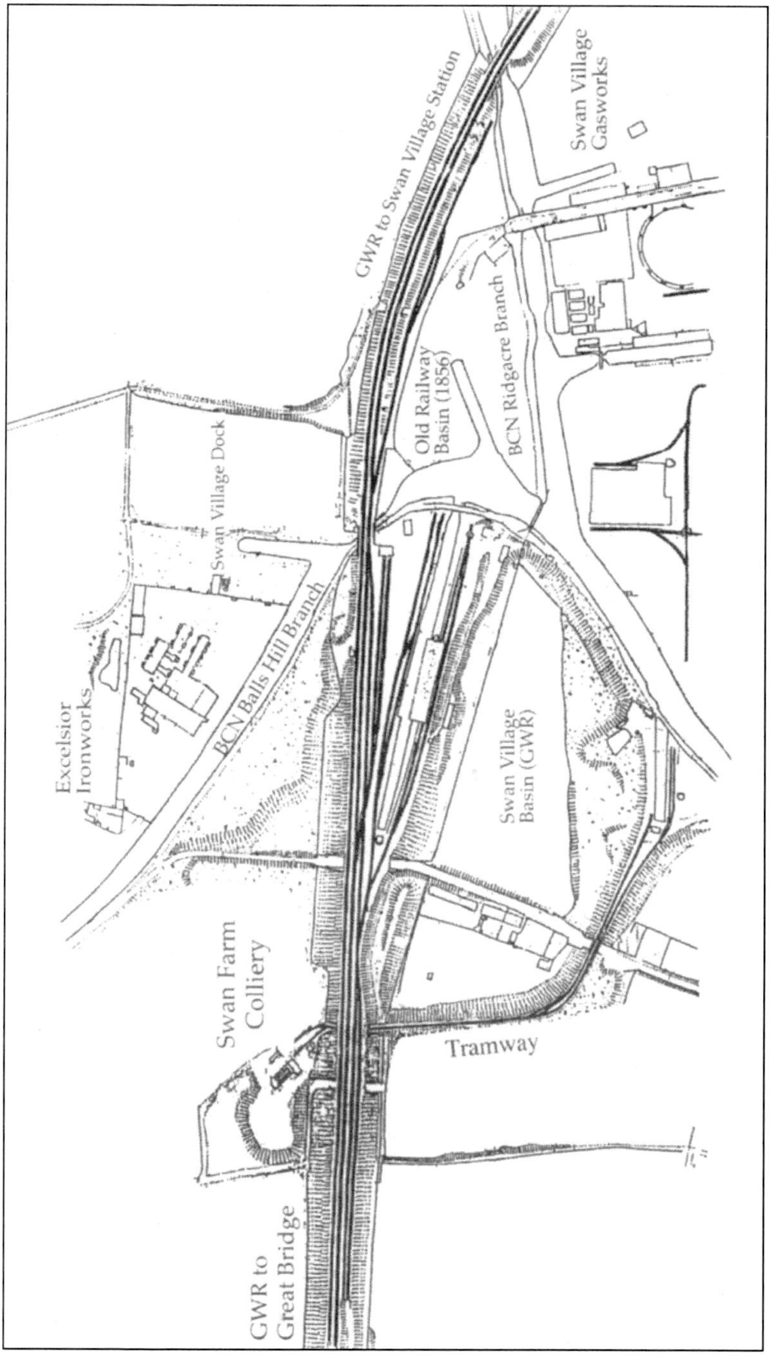
GWR to Swan Village Station
Swan Village Gasworks
Old Railway Basin (1856)
BCN Ridgacre Branch
Swan Village Dock
Excelsior Ironworks
BCN Balls Hill Branch
Swan Village Basin (GWR)
Swan Farm Colliery
Tramway
GWR to Great Bridge

TIPTON   BDJR / B&G Joint Committee, MR

The Midland Railway used a wharf at Tipton High Green c1844 -1850. It is mentioned in rate returns, but seems to have been given up at the end of 1850.

Ordered that notice be given to Mr Parkes of Tipton that the company will cease the occupation of his wharf there, Christmas Next (1).

(1)   PRO RAIL 491 /137 Midland Railway traffic minutes, Volume 1.

TURNER'S WHARF

A private wharf located beside the BCN Old Main Line at Spon Lane. It was an early wharf beside the public house which had been a boarding point for Monk's Packet Boat. The LNWR and LMS used it as a boatage depot to collect goods from the neighbouring factories.

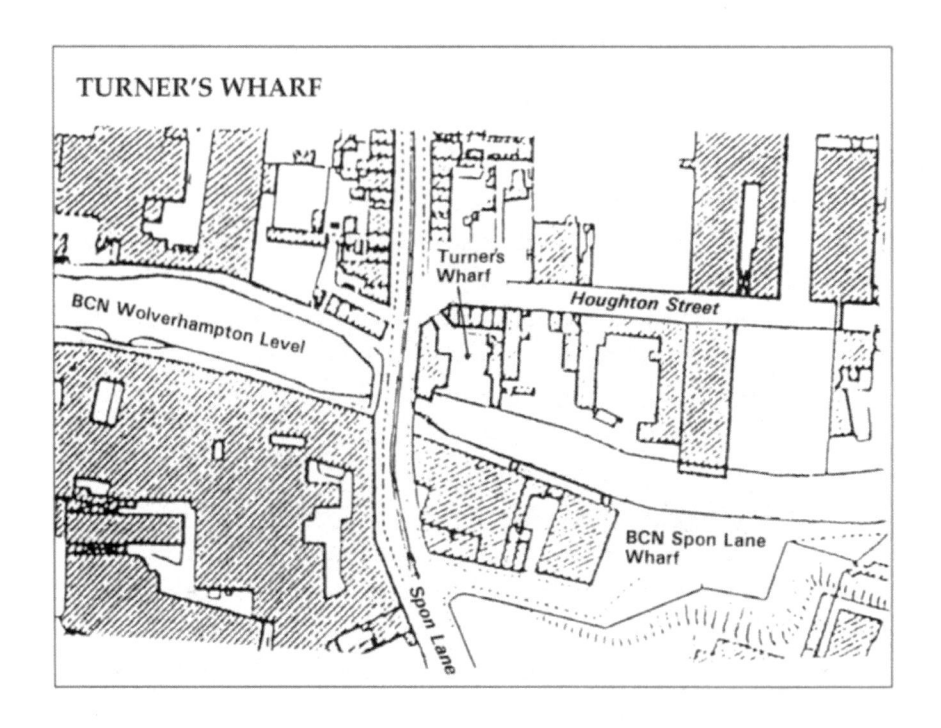

Spon Lane Bridge. The small (left hand) arch gave access to Turner's Wharf. Also through the bridge and on the towpath side is the BCN Spon Lane Wharf. Both wharves were used by railway boats in connection with Spon Lane railway basin

Sandwell Park Libraries

VICTORIA   SBR, GWR
1851-1930

A long basin which joined the BCN above the locks at Wolverhampton.

The basin was served by a short standard gauge railway that left the SBR main line to Wolverhampton before the Canal overbridge. The connection was put in during 1851 and originally only served the basin and the covered canal warehouse. In March 1852, it was decided to move the SBR goods warehouse from Stafford Road to the end of the covered warehouse at Victoria Basin in order to reduce the distance of delivering goods into Wolverhampton (1).

When the GWR chose to sell their interest in Wolverhampton (High Level) to the LNWR in 1858, it was also arranged that a new goods station was to be built at Herbert Street adjacent to Victoria Basin. Herbert Street Goods was completed in 1859 and about this time the old SBR connection was also severed with the LNWR.

The former SBR lines into Herbert Street and Victoria Basin then became a branch from the GWR at Stafford Road. Mixed gauge track was laid as far as Herbert Street. Broad gauge trains gained access to Herbert Street via the WJR and reversing on Oxley Viaduct. It has been stated by H Holcroft (2) that Broad Gauge track was laid as far as Victoria Basin, but surviving track plans for the period suggest that this was not the case (3).

The broad gauge traffic to Herbert Street ceased in 1868 and the lines were removed in April 1869.

In 1909 (4) traffic was tripped to Oxley except for the following through freights:

6.40pm Pontypool Road - Victoria Basin (arrive 4.15am)

11.15pm London (Paddington) - Victoria Basin (arrive 4.20am)

9.00pm Cardiff - Victoria Basin (arrive 6.25am)

4.00pm Gloucester - Victoria Basin (arrive 1.55am)

6.30pm Victoria Basin - Pontypool Road

8.05pm Victoria Basin - London (Paddington)

9.20pm Victoria Basin - London (Paddington) *

10.05pm Victoria Basin - Cardiff

* *Maximum Load 45 x (50/50) vacuum braked wagons hauled by County Class 4-4-0 locomotive, Monday – Friday (50 wagons allowed on Saturday only).*

In 1930 the basin was closed and partly infilled. Herbert Street was enlarged and a new goods station was constructed over the site of the old basin. The old wooden goods shed at Herbert Street had narrow platforms and goods handling there was cramped and limited.

The GWR demolished the old goods station and the basin sheds and altered the track work. Only one feature was retained, this was the three storey brick warehouse which was refurbished. The new goods depot was completed by May 1931 (3).

(1) PRO Rail 615/10. Minute dated March 3, 1852
(2) The Armstrongs of The Great Western, H Holcroft
(3) Information provided by Michael Hale
(4) PRO Rail 937/100
(5) The Great Western Magazine July 1930 and October 1931

Victoria Basin just before redevelopment at Herbert Street goods station

Michael Hale collection

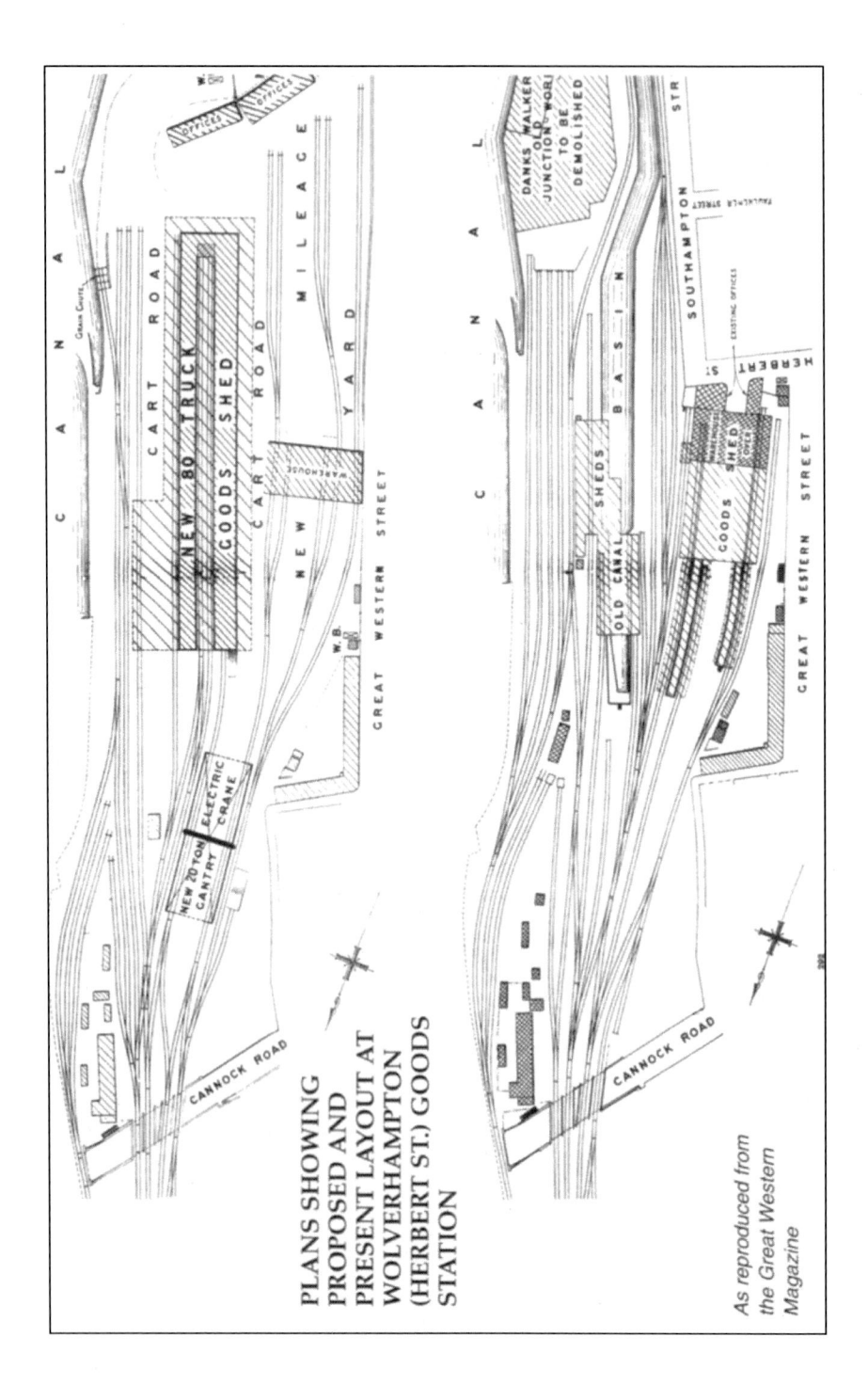

PLANS SHOWING PROPOSED AND PRESENT LAYOUT AT WOLVERHAMPTON (HERBERT ST.) GOODS STATION

As reproduced from the Great Western Magazine

WALLOWS

A private basin at the end of the Pensnett Canal that belonged to the Earl of Dudley. The LNWR used the wharf for boatage traffic to and from local ironworks.

The Wallows Wharf was an interchange basin for the Pensnett Railway. Coal brought down from the Himley and Baggeridge Collieries would be transferred into the waiting boats on the Pensnett Canal. The crane provides visual evidence of boatage traffic handled there.

Black Country Living Museum

WATERFALL LANE   MR, LMS

1877-1937

The MR had a linear wharf on the Dudley Canal north of Waterfall Lane Bridge on the offside of the towpath. This wharf was located between Waterfall Lane and Lowe's Timber Yard.

WATERY LANE (TIPTON) LNWR, LMS, BR(M)
1851-1954

Two arms of the basin joined in the centre with the Birmingham Level of the BCN south of Owen Street Bridge, Tipton.

Railway sidings were constructed on a cramped site that also served Tipton Goods. There was a single road locomotive shed that housed the locomotive that worked these siding and the traffic to and from the Stour Valley Railway.

The basin was constructed to link with the SVR and was originally intended to hold six boats.

According to the 1872 working timetable (1), only two freights called here. Both trains were in the down direction:

12.35am Camden - Bushbury (arrive 8.20am)

1.50pm Birmingham - Bushbury (arrive 2.45pm)
There was, however, an amount of trip work from other goods depots.

The basin remained after traffic ceased and was taken over by Caggy Stevens as a boat yard during the 1970s. He converted one arm into a dry dock. The future of the site is uncertain following Caggy's death in January 1997.

(1) PRO Rail 946 / 7

Canal junction at Tipton Watery Lane. The basin shed is visible on right hand side.
National Waterways Museum, Gloucester

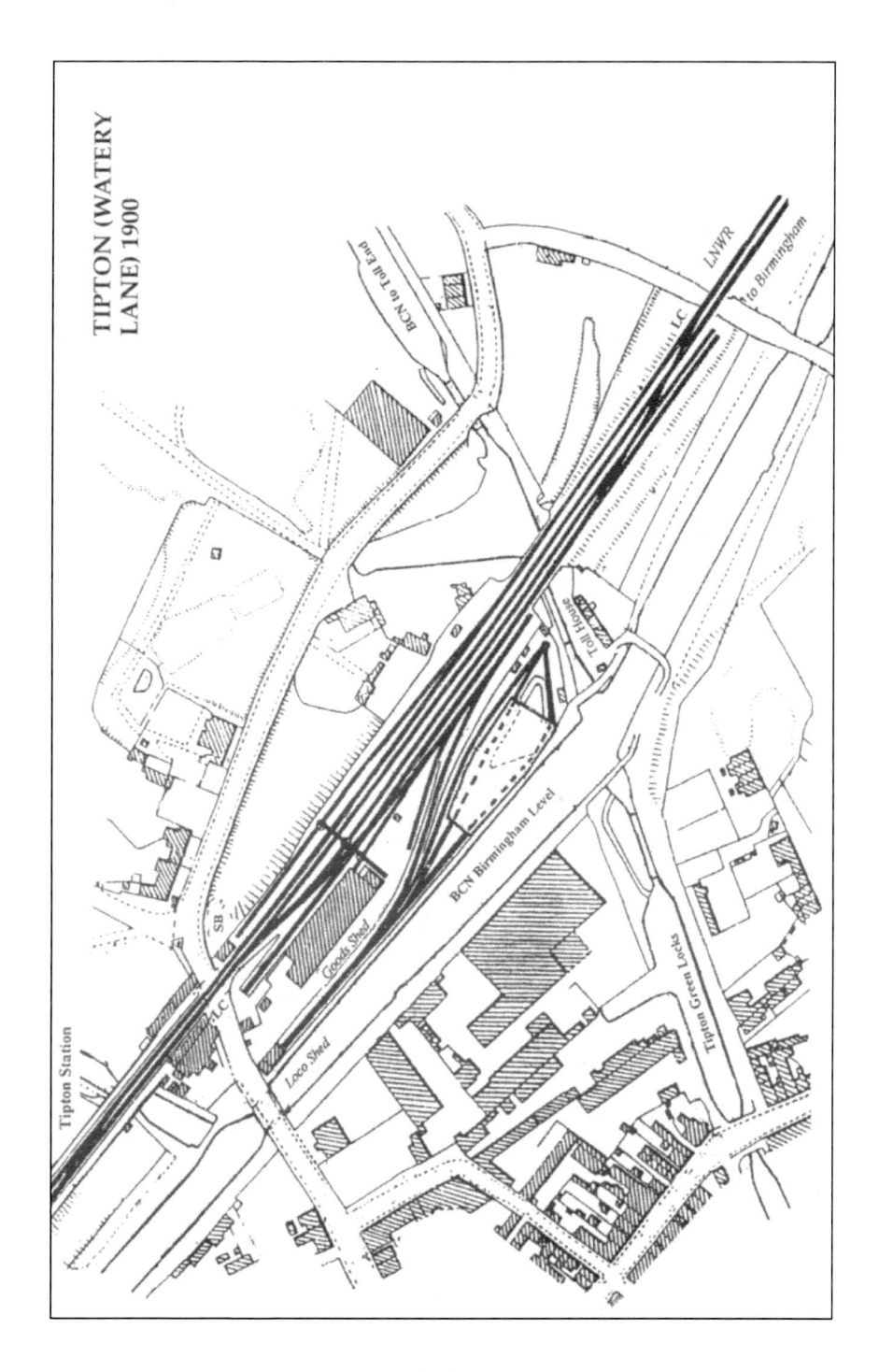

TIPTON (WATERY LANE) 1900

Tipton (Watery Lane) Basin is still in water and is now used for repairing boats

Ray Shill

WEDNESBURY (LEABROOK)   GWR, BR(W)
1855-1950

Two basins joined the Walsall Canal at Leabrook, near Wednesbury.

Standard and Broad gauge sidings connected with the GWR north of the canal overbridge. Broad gauge tracks would have been removed by 1869.

Wednesbury Basin was part of Wednesbury Goods Station, a busy traffic centre served by trips to and from Oxley and many through freights. Wednesbury had a number of industries that generated this trade. Amongst the most important were the Patent Shaft Steelworks, which had a considerable demand for high quality iron, and the various tube works which were then well established.

Services included, in 1909 (1) the 4 am Victoria Basin - Swan Village (5.13am / 6.25am), the 2.25pm Cannock Road Junction to Swan Village (3.30pm / 3.55pm) and their return workings to Oxley. Through freights included the 1.10am and 5.25 am from London (Paddington) - Oxley.

Traffic dwindled during last few years of GWR ownership. One basin was filled in and siding accommodation increased. The sidings were retained by BR after the basin traffic ceased and were later incorporated into the Wednesbury Steel Terminal. They were less used after 1980 and when the steelworks finally closed, in 1983, the basin tracks were taken up.

Present State: The surviving basin remains in water and the side bridge across the entrance is intact.

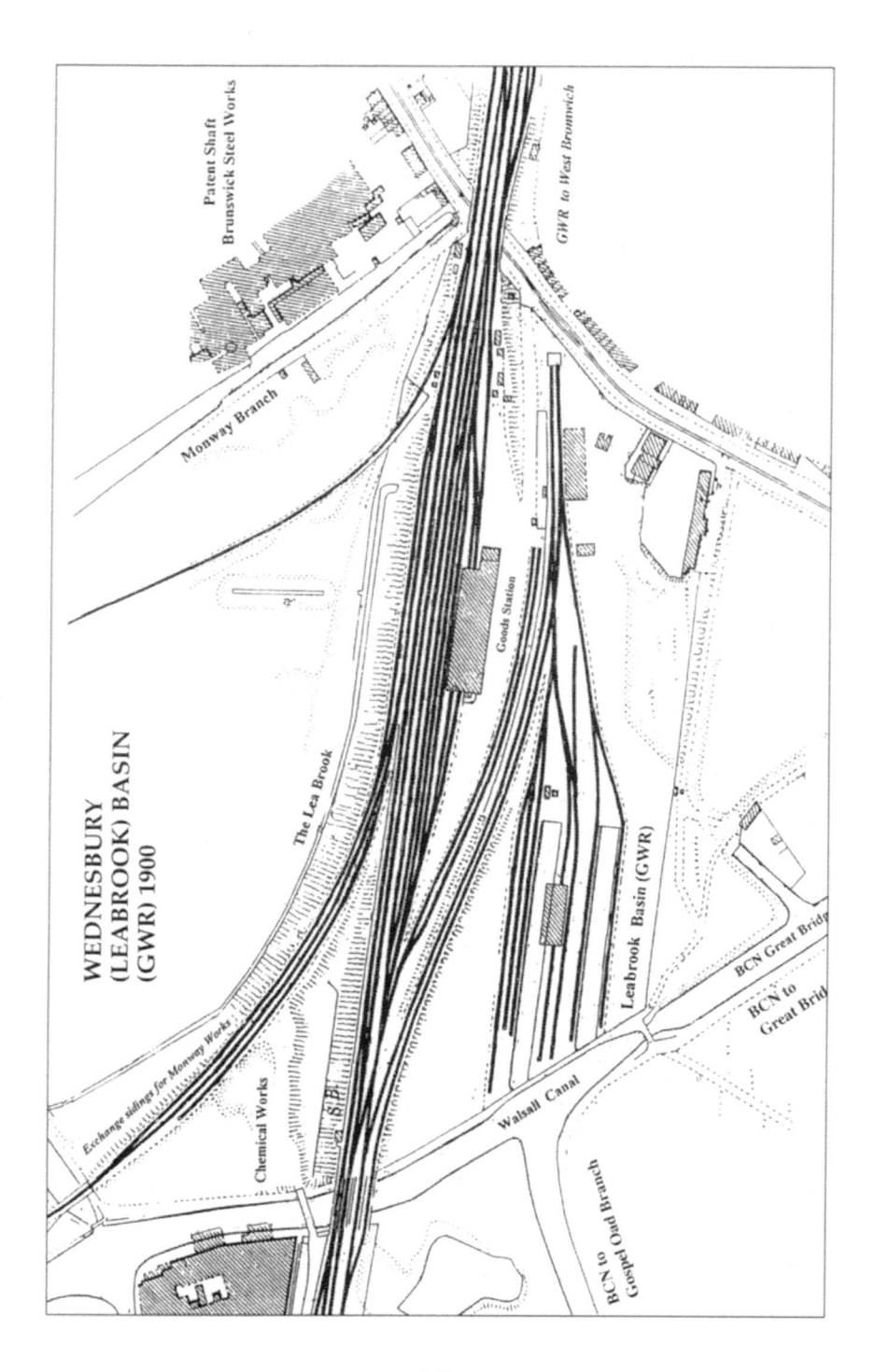

WEDNESBURY (LEABROOK) BASIN (GWR) 1900

WHEELEY'S   OWWR
1852-1858

A private wharf on the Stourbridge Canal at Brettell Lane which was used by the OWWR for boatage traffic.

WITHYMOOR (NETHERTON)   GWR, BR(W)
1878-1965

A long basin that joined the Dudley No.2 Canal at Netherton. There was also a linear wharf beside the No.2 Canal.

A standard gauge branch which served the basin connected with the GWR Dudley & Old Hill Line. The close proximity to the chain trade industry provided important traffic for the GWR for both raw materials and the finished product.

The 1909 working timetable (1) records four trips each way along the basin railway.:
  3.20pm Bordesley - Withymoor (arrive 5.35pm)
  3.40pm Oxley - Withymoor (arrive 6.15pm)
  7.30pm Rowley Regis - Withymoor (arrive 7.50pm)
  10.10pm Dudley - Withymoor (arrive 10.20pm)
  6.50pm Withymoor - Bordesley
  9.15pm Withymoor - Dudley
  10.50pm Withymoor - London
  11.35pm Withymoor - Banbury
Traffic ceased on 5th July 1965 when Netherton Goods closed.

Present state; The basin and wharf is presently used for residential moorings.

(1)   PRO Rail 937/100

WITHYMOOR   LNWR / SUR

The LNWR had a boatage depot beside the Withymoor Branch at Netherton. It was located 415 links from the junction with the Dudley No 2 canal (1), and had ceased to be used prior to 1900.

(1)   BCN distance tables 1885, PRO Rail 810 / 305.

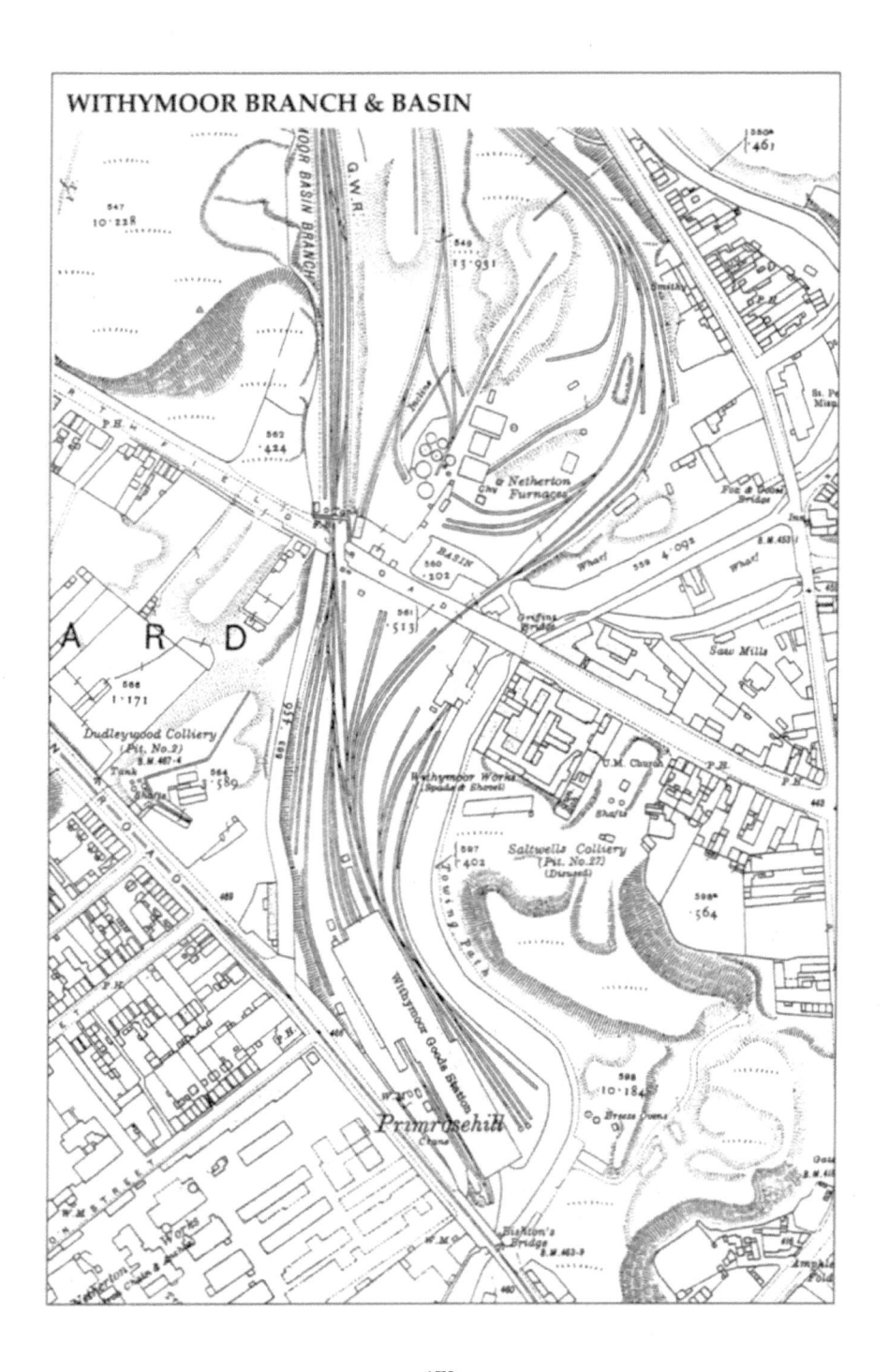

WITHYMOOR BRANCH & BASIN

Withymoor goods station. A former GWR pannier tank shunts wagons in the sidings. The interchange basin shed can be seen in the centre background

Ned Williams

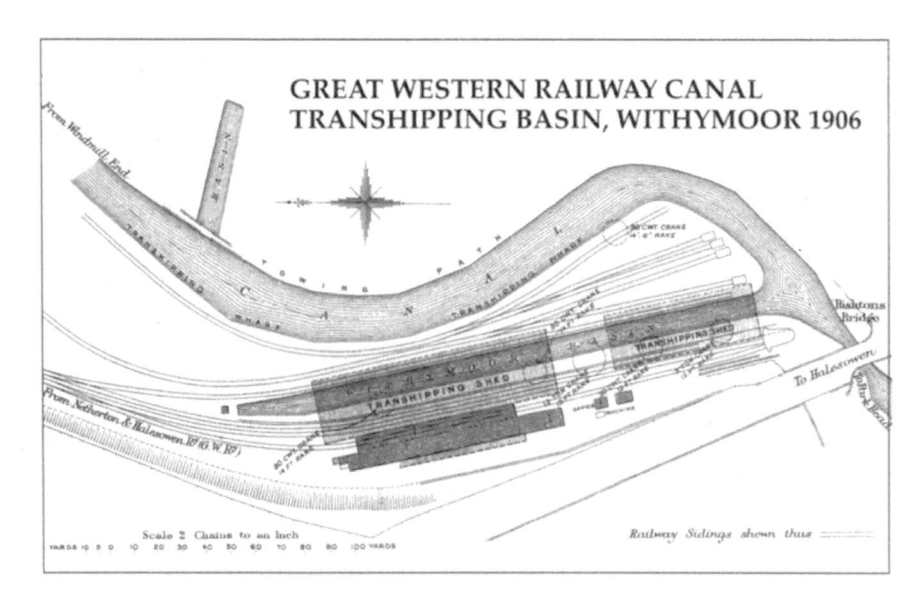

171

Chains being loaded at Withymoor Basin

Black Country Living Museum